GABEBA BADEROON

Regarding
Muslims
from slavery to post-apartheid

GABEBA BADEROON

Regarding Muslims

from slavery to post-apartheid

WITS UNIVERSITY PRESS

Published in South Africa by:
Wits University Press
1 Jan Smuts Avenue
Johannesburg, 2001

www.witspress.co.za

First published 2014
Second printing 2015

Earlier versions of some sections have appeared in *World Literature Today*,
Social Dynamics, the *Arab World Geographer*, *Annual Review of Islam in South Africa*,
African and Asian Studies, *Research in African Literatures* and *Ecquid Novi*.

978-1-86814-769-4 (print)
978-1-86814-770-0 (digital)

Edited by Helen Moffett
Proofread by Margaret Ramsay
Index by Margaret Ramsay
Cover design by Abdul Amien
Book design and layout by Abdul Amien
Printed and bound by Paarl Media, South Africa

WITS UNIVERSITY PRESS

Contents

List of illustrations

Cover: *Malay Bride* – Irma Stern. Reproduced with permission from DALRO & Irma Stern Trust © Irma Stern Trust | DALRO.

Illustrations in colour section:

P. van der Aa – *D'Almeida and his men killed by Hottentots on the shore of Table Bay in 1510 Copperplate 1707*: Source: Alfred Gordon-Brown, *Pictorial Africana: A survey of old South African paintings, drawings and prints to the end of the nineteenth century with a biographic dictionary of one thousand artists*. Reproduced courtesy of the South African National Library, Cape Town.

Hertzoggies from *The Cape Malay Cookbook* by Faldela Williams, Cape Town, Struik, 1988. Photograph by Cornel de Kock. Reproduced with permission from Random House Struik (Pty) Ltd.

George French Angas – *Cape Town from the Camps Bay Road*. Lithograph printed by Charles Lovell. Source: *The Kafirs Illustrated: In a series of drawings taken among the Amazulu, Amaponda, and Amakosa Tribes, Also, portraits of the Hottentot, Malay, Fingo, and other races inhabiting Southern Africa together with sketches of landscape scenery in the Zulu country, Natal and the Cape Colony*, 1974 [1849]. Reproduced courtesy of the South African National Library, Cape Town.

Stamps in the passport of "Auntie Galiema" on her way to Mecca in 1951. Reproduced with kind permission of "Auntie Galiema".

All pictures of the Hajji's and the pilgrimage to Mecca are from the private collection of the Haron family. Reproduced with kind permission of the Haron family.

Cape Times, 6 August 1996, "On Guard" photograph by B. Gool. Reproduced with permission of Independent Newspapers Cape, courtesy of the South African National Library, Cape Town.

The Argus, 7 August 1996, "Mass Action on Gangs". Reproduced with permission of Independent Newspapers Cape, courtesy of the South African National Library, Cape Town.

Cape Times, 12 August 1996 "Single Masked Man". Photograph by T. Dwayisa. Reproduced with permission of Independent Newspapers Cape, courtesy of the South African National Library, Cape Town.

Berni Searle – *Untitled* (1999). Reproduced with permission of the artist.

Acknowledgements

I see all the book spines there ever were,
their colours and textures like women bent in prayer on a high holy day.
My voice is small as it asks,
What will it matter to them if I make a book?

– Ladan Osman, "Silhouette"

Recently in Pennsylvania, I was recalling with a South African friend that the Afrikaans language textbook we were given at school contained the idiomatic saying: "so dronk soos 'n Kleurling onderwyser" (as drunk as a Coloured[1] teacher). Hearing this idiom – devastatingly familiar to me – my American partner felt the visceral shock of recognition of what apartheid meant. Just as education was for him a revelatory experience, for me, it was an induction into my place in a painfully and overtly unjust world. And yet it was also revelatory.

Because there was the official account – the textbook version of apartheid education – but at Livingstone High School, I was also taught the radical and progressive version. We refused the identity offered to us by the racially separate Coloured education system, of which my school was a part. As a child, I learned both what was in the textbooks and what was left out.

The idiom about the commonplace sight of a drunk coloured teacher was meant to signal the impossibility of black intellectual life. The contempt with which this saying highlighted the failure of the black intelligentsia also conveyed the heartbreak induced by apartheid's attack on all of black life. Of course, through the idiom, apartheid tried to erase the long history of black intellectual achievement in South Africa, and therefore, crucially, any resistance to apartheid had to engage in an intellectual battle too.

This book claims a modest place in such a contest.

A book is a collective effort and an intellectual autobiography. Under apartheid, an entire social infrastructure existed to turn me into a compliant subject of a racist and authoritarian state. In some ways it succeeded, and in others, it failed. The failure of the apartheid project on the small scale of one human being I ascribe to several heroic people and institutions.

I trace my genealogy to the neighbourhood pre-schools and madrassas of Athlone, a Catholic primary school named St Ignatius, and a great hive of black intellectual accomplishment called Livingstone High School (both of which were located in the segregated suburb of Claremont from which black residents were removed in the 1960s), the University of Cape Town, the University of the Western Cape, Sheffield University, Sheffield Hallam University and Pennsylvania State University. I thank all my teachers.

At Livingstone, I was seen by my teachers, some of whom had taught my mother decades before, as *clever* (an ambiguous word for a child). Thirty years before, my mother was brilliant at Livingstone, and went on to medical studies at the University of Cape Town. She told me a story about being a student there that has haunted me for long years.

I forget to look

The photograph of my mother at her desk in the fifties
has been in my purse for twenty years,
its paper faded, browning,
the scalloped edge bent then straightened.

The collar of her dress folds discreetly.
The angle of her neck looks as though
someone has called her from far away.

She was the first in her family to take
the bus from Claremont
up the hill to the university.

At one point during the lectures at medical school,
black students had to pack their notes, get up and walk
past the ascending rows of desks out of the theatre.

Behind the closed door, in an autopsy
black students were not meant to see
the uncovering and cutting of white skin.

Under the knife, the skin,
the mystery of sameness.

In a world that defined how black and white
could look at each other, touch each other,
my mother looks back, her poise unmarred.

Every time I open my purse,
she is there, so familiar I forget
to look at her.

– Gabeba Baderoon, *A hundred silences*, 2006

My mother, the luminous intellectual, countered apartheid's racist and sexist myths and allowed me to embark on that path too.

Since I was designated clever, it seemed inevitable that I too would go to medical school. However, in standard eight, two years before matric, my love of English directed me toward literary studies instead. At the University of Cape Town, I was shy, out of place, not a very good student at first, but eventually literature offered me a home and, more importantly, an intellectual community. My foundational friendships and scholarly partnerships were born at that time, both at the University of Cape Town, and its more radical and far less affluent neighbour, the University of the Western Cape.

At UCT, I was fortunate to be surrounded by a cohort of superb graduate students and my teachers and colleagues Eve Bertelsen, Dorothy Driver, John Coetzee, Stephen Watson, Abdulkader Tayob, Shamil Jeppie, Mahmood Mamdani, Amina Mama, Nigel Worden, Vivian Bickford-Smith, Ebrahim Moosa, Muhamed Haron and Johnny van der Westhuizen became lifelong influences. At UWC, the incomparable Desiree Lewis, Zoë Wicomb, Patricia Hayes, Premesh Lalu, Ciraj Rassool, Mary Hames, Suren Pillay, David Bunn and Jane Taylor were an inspiration.

In 2003 I moved to the United States. In 2007, the Africana Research Center at Penn State first welcomed me to the US academy, a hospitality I will never forget. Dayo Mitchell, Eden-Renee Pruitt and Keisha-Khan Perry were ARC Fellows whose insights shaped my work. The gifted scholars who became my friends before they were colleagues, Susan Squier and Irina Aristarkhova, have been a core of my life since.

I also thank:

Harvey Hendricks, Gail McFarlane, Rashied Omar and the much-loved Richard Dudley at Livingstone.

The friends in whose nourishing company I learned to think and write: Angelo Fick, Shaida Kazie Ali, Pumla Gqola, Rustum Kozain, Maura O'Gara, Kimberly Yates, Drew Shaw, Louise Green, Mary Watson, Roshila Nair, Maria Olaussen, Yvette Abrahams, Mary Hames, Adam Haupt, Jane Bennett, Zine Magubane, Kylie Thomas, Sindre Bangstad, Yazeed Kamaldien, Sa'diyya Shaikh, Nina Hoel, Tina Steiner, Mai Palmberg, Lesley Marx, Kelwyn Sole, Henriette Gunkel and Zethu Matebeni.

My dear colleagues and friends at Penn State and in State College: Carey Eckhardt, Carolyn Sachs, Rosemary Jolly, Tom Hale, Michael Bérubé, Jonathan Eburne, Jonathan Brockopp, Eric Hayot, Reiko Tachibana, Hester Blum, Ariane Cruz, Alyssa Garcia, Jonathan Marks, Jennifer Wagner-Lawlor, Joan Landes, Lorraine Dowler, Minnie Sinha, Melissa Wright, Lise Nelson, Terri Vescio, Tony Kaye, Lori Ginzberg, Paula Droege, Ikubolajeh Logan, Tracy Beckett, Benedicte Monicat, Robert Bernasconi, Mindy Boffemmyer, Jill Wood, Anne-Marie Mingo, Jacqui Reid-Walsh, Wanda Knight, Karen Keifer-Boyd, Erin Heidt-Forsythe, Kathy Rumbaugh, Marie Carlson, Lisa Batchelor, Staci Kelly, Maia Ramnath, Lisa Sternlieb, Charlotte Eubanks, Hoda El Shakry, Nergis Ertürk, Sarah Rich, Madhuri Desai, Clemente Abrokwaa, Tom Beebee, Shuang Shen, Mark Fisher, Shannon Sullivan, John Christman, Sophia McClennen, Patricia Jabbeh Wesley, Matt McAllister, Mary Beth Oliver, Marian Dornell, Don Kunze, Elaine Kunze, Sajay Samuel, Samar Farage, Shaoling Ma, Paul Taylor, Papori Bora, Eileen Trauth, Leonie Newhouse, Elizabeth Carlson, Chris Reed, Charles Duma, Josephine Dumas, Daniel Purdy, Jessica Johnson, Surya Parekh, Russell Frank, Sasha Turner, Janet Lyon, Deryck Holdsworth, Kevin Hagiopan, Djelal Kadir and Lovalerie King.

The graduate students in Women's Studies, Philosophy and Comparative Literature who illuminate my thinking, and my undergraduate students, who delight me in each class.

My beloved Dr Sisters: Jeanine Staples, Kathryn Gines, Solsiree Del Moral, Shirley Moody-Turner, Leticia Oseguera, Cheraine Stanford, Crystal Sanders, and Christine Buzinde.

My literature study group Josephine Carubia and Nancy Tuana.

The research toward this book was supported by a Sainsbury/Linbury Trust

Fellowship in the English department, an Associateship in the African Gender Institute, an internship in the Centre for Popular Memory and a Research Fellowship in the "Islam, African Publics and Religious Values" Project, all at the University of Cape Town; a Visiting Scholarship in the School of English at the University of Sheffield; a Guest Writer Fellowship at the Nordic Africa Institute; a Post-doctoral Fellowship in the Africana Research Center and an award of Research Leave at Pennsylvania State University. I thank the members of the above institutions and of the "Sex, Power and Slavery" conference at McGill University, the Indian Ocean Network Conference, the "Islam, Democracy and Public Life" conference and the 2011 Johannesburg Workshop in Theory and Criticism, all at the University of Witwatersrand, the conference on Religion, Media and Marginality in Africa at the University of London, and the "Genres of the Imaginaire" workshop at Vanderbilt University for their superlative scholarship and insights.

Vonani Bila, Gabriel Welsch, Ingrid de Kok, Keorapetse Kgositsile, Robin Becker, Sean O'Brien, Kim Welsch, Gus Ferguson and Kwame Dawes, poets whose delight in the word and the vivid thought have given me a home and made me a better writer.

The artists, cooks, journalists and writers who allowed me to interview them and deepened my research, and whose work sparked me into a richer understanding of history and the present.

Berni Searle, Ladan Osman, J. M. Coetzee, Rayda Jacobs, Ishtiyaq Shukri, Yvette Christiansë, Shaida Kazie Ali, Mxolisi Nyezwa, Nadia Davids, Imraan Coovadia and Zubeida Jaffer, whose words and art profoundly enrich this book.

The anonymous readers whose comments enhanced and strengthened my writing.

Roshan Cader and Veronica Klipp at Wits University Press, who gave this book a hospitable and perfect home.

Helen Moffett, my gifted editor, who is able to find the best in my writing.

Pat Rademeyer, an image visionary, with whom I share a love of cook-books.

The insightful editors with whom I worked in the course of doing the research for this book, including Desiree Lewis, Daniel Simon, Ghazi-Walid Falah, Herman Wittenberg, Sean Jacobs, Rehana Vally, Eric Worby, Elizabeth Elbourne, Gwyn Campbell, Adeleke Adeeko and Louise Green.

My supervisors Zimitri Erasmus, Richard Steadman-Jones and John Higgins.

Isabel Hofmeyr, Patricia McFadden, Chandra Mohanty, Ato Quayson, Abena Busia, Sarah Nuttall, Achille Mbembe, Pallavi Rastogi, M. Jacqui Alexander, Sylvia Tamale, Ken Harrow, Preben Kaarsholm, Scott Reese, Ridder Samsom, Monica Popescu, Jon Soske, Farid Esack, Guna Nadarajan, Shabbir Banoobhai, Shelley Barry, Elaine Salo, Melissa Steyn, Scott Reese, Heike Behrend, Uma Dhupelia-Mesthrie, Goolam Vahed, Richard McGregor, Tony Stewart and Mogamat Kamedien for generous, scintillating scholarship that has made mine better.

Auntie Galiema, Auntie Lima, Khalid Shamis and the Haron family: my deepest gratitude for honouring me with your treasured memories, photographs and words.

My family – most centrally my parents, Imran, Suleila, Nazli, Abdeya and the new generation whose life after apartheid we once dreamed for them.

Someone whose name it is a small incantation to say each day: Dorn.

Foreword

I first got to know Gabeba Baderoon in an English Literature Honours class at the University of Cape Town in 1990, where we were classmates in three seminars: one in feminist literary theory and criticism, led by Dorothy Driver; another in black South African literature of the 1970s and 1980s, led by Kelwyn Sole; and the other in the poetry of T. S. Eliot and D. H. Lawrence, led by Terry Boxall. I was struggling to find my feet in graduate literary studies – still learning its codes and protocols – in a cohort of students then considered one of the department's brightest groups.

I was constantly trying to decode other students' approaches in their seminar papers, looking for that formula or method by which I could gain power over the discipline. Of course there wasn't a formula, but there was a series of "tricks" that were akin to paradigm shifts for me at the time. Nothing about critical method – how to go about writing a critical essay – was taught or made explicit in any way. The bright students seemed to have been born prepared, while I felt like a novice trying to uncover the sleight of hand of magicians.

One of the paradigm shifts for me occurred when Gabeba delivered a paper in the Eliot and Lawrence seminar. I cannot remember whether it was on an Eliot or Lawrence poem, or both, but her presentation was framed by what at first appeared an oblique angle. She was using an article about physics – perhaps it was on Heisenberg – from *Time* magazine. Not only was it an oblique angle, but she was using a *non-literary* source – and, to me, also a "non-scholarly" source – in a class that was very traditional in its scholarship. Of course I know now that this was nothing innovative or scandalous, but to me as a novice it represented a profound shift: knowledge across disciplinary boundaries, no matter how oblique it may appear, can illuminate things otherwise obscured.

Through the years, over the course of a friendship that is unfortunately irregular in contact and communication, but nevertheless filled with intellectual delight when we do communicate, I have come to know Gabeba as a thinker who often sees things along lines of sight never considered by others – that may indeed never occur as a line of sight to others. It is an enviable intellectual habit – and one we see operative in this book – because it leads to new understanding. Here, Gabeba, a poet and a media and literary scholar, looks at the deep history of Islam in South Africa, and reconsiders the place of Islam and slavery as an integral part of that colonial blueprint that seems still to frame our contemporary relations. While a fuller social picture of the role of slavery in modern South Africa's beginnings has emerged from historians and other experts over the past three decades, Gabeba considers the lines that connect that past to our present in a broader but no less considered light: the way Islam and Muslims in South Africa have been portrayed and are portrayed in relation to our beginnings in slave society, and against the background of a deeper analysis of cultural practices and activities which underlie the stereotypes – benign and otherwise – of Islam and Muslims in South Africa.

It often still surprises me how little South Africans know about each other across our historical divisions. In general, this kind of ignorance can be attributed to uneven relations of power: those closest to economic, political and cultural power – people in the centre – care little about the lives of people further away from the centre, while those further away, on the margins, may know much more about the centre because that centre – proximity to power – is something to which most people aspire. To a small-town child, for instance, the city lights typically burn brighter; she or he will pore over maps and photographs of the city and endlessly relive visits there. In school and through media, that child will learn about political and legal decision-making that takes place in the city, about how people there dress, about social mores. She or he will learn, assimilate and mimic the codes of the city because the city represents something aspirational. The city child, on the other hand, may not even know – and may not care to know – of the existence of the small town or farm, and that his or her daily milk is produced there.

This is a fairly universal relationship – it occurs everywhere. Even the small town will have its centre and its margins. In South Africa, this uneven relationship between power and knowledge occurs on many levels and mainly fragmented along lines of race and class. This has been true for the last almost four hundred years and, considering the nature of public commentary on the internet, for instance, it continues to be so. South Africans continue to talk to each other without knowing each other, and therefore not knowing *how* to talk to each other.

Islam is one such area of culture in South Africa where even reasonably educated South Africans show a surprising lack of knowledge. In public commentary – whether formal journalism, informal internet comments or conversations overheard in a restaurant – many people pronounce on Islam and Muslims in South Africa without knowing much about Islam itself or its history in South Africa, its significance in shaping aspects of South African society, or the cultural complexity of Muslim communities in South Africa.

To a large extent this reveals the sway that the US and UK media and other cultural institutions – and our local institutions mimicking them – hold in a former British colony: media in which a link between Islam and terrorism is a constant subtext. More specifically, this "international" media tends to cover Islam only by way of spectacular events so as to confirm the subtext: protests surrounding the Danish cartoons, for instance, show Islam and Muslims to be made up of irrational mobs baying for blood. South Africans readily grab onto these frames through which to look at Muslims in South Africa. But this also happens because most South Africans don't know about the centuries-long *presence* of Islam in South Africa: a presence that belies the small number of the Muslim population and a presence that is more than the physical presence of Muslim inhabitants.

Islam is a marginal religion in South Africa, a country where the majority religion is Christian, whether publicly espoused or existing as faint traces and in highly secularised forms. While Muslim South Africans have to *know* how to fit into an unevenly secularised but largely Christian society – have to understand the codes, as it were – there is no imperative for non-Muslim South Africans to know about Islam or the culture(s) of Muslims. While there has always been a measure of interaction – some may even say a measure of intimacy – between Muslim peoples and wider South African society, that interaction has always been unequal, structured as it has been by slavery, colonialism and apartheid, on the one hand, and the closing of ranks of an embattled community, on the other. And it remains so, partly as historical and structural legacy.

This book opens up the *presence* of Islam and Muslims in South Africa in a sense far beyond the physical presence of people who are Muslim and beyond the knowledge of historians. To most non-Muslim South Africans, a Muslim presence is reduced, on the benign side, to cuisine (although differences of opinion do exist as to whether a dish is "Malay" or "boerekos"), the call to prayer (for those who, during apartheid, lived close to a "Muslim neighbourhood"), crafts like bricklaying, carpentry and tailoring, or exotic beauty and the colourful spectacle of the annual Cape Town minstrel carnival. Less benign are the reductive meanings and images linked to fanaticism and "terrorism". These stereotypes foreclose against any view that Muslims have complex interior lives that are filled (like everyone else's) with material aspirations, spiritual doubt, shifting allegiances – in short, that Muslim lives run the whole gamut of human life.

A significant gap in popular knowledge about the history of Muslims in South Africa coincides with a general lack of knowledge about the role of slavery in South Africa, even among people and communities who are the descendants of slaves. We may know that the early colonial Cape depended on slaves for labour, that the Dutch brought slaves from what was formerly known as the Malayan Archipelago, among other places and that many of these slaves were Muslim – and thus the presence of Islam at the Cape.[1]

What Gabeba's book traces, though, is the extent to which that slave-dependent economy, in general, and the place of Muslims in it, specifically, shaped initial social relations at the Cape – and, thus, racial relations throughout the history of colonial and apartheid South Africa. Benign stereotypes of Muslims are part of what Gabeba identifies as the picturesque tradition in the representation of slavery in South Africa – a mode of picturing and describing slaves and their presence without acknowledging the abuse of human rights that constituted their slavery. Put another way, the picturesque avoids the real, brutal conditions that underlie the presence of slaves in a pretty landscape painting. And if benign and contemporary stereotypes of Muslims can be traced back to slavery in South Africa, so too can contemporary representations that associate Muslims and terror.

Many of us will be surprised to learn, for instance, that the association between Muslims and the threat of mob violence has early, local precedence. Part of the impetus behind this study was exactly the way in which images of protest marches by People Against Gangsterism and Drugs (Pagad) in the 1990s, for instance, conformed to the contemporary framing of Islam in US and European media – mobs of Muslims bent on mayhem. But surprisingly, a similar media association between Muslims and violence is here traced back to the nineteenth century, shortly after manumission.

This threat of violence is the flip side of the more benign stereotype of the excellent cook or tailor, the obedient and honest slave or servant. And so this book identifies a continuous ambivalence – from the days of slavery to the present – in the representations of Muslims and Islam in South Africa by those with the power to represent: Muslims either are docile slaves or the agents of subversive violence.

I think it's important that this *primal scene* of modern South Africa – the roots of our social relations in slavery – is excavated for an audience wider than historians. While historical work over the past thirty-odd years has done much to illuminate South African slave society, Gabeba's book does a lot more in showing how that society remains present and reflected in present-day South African culture.

In tandem with her analyses of the history and politics of *mis*-representations of Islam and Muslims in South Africa, Gabeba also explores contemporary *self*-representations by Muslims, ranging from cooks to visual artists to writers. This reveals a complex, contradictory culture which belies one-dimensional stereotypes, especially those which cast Islam and Muslims in South Africa as something exotic and mysteriously Eastern, as something unknowable. Muslims in South Africa are South African Muslims. As much as Muslims and Muslim slaves have shaped this country's history over more than three hundred years, South African history has shaped Muslims here. It is this kind of inter-connectedness that the book ultimately unravels and which is its salutary contribution to a dialogue about South Africanness that, I believe, still needs to happen.

Rustum Kozain

Introduction:
Beginnings in South Africa

Since the colonial period, popular culture has trained a fascinated and uninhibited gaze on Muslims in South Africa, evident in the abundance of images of "Cape Malays" (a term for Muslims which I discuss below) in travel writing, cartoons, paintings, caricatures and cookbooks produced from the eighteenth century onward. In these images, Muslims are typically presented as exotic, submissive and static, and the representations are overwhelmingly associated with the past. Revealingly, even in the earliest cookbooks published in South Africa, writing about Muslim food is almost always characterised by nostalgia, a longing for what is nearly lost or on the point of being forgotten. Such picturesque Muslim figures thus imply pastness, evoking not only what is to be remembered, but what is to be forgotten. In this book, I argue that this conventional portrayal of Muslims *enables* certain histories to be forgotten.

An extensive record of cartoons, popular paintings and cookbooks has created a familiar repertoire of Muslim figures in the South African imagination, a repertoire infused with larger political meaning. Images of kindly Malay washerwomen and cooks and submissive Malay men reflect a comfort with the intimate presence of Muslims, but also erase the trauma of slavery – through which Islam first entered the South African colonies. While the topic of slavery and Islam has receded in other arenas of public culture, popular culture has continued to linger with familiarity and even pleasure on images that allude obliquely to slavery. Through a charged play of visibility and invisibility, the long fascination with images of Muslims in the popular realm thus holds a revealing diagnostic power.

"To regard" denotes both "to look" and "to respect", "to stare" and "to contemplate", "to gaze" and "to consider". These dual meanings suggest the act of looking thoughtfully, of reflecting, with an attitude either of intimacy or distance. The title of this book uses the word "regarding" in the present continuous form, intending the act of looking to be sustained and critical. "Regarding" also suggests being at a certain remove – that the perspective

1

taken in the book stands back from Muslims and is about, or in connection to them, which connotes a broader and looser relation. The title therefore signals the act of looking directly and continuously at Muslims, yet it also includes a more diffuse meaning. By invoking a direct focus as well as a more expansive scope, *Regarding Muslims* encompasses both the specific and the general.

The specific concerns the mode of looking that arose in the Cape Colony in relation to Muslim slaves. The more general sense suggested by the title is the role of representations of Muslims in shaping concepts of race, belonging and sexuality in South Africa, and beyond. Drawing on an extensive popular and official archive, *Regarding Muslims* explains the crucial place of Muslims in the history of slavery, colonialism, apartheid and post-apartheid life in South Africa, and suggests the resonance of these discussions beyond the country.

The sustained appeal of images that obliquely or directly figure slavery signals a demotic grappling with history. Popular images of Muslims from the nineteenth into the twentieth centuries show similar themes: alluring Malay women, abundant food, religious festivities and pilgrimage. These can be seen as a barometer of a legacy that official culture suppressed or sought to redirect into the racial project of apartheid. But unofficial culture has continued to retain the reassuring spectacle of placid Malays, producing a distorted mirror in which we can read history obliquely.

This oblique relation to history is reflected in the following three stories of looking.

Since the colonial period, the vantage point on Signal Hill above Cape Town has been a site from which many landscape paintings of Cape Town were painted (Murray: 2001). It is also the location of the oldest slave graveyard in South Africa, named Tana Baru, the term for "New Place" in Bahasa Melayu, a lingua franca among enslaved people in the Cape Colony. The urbane and aesthetically pleasing city represented in colonial-era paintings was therefore literally founded on slave bodies and their labour, but the picturesque landscape rendered the violence of enslavement invisible. This shows not simply how Muslims are represented in visual art, but that they are present in the *making* of a South African visuality. The very conception of landscape, and related notions of nativeness and belonging, have been shaped by the presence of enslaved Muslim bodies.

This play of visibility and invisibility is further conveyed in a second story. In 1998, I was a graduate assistant at a conference in Cape Town to mark the centenary of the publication of Joseph Conrad's *Heart of Darkness*, which was attended by eminent scholars in the field. On the cover of the conference programme was a small decorative figure. This emblem had no real relation to Conrad, although it was suggestive of the nineteenth century and the colonial history of the Cape, and was to be glanced at briefly before one went on to the substance of the programme. The small motif was an aesthetic gesture that barely merited attention, but it caught my eye. It was a picturesque figure of an enslaved person.

On reflection, it struck me that the significance of such figures eludes recognition even when they are in direct view. I began to see them as a mechanism for shifting what *can be seen*, for establishing what is normative and central, and what is marginal and insignificant. To invite a brief glance before the gaze moves on to matters of substance is, I believe, the function of the picturesque view of slavery in South Africa. This aestheticised view of the founding institution in colonial South Africa has been used to create a normative and generalised history in which white subjectivity is central and the violence of slavery is impossible to recall. I explore this idea by examining the constitution of several arenas of normativity in South Africa, through discourses of landscape, food and sexuality, among others.

In some ways, one can argue that the above convention for portraying Muslims can be classed as kitsch art. Kitsch refers to highly consumable art with an immediate and almost calculated popular allure. The popular meaning of kitsch as cheap, consumable and lacking in aesthetic value is countered by the view that such art has in fact an important diagnostic value and is "a phenomenon of utmost political significance" (Menninghaus 2009: 42).

Kitsch brings a frisson of pleasurable recognition that works to circumvent critique, a sentimental and reassuring set of visual tropes that requires no further thought. Many popular images of "Malays" – found in calendars, postcards, cartoons, popular paintings and cookbooks – fall into the mode of kitsch. They are kept in the home, where they act as an intimate "list of curiosities" (Menninghaus 2009: 43). The satisfying immediacy of kitsch images asks no questions and closes the distance of critique. It "offers instantaneous emotional gratification without intellectual effort, without the requirement of distance, without sublimation" (Menninghaus 2009: 41).

Kitsch is suggestive for my discussion of the plethora of popular representations of Muslims because such images make no demands and circumvent unsettling questions; their appeal resides in the familiar, and their immediate confirmation of conventional thought. Clement Greenberg argues that kitsch relies on and therefore illuminates specific cultural phenomena because it operates through "the availability close at hand of a fully formed cultural tradition, whose discoveries, acquisitions and perfected self-consciousness kitsch can take advantage of for its own ends" (1939: 40). This is indeed the power of kitsch. Following Walter Benjamin, John McCole suggests that "ornamental kitsch provided models for detecting the latent presence of archaic forces in modern experience" (1993: 214). Therefore one can read kitsch as a diagnostic tool for thinking through such a "fully formed cultural tradition". This is particularly suggestive for contemplating the meaning of the extensive archive of popular portrayal of Muslims as "quiet, kind, slow-speaking, fatalistic and passive" (Jeppie 1988: 3). These familiar images of "Malays" therefore construct Muslims as an instantly recognisable phenomenon.

At the same time, I do not wish simply to dismiss the phenomenon of popular fascination with images of Muslims in South Africa. There may in fact be a "folk critique" at work in these images. The repeated circling back to certain soothing images of enslaved Muslims at a time when dominant culture was suppressing allusions to the brutality of slavery, the intimacy of many with these images, and the insistence that they are harmless, comforting and pleasurable, is richly suggestive. What do these images offer solace from? How do they relate to "folk amnesia" regarding memories of slavery (Wicomb 1998: 100)? The throwaway, disregarded and overlooked presence of kitsch images of Muslims can therefore be read not only as a reflection of a culture, but as an insistent and revealing relation to it.

Do I seek in this book to trace images that "speak back" to the history of infantilising, quietist and picturesque images of Muslims? To render visible previously overlooked experiences is a venerable aim in postcolonial writing, yet I do not limit myself to this. Instead, I explore how the imperial script about Islam became normative. This complex challenge is conveyed in the last story of looking I describe here.

In an intriguing trope, the cooks I interviewed for the chapter about Muslim food revealed in their descriptions of learning recipes a kind of gaze turned back, but obliquely, without being seen to look, a technique of simultaneous observation and subversion they described as "stealing with the eye" and "catching with the eye". This agile and questing gaze is suggested by the image of the woman on the cover of *Regarding Muslims*, a "Malay Bride" portrayed by the South African modernist painter Irma Stern, whose sideways glance is complex and questioning, refusing to easily accept the regard of the viewer.

Drawing on these stories of looking, I argue that South African popular culture's long fascination with images of Muslims and the various ways in which these images have been resisted and transformed, reflects a demotic grappling with history. Hence my exploration of practices of regarding Muslims and their role in shaping the country's history and culture.

Recursive beginnings

Political time is short. Cultural time is ... glacial.

– Stuart Hall (cited in Frankenberg and Mani 1993: 304)

On 5 August 1996, the front pages of the *Cape Times* and *The Argus* newspapers in Cape Town were dominated by a story about the murder of a gang leader named Rashaad Staggie, allegedly by members of a vigilante group called People against Gangsterism and Drugs (Pagad).[1] In the preceding months, Pagad had established a public presence through a series of marches by thousands of its members through the city, simultaneously proclaiming a broad, pan-religious appeal while also drawing on specifically Muslim prayers and iconography in its activities. The news stories about the 4 August slaying and the role of Pagad contained striking photographs of Muslims that diverged strongly from the picturesque convention usually used to frame Islam in South Africa. As noted above, while Muslims were generally presented as benign, exotic and decorative, the Pagad images showed them as masked, militant and threatening.

The Pagad images in August 1996 were extraordinarily vivid and powerful, and their appearance on the front pages helped several national newspapers to sell out their print runs in the week that followed.[2] The effect of the photographs was due partly to their inversion of the picturesque. They jarred loose a centuries-long pattern of discourse depicting Muslims as passive and submissive. Yet, as I show in Chapter 5, the vision of Islam in the Pagad images also accorded with a powerful international idiom about militant Islam. This took hold in the South African media after the country's isolation came to an end in 1994, when international investment in local media subjected news organs simultaneously to the pressures of political transformation and the commercial imperative to increase revenues. The effect of the images also stemmed from a long-held local anxiety about the place of Muslims in South Africa. The Pagad photographs are therefore a palimpsest of the country's conventions for viewing Islam and prompted the research that led to this book.

Islam poses a paradox in South Africa. Today, Muslims form an integral part of the post-apartheid nation and are visibly represented in politics, education, business, the media and the arts, even though they make up less than two per cent of the country's population (Tayob 2002: 20). Despite this significant public profile, the history of Islam in the country is not widely known and Muslims are often portrayed in circumscribed ways in South African popular culture. The paradox of being disproportionately visible yet strangely overlooked gives Islam an *ambiguous visibility*. The form of such visibility is also distinctive. In images of weddings, funerals and pilgrimage, Muslims have been staged since the eighteenth century as marginal and exotic, yet paradoxically also necessary figures in the colonial and, later, the national imaginary. South African cookbooks, popular histories, cartoons, travel writing and news stories often feature picturesque and tranquil Muslim figures. However, Islam is also associated with anxieties around coded and occult practices, reflected in long-held beliefs in Muslim women's ability to "gool" (use magic powers) and the tendency of Muslim men toward sudden violence, or running "amok". This conception of Muslims as alternately benign and threatening resonates in some ways with international conventions for portraying Islam, but the pattern in South Africa has distinctive features.

In this book I show how the portrayal of Muslims as placid and marginal has served a crucial rhetorical function. I also explore the largely unremarked role that Muslims have played in the formation of South Africa's history and culture. It is not possible to fully understand enduring concepts of race, sexuality and belonging in the country today, I argue, without attending to the crucible of colonialism, slavery and Islam in which they were formed.

In rewriting the place of Muslims in South Africa, I revisit the concept of "beginnings" in the sense proposed by Edward Said, who theorised a distinction between *beginnings* and *origins*. He asserts that origins derive their authority from being "divine, mythical and privileged", while beginnings are "secular and humanly produced" (Said 1975: 373). Bearing an inherent claim to authority, "an origin centrally dominates what derives from it whereas a beginning ... encourages nonlinear development" (Said 1975: 373). This distinction is critical to my project. South Africa's history is viewed largely through the prism of apartheid, the devastating system of legislated racial discrimination that operated from 1948 to 1994. The impact of slavery has receded behind these crucial and more recent traumas. Consequently, the colonial period is seen as "a mere prologue to the more interesting and more important and dramatic forging of a modern capitalist economy" (Worden and Crais 1994: 2). Given that the Cape was colonised two centuries before the northern part of South Africa, a period during which slavery shaped all social and economic relations, it is hard to overstate the importance of the institution of slavery for shaping the colonial and, later, the apartheid history of the country (Worden 1985: 4). I revisit this origin and demonstrate the significance of slavery and the colonial period for apartheid and the contemporary era.

It is in this mode of rethinking founding narratives that this book claims South Africa's relationship to Islam not as an *origin* but as a *beginning*. I consider the role of Muslims in the formation of the country's racial and sexual codes during the colonial period in South Africa, a traumatic beginning that is often overwritten by other narratives. I do not question the significance of apartheid; rather, I attempt to articulate its crucial continuities with the colonial period. This book writes Muslims into a new beginning for South Africa, not through an additive approach that inserts them into the formation of the South African "rainbow nation", but by showing that in addition to land displacement, war and the genocide of the Khoisan, the country was fundamentally shaped by the convergence of slavery and Islam. I explore the role of Muslims in the "primal scene" of slavery in South Africa, and propose that slavery and Islam combine to form a South African *beginning*.

Slavery as a starting point

Slavery and Islam are intricately connected in South Africa. Muslims first arrived in the Cape Colony in 1658 as slaves and free servants of the Dutch, only six years after the Colony's founding. This makes slavery and the arrival of Muslims coterminous with the beginning of colonial settlement in South Africa. However, slavery is not just the temporal starting point for this study. The historian Nigel Worden points out that slavery shaped all social relations in the Cape Colony and its hinterland; for significant periods between 1658 and emancipation in 1834, slaves in fact formed the majority of the population of the Cape Colony (Worden 1985: 4; Dooling 2007: 7).

Islam arrived in South Africa in the context of colonial settlement and slavery. In 1652, the Dutch East India Company (Verenigde Oostindische Compagnie or VOC) established a refueling station at the Cape to serve its trade in spices from Asia. Importantly, the Cape also marked a crucial point on the slave route from East Africa to the Americas (Da Costa and Davids 1994: 3). Unlike colonies in the New World, the Cape settlement was not initially aimed at colonial expansion; its purpose was solely to provision ships engaged in the Dutch shipping routes to the East (Worden 1994: 9). However, the activities of the Dutch soon encroached on the land of the Khoi and San, the indigenous people of the Cape, who resisted the latter's attempts to conscript them as labour for the Company. Because the VOC forbade the *enslavement* of indigenous people, the Company resorted to the use of imported slave labour, and enslaved people were brought to the Cape at first from West Africa, and subsequently from territories around the Indian Ocean (Worden 1985: 7).

The first Muslims to arrive at the Cape in 1658 were the Mardyckers of Amboya in the East Indies, who were brought as soldiers to support the Dutch in the face of Khoisan resistance (Tayob 1999: 22). However, it was as slaves that the vast majority of Muslims were deployed to the colony. Initially, the VOC acquired slaves from the Dutch West India Company, which was deeply involved in the slave trade to the Americas. Most of the enslaved people were brought to the Cape Colony from the Indian Ocean region, including from East Africa, the African islands of the Indian Ocean, and South and South-east Asia (Worden 1985: 8). The Dutch exploited nodes of an existing slave trade established by the Portuguese, and people were captured as slaves in Mozambique, Madagascar, India and territories in South-east Asia to be brought to the Cape (Bradlow and Cairns 1978; Botha 1969 [1928]). Over the course of almost two centuries of slave-holding society at the Cape, the enslaved population came to number more than 60 000 people (Ross 1999: 6).

Islam was the religion of most enslaved people at the Cape; in addition, there was a high rate of conversion among indigenous people, who were subject to conditions as brutal to slavery (Bradlow and Cairns 1978). According to Worden, Islam offered enslaved people "a degree of independent slave culture" separate from that of slave-owners (Worden, 1985: 4). Andrew Bank found that slaves created spaces outside of the paternalistic slave household in which to exercise agency, including through the practice of Islam (1995: 184). For instance, "ratiep", a ritual piercing of the skin by adepts who appeared to feel no pain , could be read as "an active expression of control over the body through denial of physical pain" (Bank 1995: 184). Even more powerfully, "ratiep" could be seen as a coded "rejection of their owners' claims over their bodies" (Mason quoted in Bank 1995: 184). Islam and slavery were so intimately connected in this period that the word "Malay", which refers to the lingua franca of Bahasa Melayu spoken by enslaved people at the Cape, who had come from different territories around the Indian Ocean, became the word for "Muslim" at the Cape. Because of this history, slavery remains central to the meanings that Islam holds even in contemporary South Africa.

During the period of Dutch control at the Cape, enslaved people were owned by the VOC, with some the private property of free burghers. In addition, there was a small number of "Free Blacks" in the Cape, who were either manumitted slaves or people who had arrived as free servants from Batavia, the VOC headquarters in Asia (Worden, Van Heyningen and Bickford-Smith 1998: 64). Included among Muslims brought to the Cape were leaders exiled from South-east Asia, where their role in driving resistance had proved an obstacle to Dutch trade and colonial expansion. Among these leaders was Sheikh Yusuf, who arrived in the Cape in 1694. Exiles such as Sheikh Yusuf were isolated in remote areas outside Cape Town to reduce the risk of their influencing Muslim slaves. Despite this, according to oral tradition, these figures became beacons for runaway slaves, and "the memory of these political exiles and prominent personalities became an important part of Muslim religious consciousness and practices" (Tayob 1999: 23).[3] Abdulkader Tayob points out that 1694 was the date chosen by local organisers to mark the three-hundredth anniversary of Islam in South Africa, rather than the date of the earlier arrival of the Mardyckers, a sign of the complexity of the place of Islam in South Africa.

This history includes both resistance to colonialism and the recruitment of Muslims to enforce colonial rule (Tayob 1999: 23). While the vast majority of Muslims were brought to the Cape as slaves, the Mardyckers arrived as soldiers to support the Dutch against Khoisan resistance. According to Tayob, the mass celebrations of the tri-centenary anniversary were "a significant indication of how Shaykh Yusuf had been adopted as a symbol of Muslim presence in the country and Islamic resistance to colonialism and apartheid" (1999: 23). The earlier presence of the Mardyckers, on the other hand, signalled a more ambiguous role, in which complex local politics led to both resistance to Dutch settlement and collaboration with it.

The way in which slavery has been remembered in South Africa is a crucial subject, addressed in Pumla Gqola's ground-breaking study *What Is Slavery To Me? Postcolonial/slave memory in post-apartheid South Africa* (2010). Gqola gives nuanced attention to the shifting meanings of memories of slavery and their articulations with race and sexuality in the post-apartheid period. Studies of South African history written before 1980 assumed that the role of slavery in the Cape was minor and its character relatively "mild" (Keegan 1996: 16). A range of popular texts from cookbooks to landscape paintings also reflected this benign view of the colony's system of forced labour. It was only in the 1980s that significant new scholarship on slavery in South Africa countered these assumptions and demonstrated that slave labour was in fact central to both the economy and the culture of the Cape Colony (Worden 1985: 7). Because of the high proportion of male slaves to male colonists, colonial society at the Cape had an intense fear of slave resistance; consequently, slaves were disciplined through "the massive use of judicial force" (Ross 1983: 2). Enslaved people owned by private burghers were subjected to "violent and extreme" punishments (Worden 1985: 4). Thus it is notable that a system characterised by the exercise of brutal control was portrayed as mild and picturesque, a system of representation I analyse in Chapter 1.

Historical records show that colonists had a compulsive anxiety about slave rebellion, poisoning and theft, though the most common forms of slave resistance were escape and flight (Dooling 2007: 12; Penn 1999). Nonetheless, insurrection remained a "paranoic fear" among Cape slave-owners and, as a result, they often used brutal displays of violence as a disciplining mechanism (Hall 2000: 24). In 1754, a slave code based on the Batavian model (also known as the Statutes of India) was instituted in the Cape Colony to control the perceived dangers posed by the slave population (Worden, Van Heyningen and

Bickford-Smith 1998: 60). In an attempt to "curb plots", the code stipulated the numbers of slaves who could gather together. Slaves were also required to carry "passes" signed by their masters to enter the town or ascend Table Mountain (Worden, Van Heyningen and Bickford-Smith 1998: 60). This means of surveillance and control over the movement of black people later became the basis of laws that constricted mobility in the apartheid era, when all black men (and later black women) were required to carry passes in one of the most intrusive and destructive elements of the apartheid system.

To the colonial gaze, the sight of large numbers of black people thus evoked the unsettling trope of slave rebellion. Such anxieties helped to shape not only social relations, but the built environment of the colony. John Mason confirms that slaves at the Cape were subjected to "almost constant surveillance" (2003: 110) and kept "within the reach of their masters' and mistresses' eyes, tongues, and hands" (2003: 108). In an "archaeology of absences" conducted into the colonial Cape, Martin Hall showed that the intimate presence of slaves and Khoisan serfs shaped the architecture of colonial-era farms and the city. The fear of arson by runaway slaves influenced both the built and natural environment on farms, including the placement not only of houses and slave quarters, but also trees, rocks, and crops (Hall 2000: 198). The landscape of the Cape was thus marked by the anxiety generated by the presence of enslaved people.

Prior to 1804, the public observance of Islam under the Batavian Code was severely constrained, although the Dutch eventually tacitly tolerated Muslim practices. Many burghers encouraged the conversion of their slaves to Islam, as the law of matrilineal descent allowed the enslavement of children of Muslim slaves, but not Christian ones (Shell 1997: 272). Slave-owners also believed that Muslim slaves were more reliable and "less unruly" due to Islam's prohibition on the consumption of alcohol (Ross 1993: 17). Nevertheless, precisely because Islam offered enslaved people the possibility of an interior life and a communal space outside of the control of slave-owners, the observance of the religion was regarded with ambivalence by the Dutch, and the public practice of Muslim rituals was punishable by death (Theal 1905: 1–2; Worden, Van Heyningen and Bickford-Smith 1998: 77; Tayob 1999: 24, Ingsoll 2003: 375). In this context, Islam survived through hidden practices that shaped communal relations, language and food rituals that survive among descendants of slaves and in the broader South African culture even today. The nature of the relation between internal practices and their larger meaning is of particular interest in this book.

The hidden nature of Islamic observance changed in 1804 when the Dutch colonial authorities, seeking the loyalty of Muslims in the face of an impending British invasion, granted them freedom of religion for the first time. According to Tayob, despite the constrictions that Muslims faced during the colonial period, they developed institutions such as the first school for black people in South Africa, established in 1793 (1999: 28); the first mosque (the Awwal mosque) in 1798 (24); and the first written texts in Afrikaans, using Arabic script, in 1856 (28). With this history of deeply coded rituals, and because of the conventional tradition of representing slavery at the Cape in a picturesque tradition, representations of Islam in the colonial context must thus be read critically.

In the dominant picturesque mode seen in landscape paintings in the nineteenth century, the violence of the slave-holding Cape Colony was rendered into a pleasing and domesticated view. In contrast to indigenous people, who resisted forced labour and were consequently decried by settlers as "idle" and "volatile", "Malay" slaves were portrayed in such paintings as skilled, reliable and compliant, while also mysterious and exotic (Coetzee 1988: 28). An over-determined visibility of Islam through which Muslims were represented as complicit with the desires of white colonists became crucial to the conventional portrayal of a pleasing colonial cityscape. The picturesque tradition led to a heightened but ambiguous visibility for Islam in the Cape and continued into the mid-twentieth century. In the chapters on landscape painting and food that follow, I trace the limited repertoire of images of Muslims that arose during the colonial and apartheid eras, and show the development of an increasingly complex view of Islam in the post-apartheid period.

Islam and race

Islam has an intricate history of race in South Africa. Given that slave labour was crucial to the survival of the colony, the impact of slavery on the practice of Islam and on the subsequent history of South Africa has been profound. The Muslim community at the Cape developed its character and practices under conditions of enslavement, enforced prostitution, colonial rule and the fraught post-emancipation period. Islam became a refuge for enslaved people as well as for indigenous Khoi and San people, who consequently formed a creole slave and indigenous Muslim community at the Cape. The ability of this community to absorb people of different origins has left a legacy of racial indeterminability in the South African meaning of the word "Muslim". However, this inclusive history was subsequently overwritten by the racialising imperatives of Dutch and British imperialism and, later, apartheid – during which Muslims became subject to shifting discourses of race.

The enslaved people brought by the Dutch to the Cape became known as "Malays"; even today, the descendants of slaves at the Cape are often called (and name themselves) "Cape Malays". While this suggests a geographical origin in Malaysia, the term has a more complex set of connotations.[4] Enslaved people at the Cape were brought from several territories around the Indian Ocean, including Mozambique, Madagascar, India and South-east Asia, and spoke a variety of African and Asian languages (Shell 1994: xxv; Bradlow and Cairns 1978). As noted earlier, Bahasa Melayu was a lingua franca in the Indian Ocean region and also became a common language among slaves in the Cape. Several strands of meaning therefore converge in the eventual use in the Cape Colony of the word "Malay" for Muslim. As Kerry Ward points out, "[a]t the Cape, the term Malay could mean Muslim, or could refer to a linguistic group, or could be a geographical designation of place of origin. It was only by the end of the VOC period that the term Malay began to lose its direct link to forced migration and became more exclusively tied to the fact of being Muslim" (2012: 86). Derived from the use of Bahasa Melayu and eventually coming to mean "Muslim", the term "Malay" is also shadowed by the history of enforced migration and enslavement.

The use of the word "Malay" for Muslim during the colonial period is distinct from its use under apartheid as the racial category "Cape Malay" or "Malay". In this book, I use the term "Malay" for Muslim in its historical context, specifically alluding to the relation of slavery to Islam. I do not intend to connote its contemporary meanings, which place "Malay" within the apartheid racial category of "Colouredness", and which is consequently used to distinguish between "Indian" and "Malay" Muslims. In addition, I do not intend my use of the historical term "Malay" (which included people from East Africa, India and South-east Asia) to suggest that the people known as "Cape Malays" in contemporary parlance are the exemplary Muslims in this book, nor that the Western Cape, the home of most people who were categorised as "Cape Malay" under apartheid, is the representative space of Islam in South Africa. I do show, however, that the Western Cape province, which covers most of the historical territory of the Cape Colony, was the locus of colonial slavery and (not coincidentally) is the province where most, but not all Muslims in South Africa live. Unreflective extrapolation from the Cape to the whole of South Africa is a legitimate concern and overwrites the different regional histories of Islam.

Cape exceptionalism and overgeneralisation are serious problems for grappling with the history and contemporary impact of slavery (Jeppie 2001: 81; Jacobs 2002: online). This book focuses on images of Islam in the Cape, but does not claim that these discussions are representative for the whole of South Africa. On the other hand, I find an equal danger in regarding the Cape as exceptional and marginal, which has resulted in the neglect of slavery in conceptions of broader South African history. Such neglect does a grave injustice to a critical part of the country's history, and has had the effect of rendering indigenous and enslaved people's experiences during the colonial period marginal and invisible. This runs the risk of transforming slavery and the genocide of the Khoisan into minority topics, viewed as not authentically "African" or "South African" enough and a superficial distraction from the needs of the African majority. Rather, the current racialisation of Muslims is a *consequence* of the colonial period, and the fact that South Africa's experience of slavery is characterised by specificity is simply one more reason to address its complexities. Both exceptionalism and overgeneralisation of the Cape are therefore problematic phenomena which I take care to avoid. I demonstrate below how a picturesque view of slavery and Islam, which constituted a sense of exceptionalism and exoticism about Muslim slaves, has helped to mute public understanding of the role of the crucial phenomenon of slavery in constituting contemporary South Africa.

Slavery in the Cape was abolished in 1834 under British rule. Vivian Bickford-Smith shows that in the post-emancipation period, factors such as economic hardship, the impact of white exclusion, and laws such as the Liquor Act combined to undercut the development of a unified black identity in Cape Town and instead encouraged separate "Malay", Coloured and African identities (1995). Black Capetonians were legally divided into enslaved and enserfed people, but nonetheless found grounds for connections under similar conditions of labour, oppression and violence (Jeppie 2001: 83). However, Shamil Jeppie notes that post-emancipation official discourses concerning religion overrode such relations, and "all the evidence of creolisation, ethnic interaction, cultural exchange between the slaves, and newly-forged identities in the setting of the slave society of urban Cape Town was rejected" (2001: 84). Instead, a sense of ontological differences among blacks was encouraged. As a consequence, despite extensive relations during enslavement, as a result of the use of religion as a mechanism of racial division in the period after emancipation, a sense of immutable difference developed between "Muslims-as-Malay" and "Christians-as-Coloured" (Jeppie 2001: 83).

Images of "Malays" played a significant role in the constitution of such differences. In the course of the nineteenth century, "Malays" were increasingly portrayed as quaint, enigmatic and distinct from others (Jeppie 1988: 8). Robert Ross confirms that from the mid-nineteenth century, popular portrayals featured "the growing image of the 'Malays' ... as mysterious and exotic" (1999: 140).

The construction of separate racialised religious identities in the nineteenth century was followed in the twentieth century by the "reinvention" of "Malays" along racial lines, particularly in the Cape, a project to which the work of the Afrikaans linguist and folklorist I. D. du Plessis was central (Jeppie 1988: 8). In his popular book *The Cape Malays* (1972), Du Plessis articulated a racial theory of the "Malays" which he extrapolated from descriptions of the body to the mind to the constitution of a "Malay" race. This theory was given a sense of historical depth through the use of nineteenth-century paintings of picturesque "Malays" from George French Angas' *The Kafirs Illustrated* (1849). Far from simply purveying a harmless romanticism, Du Plessis's work disrupted the furthering of a broader black identity and helped to "fragment the development of autonomous political movements among the coloureds" (Jeppie 2001: 88). The ethnicising and racialising of Islam that had started in the immediate post-emancipation period thus foundered in the face of the racial instability of the term "Malay", but it has had lastingly damaging effects.

In 1950, the Nationalist government passed the Population Registration Act, the foundation of apartheid, which created three legal racial categories: white, Coloured and native, into which all South Africans would be assigned.[5] According to the 1959 extension of the Population Registration

Act, four groups were established: white, Coloured, Indian and native, and the sub-category "Cape Malay" fell into the "Coloured" racial group. While the post-apartheid censuses have continued the use of racial categories inherited from apartheid, there is a danger in retrospectively racialising and ethnicising Islam. Islam was first practiced in South Africa within a creole slave community subjected to systemic sexual violence through the enforced prostitution of female slaves in the Slave Lodge. As a consequence, racial heterogeneity was structured into the experience of being Muslim and enslaved. Both colonial and apartheid-era accounts confirm Islam's confounding effect on race due to racial heterogeneity and conversion, through which anyone could become "Malay" through professing adherence to the tenets of the religion.[6] During apartheid, the phenomenon of conversion highlighted the problem of drawing lines of race by means of religion, since whites who converted to Islam lost their whiteness (Posel 2001). While this demonstrates the apartheid government's keen interest in protecting the purity of whiteness, the idea of pure blackness is also troubled by the malleability of Muslim identity caused by conversion. Because of this history, the topic of Islam and race cannot be approached in a solipsistic manner.[7]

The racialisation of Muslims as "Coloured", "Indian" or "Cape Malay" has had the effect of transforming slavery, which was the dominant social force in colonial South Africa for 176 years, into a minority, and therefore minor, subject. Cast as a "Malay" or, at most, a "Coloured" issue, slavery has been seen as exceptional to broader South African history. In a historic injustice, this "minor" status gives to slavery connotations of pathos or exoticism, and diminishes its general and national significance even further. As a result, slavery has been seen as part of a distant and picturesque past that turns slaves into exotic and "timeless" people, rather than "the first modern people" of southern Africa (C. L. R. James cited in Hofmeyr 2007: 5). In addition to misrepresenting a crucial part of the country's history, this poses the risk that people classified after emancipation as "Coloured" are not fully included in the national South African narrative, which can generate self-ethnicising and further fracture. In fact, South Africa has a uniquely inclusive history of Islam – and an informed debate would embrace the complexities of this beginning. To retrospectively assign a race to Muslims is to accede to apartheid's fantasy of racial separateness. The danger of minoritising slavery and ethnicising Islam is that it undermines a general and critically important history.

To make this argument does not mean one can ignore the fact that the lives of Muslims in South Africa are crucially influenced by race. Abdulkader Tayob points out that race significantly shapes the experience of being Muslim in South Africa. Islam is frequently assumed to supersede the influence of class, language, ethnicity and history – as though Muslims are somehow exempted from such factors. Erasing attention to specificity and variation among Muslims creates the erroneous perception of a singular Muslim community. Instead, as Tayob notes, "Muslims in the various racial categories of apartheid South Africa experience Islam in very different ways" (2002: 20; Bangstad 2007).

I use the term "Muslim" without intending it to mean "Malay" in the apartheid sense, and place the latter in quotation marks to highlight its sensitive and contentious history. At the same time, following Tayob, I do not claim a uniform experience for all Muslims in South Africa. Historically, one third of those labeled "Malay" had East African origins; another third came from South Asia (India), and the last third from Indonesia and Malaya. Given the layered meanings to the words Muslim and "Malay", I do not use the latter as an exclusionary measure to ignore the contributions of "Indian" Muslims such as the writers Zuleikha Mayat, Shaida Kazie Ali and Imraan Coovadia, nor African Muslims such as Mphutlane wa Bofelo and Malika Ndlovu. Instead, I follow the argument of Zimitri Erasmus that colouredness in South Africa is a "kind of black[ness]" that encompasses specific histories and experiences within the larger category of "black" (Erasmus: 2001b). I regard the contemporary terms "Malay", "African" and "Indian" Muslims as referring to *kinds of Muslimness*. The writers I discuss in this book have been variously labeled Indian, coloured, white and "Malay", demonstrating that the terms "Muslim" and "Malay" have very permeable boundaries. Nadia Davids and Zubeida Jaffer do not identify with being either "Malay" or Indian, although their family histories mean that they could qualify as both. Rustum Kozain's mother is a convert to Islam from Christianity (under apartheid, she would have been classified as "Coloured" and, with conversion, become "Malay"). When he converted to Islam in 1964, Tatamkhulu Afrika reclassified himself from white to "Malay".

Islam as racial instability

The relation of Muslims to race continues to be shaped by tropes established under apartheid. This has to do with a paucity of knowledge about the history of Islam in the country, and the complexity of the term "Coloured", under which most Muslims were categorised after emancipation and under apartheid. In the racial hierarchy of apartheid, "Colouredness" formed the interstitial zone between "native" and "white". A site of acute anxiety, this zone was intensively policed. Its apartheid definition was as follows: "A Coloured person is a person who is not a white person nor a native". Defined solely through negatives, "Colouredness" was imbued with ambiguity. Islam gave added detail to the meaning of this interstitial racial category.

To grasp the investment in racial purity and separateness during the later colonial period and apartheid, one has to recall the unprecedented racial heterogeneity that resulted from the diverse origins of the Cape's populace, and the sexual violence of the slave-holding system. The population of the Cape and particularly enslaved people in the Colony constituted one of the most racially heterogeneous communities in the world at the time. The term "Coloured" had been used since the beginning of the Colony to refer to a group of people consisting of Free Blacks, manumitted slaves and the Khois-an community during slavery. After 1834, this group burgeoned to include former slaves. In the post-emancipation period, the much larger number of people included in the category meant that Colouredness became laden with disquiet for white colonial society, particularly because of the political rami-fications of a coalescing black identity.

"Colouredness" in South Africa has always exemplified unease around "race purity" and identity (Posel, 2001: 56). Through the Population Reg-istration Act, the apartheid government attempted to give finite meanings to the terms white, Coloured and native, but it immediately faced the ad-ministrative and discursive elusiveness of naming and fixing race. After the passage of the Act in 1950, the task of assigning a legal racial category to twenty million South Africans was given at first to census-takers, but the scale of the undertaking soon meant that the government assigned all public servants to administer the labelling of race (Posel, 2001: 58). The use of poorly trained bureaucrats heightened the arbitrariness of decisions about racial classicification, and the apartheid state struggled particularly with the legal implications of "Colouredness". The term's blurred edges created the possibility of "reclassification", or the movement from one racial identity to another. In effect, "Colouredness" was the *fluid middle* of the racial hierarchy in South Africa that revealed the permeability of whiteness and blackness.

Thiven Reddy argues that apartheid's hierarchical system of racial cat-egorisation, with white and black at its furthest extremes, was paradoxically both subverted and sustained by the indeterminacy of the term "Coloured" (2001: 65). In contrast to the proclaimed stability of blackness and whiteness, Colouredness represented the "'impure', mixed, the borderline, the unclas-sifiable [and] the doubtful" (2001: 68). To Reddy, the category was therefore both "the extreme Other of dominant racial discourse in South Africa, and also ... its very ambivalent core" (2001: 68). In this formulation, Coloured-ness stood for the stresses, contradictions and evasions produced by the impossibility of racial purity, and its indeterminacy provided a despised but necessary flexibility that absorbed the strains of the system. Coloured people were seen as "residual, in-between or lesser ... lacking, supplementary, exces-sive, inferior or simply non-existent" (Erasmus 2001a: 15). Both because it was central to the system of racial classification, and because it was inherently destructive to this system, "Coloured" identity was among the most heavily policed concepts during apartheid, and, significantly, also during the earlier colonial period. In fact, Reddy argues that there was an important continuity between the colonial and apartheid systems of race classification (2001: 65). Under the British, the shifting but nonetheless carefully marked differences of colour in the Cape were given legal status that "formalised" these differences into racial ones (Keegan 1996: 24). In 1959, the apartheid government refined its definition of this interstitial category, dividing the term "Coloured" into "Cape Coloured, Cape Malay, Griqua, Indian, Chinese, 'other Asiatic', and 'Other Coloured'" (Reddy, 2001: 75). The proliferation of terms for naming race only emphasised the tenuousness of racial classification.

While "Coloured" skin was the focus of anxious vilification for marking racial impurity and embodying the instability of race, Islam provided a small but crucial detail to this picture. Muslims formed part of the "Coloured" centre that was intended to stabilise the meanings of blackness and whiteness; however, in the official apartheid view "Malays" signaled a promise of purity, rather than the despised "mixedness" of "Colouredness". Compared with the supposed "lack" of Colouredness, Malays were associated with a *plenitude* of meaning. The rituals of "Malay" life, from clothing to festivities, were used to assert a sense of the cultural and *racial* distinctiveness of the "Malays" (Jeppie 2001: 87). However, the racial indeterminability of Muslims also formed part of the uneasy indeterminability of Colouredness. In the official discourse,

19

"Malays" functioned as benevolent fillers between whites and "natives," continuing a role established during the colonial period. As noted above, the 1959 Extension of the Population Registration Act also created the separate category of "Indians", who had previously been included in "Colouredness". Muslims could be either "Indian" or "Malay". The similarly complex racial term "Indian" was also envisioned as a buffer between native and white.

The terms "slave," "Free Black" and "Malay" (Muslim) thus introduced a critical racial instability into South Africa, which was carried in the post-emancipation period by the label "Coloured". Due to Islam's racial heterogeneity as a result of sexual violence under slavery and the encouragement of conversion, being Muslim could include enslaved, free, black, slave-owner, burger, white, Coloured, Dutch, British, indigenous, African, Asian and European people. The question "who is Muslim in South Africa?" thus carries with it a founding (and confounding) racial puzzle.

Belated conversations and critical interruptions

Conversations about slavery in South Africa are perennially belated (Worden 1985), with Pumla Gqola's trailblazing work the first full-length study of the cultural legacy of slavery in South Africa. Her book extends the insights of an exceptionally strong tradition of radical history in South Africa into the area of culture. Gqola is not alone in such complex analyses; she joins the ranks of historians who have given the most sustained and theoretically sophisticated attention to slavery (their work was also central to resisting apartheid as an intellectual project).

The University of Cape Town is a renowned centre of scholarship on South African slavery, and historians at the university have fundamentally shaped the field.[8] In the face of the stubbornly trivialising tone of images of slavery in popular culture, their work and that of others has been central to asserting the importance of slavery as a force in South African history and as a scholarly field.

Even in history, however, scholarship on slavery in South Africa has trailed at least thirty years behind that of revisionist work elsewhere (Worden and Crais 1994: 3) and despite the excellent record of recent South African historical scholarship, the role of slavery and Islam in the country's formation remains little discussed today outside the academy, a situation that has had grave consequences. The relative invisibility of slavery is exacerbated by a discursive problem. The unique features of slavery in South Africa, including the fact that two-thirds of the enslaved people at the Cape came from Asia, have made slavery subject to the problem of exceptionalism, in the sense that South Africa's experience of slavery appears to be an Asian rather than an African phenomenon. The specific nature of slavery at the Cape has been used to portray it as atypical or unrepresentative of South Africa. As a result, it has been hard to show that slavery is an integral and fundamental part of the country's history. The dominant Atlantic mode of slavery studies has only recently been supplemented by attention to the history of slavery in the Indian Ocean region, which has bolstered interest in this element of South Africa's past.

The most important reason for this neglect of slavery, however, is the trivialising effect of the picturesque mode, an aesthetic tradition that has ensured that the brutal system of slavery at the Cape continues to be seen as "mild" and to confer a benign beginning to colonial settlement in South Africa. Thanks to the prevalence of the image of the submissive "Malay" slave in the visual tradition in South Africa, enslaved people have been envisioned as figures of exoticism or pathos, abstracted from history and functioning solely to add depth and distinctiveness to white subjectivity. The power of these colonial-era discourses is still evident today, aided by the myth of an "empty land", which denied the presence of indigenous people before colonial settlement.[9] It is a major aim of this book to critique the effects of the picturesque mode and demonstrate the necessity of reading slavery differently.

To counter the silences about slavery, I engage in a respectful "argument with history", defined by the poet and literary scholar Yvette Christiansë as a way "to bring to the fore a voice for which there is no discursive place in any formal history" (2006: 303). This approach is exemplified in the work of feminist literary scholars such as Zoë Wicomb, Pumla Gqola and Meg Samuelson and engages with the cultural significance of slavery by drawing on historical scholarship without ceding authority to the latter. Both literary scholars and historians acknowledge generative relationships between the disciplines.[10] Productive interactions between literature and history include Pumla Gqola's 2010 study, which theorises a radical role for memory and imaginative reclamations of slavery, Sarah Nuttall and Cheryl Ann Michael's application of Robert Shell's historical scholarship in formulating their concept of "intimacies" in South African culture (2000) and the novelist Zoë Wicomb's rewriting of both literary history and historical scholarship on colouredness in her novel *David's Story* (2001).

It is apposite to consider the role of literature in public knowledge about slavery. Literary studies can contribute significantly to current debates on slavery and Islam in the context of enormous gaps in the documentary sources on slavery – for instance, the near complete absence of slave narratives at the Cape.[11] Literature offers a capacity to read absence and trace, treating the lessons of etymology and fiction as serious textual sources. Few can doubt the profound intellectual contribution of fictional works such as Toni Morrison's *Beloved*, Bessie Head's *A Question of Power* and Zoë Wicomb's *David's Story* to our understanding of the past through their powerful subversion of nationalist histories and fiction.[12] Literature is hospitable to the "the everyday, the ordinary and the seemingly insignificant", and imaginative works "shed light on broader questions of subjectivity and political expression" (Lewis 2002: 392). The literary realm derives acute insights from what may be envisioned from traces and fissures, even the "illegitimate meanings" that emerge from them (Wicomb quoted in Woodward, Hayes and Minkley 2002: xxxi). Poets, novelists and literary scholars have generated new theoretical insights by crafting imaginative works from historical archives and the voices absent from them. Such scholars have written insightfully about the necessary expansiveness of literature in overcoming the distortions of the archive, while also cautioning against the risks of writing "redemptive" narratives about subaltern subjects and treating "private" archives simply as positivistic data (Wicomb 1998; Christiansë 2006).

Literature cannot claim the exclusive ability to engage productively with silence, as J. B. Harley's "cartographic silences" and Martin Hall's "archaeology of absences" demonstrate. But radical feminist theatre, fiction and literary criticism have highlighted neglected elements of the past – such as slavery's legacy of sexual violence – and, importantly, brought them to a broader audience.[13] Literary scholars have critiqued history's "assurance" in speaking about the past, and the self-validating and unreflective stance of some social history scholarship (Lewis 2002: 267). Like Lewis, Nuttall and Michael charge some historians with "play[ing] down their presence, reflecting a romance of authenticity in which intellectuals begin to consider any intervention or mediation a betrayal of the subaltern consciousness or voice" (2000: 11). Perhaps the relation between history and literature might better be seen, following Gayatri Spivak, as a process in which the two "critically 'interrupt' each other, bring each other to crisis, in order to serve their constituencies, especially [that which] each seems to claim all for its own" (Spivak quoted in Woodward et al. 2002: xv).

My method of constituting the texts and reading practice for this book was to trace the trajectory of South African visual representations of Muslims in popular and literary fiction, travel writing, cookbooks, folktales, media and paintings. These texts include both formal and interstitial genres that hover between fiction and fact, and generate the kind of knowledge that fills in the spaces between more authoritative sources. I sought images of Muslims in little-noticed parts of South African culture and conducted interviews which drew forth views that otherwise would not register in the official archive on Muslims in South Africa. By attending to different forms, I was able to access a sense of the "voices and process through which Muslims imagined and constructed their own sense of community" (Jeppie 2001: 94). The stories, memories and jokes elicited in the interviews constitute parallel archives that show Muslims as complex figures, as makers rather than simply objects of meaning, and revealed how the "palimpsestic narrative of imperialism" became normative (Spivak 1988: 281). These texts operate between the evanescent and the concrete, and require a nuanced set of reading practices.

How not to be left with a simple picture

Drawing on both official and alternative archives, this book offers a long reading of the portrayal of Islam in South Africa. The aim is not simply to insert Muslims into South African history and culture, but to bring to the fore the role of slavery in the formation of South African culture. Revisionist projects such as this one face the unconscious temptation of redemptive narratives. Redemption, however, is always conditional. In this project, it would require Muslims to become impossibly pure figures and exemplary citizens at the risk of invisibility or exclusion. Indeed, as Arjun Appadurai argues, in the era of globalisation, the requirement of purity from minorities can become a motor of nationalist anxieties and violence (2006). However, myths about

Islam cannot simply be reversed by telling "truths" about Muslims. Indeed, as Mahmut Mutman observes, "Orientalism should not be understood as 'a structure of a lies or myths', which, once the truth about them were told, would simply go away" (1994: 24). To seek to correct images of Islam and abolish its impenetrability is part of the Orientalist fantasy, because it repeats the formula of linking Islam to inscrutability or violence, and embodies the very anxiety that it is trying to alleviate.

This book seeks neither form of redemption. Instead, I aim to offer a historically informed and complex view of Islam, neither picturesque nor redemptive, and through it, a fuller understanding of the making of contemporary South Africa. Consequently, I do not convey a heroic, nationalist counter-portrait of Muslims solely as part of anti-colonial resistance, the anti-apartheid struggle, or a contemporary anti-imperialist project. The picture of Islam in South Africa is in fact more complex and uneven.

What might a nuanced vision of Islam look like? In the book as a whole, I examine the history of representations of Islam in South Africa and tell a complex story of the place of Muslims in the South African national imaginary. I explore how the founding system of slavery in South Africa, which lasted from 1658 to 1834, came to be seen as marginal and exceptional to the national narrative. The book seeks to counter the invisibility of slavery in the public sphere and to revisit the place of Islam in the making of South African history and identity. I discuss slavery and Islam simultaneously, and sometimes apart.

There are always multiple aesthetic practices with their own intricate relations to history, of course. Certain representations of Islam resonate strongly with the history of images I outline above, others do not align with it, and some contest it. Already during the colonial and apartheid era there were other ways of speaking about Islam. Some of the texts I examine show that Muslims created alternative temporalities and spatialities during slavery, and that images of exotic Muslim food are haunted by a fear of poison and magic. Other texts speak in mobile registers, including satirical and experimental forms, and engage with the politics of a multi-polar world in which Islam is productively decentred without being marginalised.

In Chapter 1, I approach etymology as a set of linguistic landmarks and histories, pointing to the role of the racist term "kaffir" during the colonial period in rhetorically recasting indigeneity as corrupt and unfit, and delegitimising indigenous people's claim to the African landscape. Through this example of a word derived from Islamic practice but used as a racial label *for* Muslims, I show how the meanings and experiences of Islam have been transformed by the specific context of South Africa. I also demonstrate how the colonial view of Muslims evolved into the lexicon of apartheid and lingers in the post-apartheid period.

The political effects of the longstanding convention of a picturesque Islam portrays Muslims as perpetually exotic, abstracted from history, timeless and marginal. I show that since the colonial period, the figure of the picturesque "Malay" has helped to secure a sense of belonging for white settlers in the South African landscape. Characterised as industrious, placid and picturesque, the icon of the tranquil "Malay" slave anchors the myth that Cape slavery was "mild" and helps to craft an innocent beginning for colonial settlement.

In a discussion of Muslim food in Chapter 3, I explore tropes of spices and secrets, and demonstrate that the cuisine articulates dissonant meanings; for instance, the political history embedded in the Hertzoggie biscuit.

Chapter 4 discusses the impact of slavery on contemporary concepts of sexuality and gender, examining innovative visual and literary texts that unflinchingly confront slavery's sexual violence. The texts reveal the damaging and unaddressed legacy of slavery for concepts about sexuality for both women and men and shows that this has detrimental consequences for the country as a whole.

In 1996, news stories on Pagad created a frisson of recognition by overturning the picturesque mode and reviving the nineteenth-century image of the "fanatical" Oriental running "amok". The Pagad photographs articulated both a new and an old vision of Islam, while also drawing on an anachronistic international idiom focused on extremism and alienation. To better understand the impact of these images, Chapter 5 analyses the Pagad images and draws on interviews with journalists to understand the century-long oscillation between the images of the picturesque "Malay" and the "Oriental fanatic". This research establishes the influence of the Pagad stories on subsequent representations of Islam in South Africa, as well as the broadening of subsequent discussions.

In the last chapter, I explore artistic visions of Islam that connect with earlier dissident trajectories that deconstruct historical and colonial tropes. Such texts decline to create virtuous and redemptive Muslim figures and instead

re-imagine the place of Islam in a South African history and present. I conclude with an analysis of literature and art that re-imagine Islam in South
Africa in critical and provocative ways. Shaida Kazie Ali's *Not A Fairytale* and
Nadia Davids' *At Her Feet* craft feminist critiques of nationalist South African narratives and of patriarchy within Islam in politically ambitious and
formally innovative works. Rustum Kozain's poetry articulates a vision of
Muslim belonging in the South African landscape that does not claim prima-
cy over other communities. The book ends with Tatamkhulu Afrika's memoir
of his self-made Africanness, envisaged not as ethnocentric nor reliant on
skin colour, but as a reciprocally formed humanity attained through empathy, selflessness and activism. Afrika's memoir ultimately decentres Islam and
places the truly marginal, those who lack the redemption of either political
affiliation or religion, at the centre of his conception of justice and identity.

CHAPTER 1

Ambiguous Visibility:
Muslims and the making of visuality

Africa was not a new world.

– J. M. Coetzee (1988: 2)

Regarding the South African landscape

In *White Writing*, his influential study of landscape in South African literature, J. M. Coetzee argued that European colonists held an ontologically
tenuous grasp on the land. For settlers in South Africa, the landscape refused
to be blank and inscribable, denying a fantasy of a new Eden. Instead, the
African landscape was riven by a stubbornly anterior indigenous presence
that transformed colonists in South Africa into *belated* arrivals – newcomers,
temporary, passing. As a consequence, Coetzee observed, they were pecu-
liarly "unsettled settlers" (1988: 8).

This unsettling relationship is encoded in one of the earliest portrayals of the Cape after settlement began: a 1707 copperplate by P. van de Aa
titled *D'Almeida and his men killed by Hottentots on the shore of Table Bay
in 1510*. The image depicts a battle at the Cape almost two hundred years
before, provoked when Portuguese sailors kidnapped Khoi children and
stole cattle during negotiations about provisions (Gordon-Brown 1975: 5).
In the resulting battle with Khoisan warriors, the feared Portuguese general
Francisco D'Almeida, who had conquered much of the East Coast of Africa,
as well as parts of the Indian sub-continent for the Portuguese crown, was
killed, along with sixty-four of his sailors.[1] The battle reverberated in the European imperial imagination, creating an association of peril with the Cape
that kept the Portuguese from stopping at Table Bay for decades (den Besten

2013: 449). In many ways, therefore, this Dutch image of a Portuguese battle inaugurates a European conception of the South African landscape as perilous and threatening.

The perspective of the engraving is framed by three ships in the lower left corner in the foreground, separated by blustery seas from the shore in the upper right hand corner, where hundreds of Khoisan warriors are gathered, equal in proportion to the ships, brandishing spears and bows against the small figures of five unarmed Portuguese sailors. The print's strongest lines and darkest textures are found in the ships and the formation of Khoisan figures. The ships appear ordered but static, the angles of their masts, sails and flags contrasting with the choppy water. The waves near the ships are heavy and detailed but gradually lose definition and only at the shoreline do the human figures become more distinct. The Khoisan fighters are clearly delineated; by contrast, the Portuguese sailors are fainter and partly disappear beneath the surface of the water. The Khoisan soldiers are moving forward and some are aiming their spears at the Portuguese sailors, one of whom is falling backward into the waves. Two sailors are standing waist-deep in the water, their arms raised as though in surrender.

As in all engravings, a series of translations is at work: from experience into narrative, from narrative into painting, from painting into copper engraving, and from engraving into print. In this process, many mistranslations and "mistake[s]" can occur (Gordon-Brown 1975: 5). In addition to the slippages of translation, a market had developed for images of far-off lands in the metropole, and the exotic aspects of such drawings were often intensified during the production of the prints (Landau 2002: 4; Klopper 1989: 71). Therefore, although Van de Aa's work referred to a historical event, the metaphorical meanings of its configuration of sea, land and conflict are compelling.

The lines, shadows and textures of the copperplate aid a sense of division and fragility in the image. The bay between the ships and the shore recalls both the link to Europe and the riches of the East. In addition to distance, differences in scale and definition confirm that the sailors are far beyond the reach of the safety of the ships. On the shore, the Khoisan warriors form an impenetrable barrier to the land. The "eye" of the painting lies in the protective refuge of the ships, helplessly watching the defeat on shore.

In this early representation, the Cape thus enters the European visual imaginary through a representation of treacherous natives and a hostile landscape, a theme that would continue to characterise white portrayals of South Africa into the twentieth century, as Coetzee notes. The literary scholar Robin Visel had observed a similar anxiety: "According to Schreiner and her white literary descendants who enlarge upon her portrait of alienation, Africa is inimical to the settler; the land embodies the hatred of the native people for the invaders" (Visel 1990, 118). Similarly, David Bunn finds in colonial poetry about the Eastern Cape, where Nguni people resisted colonial displacement, that "the superficially picturesque encircling landscape is a place of deep menace" (2002: 61).

Yet, by the end of the nineteenth century, history textbooks in the South African colonies articulated a different vision of the land: that its history *began* in 1652 with the arrival of Jan van Riebeeck, the Dutch commander of the provisioning outpost established at the Cape. School history books asserted that Van Riebeeck was "the first human" to live in South Africa (Witz 2000: 324). This was a rhetorical declaration of settler belonging so profound it claimed that nothing *existed* before. How was this achieved?

The history of a painful word

Along with the brute power of war, displacement and genocide, this sense of belonging was realised through two discursive mechanisms: the first evident in etymology, and the second in representations of landscape. The first mechanism for securing colonial belonging was through naming the people who preceded European settlement as profoundly *other*, as lacking in fit and significance. This Adamic project of naming is recounted in the nine pages of the longest entry in the *Dictionary of South African English on Historical Principles* (1996). This entry delineates the meanings and usage of the most notorious word in South African history, known for its license of violence towards blacks during apartheid, but first used during the colonial period. The word is "kaffir".

> "kaffir" noun and adjective. *Offensive* in all senses and combinations. Also with initial capital, and (formerly) cafar, caffer, caf(f)ir, caffre(e), cafre, kaffer, kaffre. [ad. Arabic *kafir* infidel. The form *kaffer* is influenced by Dutch (and subsequently Afrikaans).] (1996: 342).

As the *Dictionary of South African English on Historical Principles* (hence-forth *DSAE*) conveys, "kaffir" is a comprehensively abusive word used to denote black people in South Africa, exemplary of the denial of black people's humanity under apartheid.[2] Offensive to the extent of being unsayable today (in fact, its use constitutes a hate crime in South Africa),[3] the word is un-pardonably painful and violent, and I wish to give it neither currency nor recuperation here. Entries in the *DSAE* show that not all meanings of the term were derogatory,[4] but even during the colonial period there was resistance to the use of the term by people to whom it was applied (*DSAE* 1996: 342). However, because of the language and tradition from which it is derived (and from which it has widely departed), the provenance of the word reveals a subsumed history of race, religion, landscape and belonging in South Africa.

The word "kaffir" is derived from an Arabic root word meaning "closed," and connotes someone who has closed his or her heart to the truth of Islam (Qibtiyah 2004: interview).[5] Derived from this root, the general meaning of "kaffir" is "non-Muslim". The term has related meanings of "non-believer" or "infidel," often rendered in English as "kaffir".[6] With a Muslim presence in South Africa dating from 1658 (when the Dutch first brought Muslims to the Cape), it is reasonable to assume that Islam delivered the word to the colonial lexicon. However, the use of the word to describe people in South Africa *predates* the arrival of Muslims in the colonial territories. According to the *DSAE*, the first recorded use of "kaffir" applied to southern Africa (in the form of "caffre") appeared in Richard Hakluyt's *The Principal Navigations, Voyages, Traffiques and Discoveries of the English Nation*, the first volume of which was published in 1589. George Theal asserts that European settlers in South Africa adopted the word from its use by East African Muslims for "infidels" in the southern part of Africa (*DSAE* 1996: 347). Henry Lichtenstein writes in his *Travels in Southern Africa*, "[b]eing Mahommedans, they gave the general name of Cafer (Liar, Infidel) to all the inhabitants of the coasts of Southern Africa" (1928: 241).

What are the implications of this provenance of the word "kaffir" in South Africa? One is that developments in the colonial period were essential to the terminology and ethos of apartheid South Africa. Second, before European settlement, southern Africa was part of a geography (and cosmology) created by the connecting tissue of the Indian Ocean. Before the word became associated with Dutch and British relations with Nguni polities in the Eastern

Cape, the use of "kaffir" applied to southern Africa carried with it a history of relations with East Africa and the Indian Ocean, between Swahili- and Arabic-speaking traders and Portuguese explorers.[7] Third, while today Muslims constitute a minority of South Africa's population, examining the history of Islam in South Africa engages with the core of the country's history – its very beginnings, in fact.

The role of Islam in this formulation is complex, however, as the subsequent career of the word "kaffir" in South Africa suggests. Demonstrating its divergence from an original Islamic meaning, the word would also come to be applied *to* Muslims, as the name of slaves who performed the duties of policemen during the Dutch period (Worden, Van Heyningen and Bickford-Smith, 1998: 61), and with the inclusion of Muslims in the well-known book of prints and essays titled *The Kafirs Illustrated* (1849) by George French Angas. This complex trajectory confirms the tangled racial meanings associated with Muslims.

While its starkly declamatory use during apartheid was mostly as a noun, I draw attention here to the use of "kaffir" as an adjective. During the nineteenth century, settler society used this modifier to name indigenous fruit, birds, trees, paths, food, tools, as well as what they perceived to be the behaviour, mentality and sense of time of indigenous people – everything anterior to them.[8] Both Dutch and British settlers used the term with a range of connotations, not all necessarily derogatory, according to the *DSAE*, although that sense hovered near every use of the word.[9] Crucially, whether or not it was a neutral designation, the adjective performed the function of disarticulating the naturalness of fit between the concepts it described, and the place in which they occurred.

The nine pages of the *DSAE* listing the uses of the word thus constitute an immense catalogue of renaming and remaking "nativeness" into "otherness". The use of the word "kaffir" to name South African flora and fauna denotes "indigenous'" and "wild" (*DSAE* 1996: 343). Tied to the increasingly common derogatory meanings of "kaffir," indigeneity itself, rather than conveying inalienable belonging, became a belittled concept that connoted corruptness and lack of fit. Once the landscape was designated "barren" and "wild", it could also be deemed "empty" (Witz 2000: 324). The proliferating use of the word "kaffir" therefore asserted that events that occurred prior to European arrival had no meaning, or were "uninscribed," a process of *emptying* the land and remaking it into an object of the imperialist gaze that Gayatri Spivak asserts is central to the project of empire.[10] She argues that:

> the notion of textuality should be related to the notion of the world-ing of a world on a supposedly uninscribed territory. When I say this, I am thinking basically about the imperialist project which had to assume that the earth that it territorialised was in fact previously un-inscribed. So then a world, on a simple level of cartography, inscribed what was presumed to be uninscribed. Now this worlding actually is also a texting, textualising, a making into art, making into an object to be understood (interviewed in Mutman, 1994: 35).

Spivak shows here that the imperialist project required that the world be re-made as empty or "previously uninscribed" so that it could be "inscribed" by European occupation. She contends that such remaking is centrally achieved by writing and art that inscribe the land with new meanings. Art rendered the occupied territory into an object that could be understood, and therefore naturalised imperialism's assertion of ownership over what it proclaimed to be an "uninscribed" land. I explore this mechanism by continuing to analyse colonial-era landscape paintings of the Cape below.

The *Oxford Universal Dictionary* (1944) shows a similar impact of colo-nialism on the meaning of the word "native". In 1535 "native" meant "one born in a place"; or, legally, "one whose parents have their domicile in a place." In 1603, after the consolidation of European exploration and colonial settle-ment, "native" meant "one of the original or indigenous inhabitants of a country; now *esp. 'one belonging to a non-European or uncivilised race'"* (em-phasis added). Deprecating connotations in this vein can be seen in the use of the word "native" under apartheid.[11] The word performed an agile func-tion in the making of race, since it also helped to secure white belonging in colonial contexts. In Australia in 1861, "native" meant "a white person born in the country". The evolution of the meanings of "native" points to the claim of *native* belonging by whites as an element of settler identity in Australia and South Africa. Here too the claim of white "indigeneity" operates through the empty land myth described by Spivak (Mutman 1994) and Marks (1980).

In the course of the colonial period, the use of "kaffir" as an adjective pro-liferated into a multitude of terms, so much so that "the word became strongly associated with South Africa [itself]" (*DSAE*, 1996: 347). The meanings and uses of the word "kaffir" listed in the *DSAE* have no prevalence outside of southern Africa (Pechey 2002: 14). The wide utilisation of the term in the colonial territories had three main outcomes, all intimately linked.

Firstly, the term had an ontological function. Settlers appeared to name as "kaffir" what had to remain separate from them, clearing a space for a selfhood that was defined against the African other. As Edward Said argued in *Orientalism*, the creation of otherness is a formula for the creation of the self (1978: 60). Orientalism constantly confirms the sameness of the Orient. However, it is "productive, not unilaterally inhibiting" and produces the delight of discovery and connectedness (14). Said noted that the idea of the Orient as other was central to the constitution of a Western subjectivity: "the idea of an Orient exists to define the European" (60). Crucially, this is not a purely additive or subtractive model, in which the West is simply opposed to a pitiful and lacking East. Instead, Orientalism *produces* the Western subject just as much it creates the Oriental. Indeed, the function of Orientalist discourse is "*the centring of the Western self*" (Mutman, 1994: 3, emphasis in original).

The alternative to the separation of the self and the other appears to be the threat of being consumed by indigeneity, suggested by the insidious African sense of time in a "kaffir appointment" (for which one need not be punctual), becoming a "kaffirboetie" [little brother] by feeling a contaminating sympathy for the despised group, or "to go to the kaffirs" (to degenerate).

Secondly, the word "kaffir" also functioned to remake the landscape. In colonial South Africa, this derogatory modifier metastasised into a vast naming that *forced* newness onto a world that was not new. The landscape was named in a way that enabled it to be possessed by Europeans. "Kaffir" labelled as unnatural the connection between indigenous people and their claim to the land. Instead, this relationship was portrayed as distorted, corrupt and unfitting. Blanketed by the adjective "kaffir", the South African landscape was "saturated with meaning" and turned into a stage upon which Europeans would be central actors while indigenous people would be acted upon (Said 1978: 84). Paul Carter theorises this erasure of prior meanings by new, imperial ones as "the theatricalisation of the ground – its transformation into the *tabula rasa* of space which, by virtue of its emptiness, licenses the colonist's usurpation of it" (1996: 24). Such a vision enabled European settlers to proclaim their own more fitting relationship with the African landscape.

The third, and crucial, function of the word "kaffir" was that it signalled a boundary of *time*. The extraordinary fecundity of the word was tempered in the colonial setting into a formula for the creation of a *beginning*. If "kaffir" marks corrupt indigenous meanings, then the settler relationship with the land inaugurates a new beginning. By marking the landscape, "kaffir" causes history to commence with settler arrival. At first the word looks like a spatial gesture, but in fact it is also a temporal one. Symbolically, "kaffir" not only announces a claim to land, but also marks a beginning of history.

This reading of "kaffir" shows how racial identities became marked onto bodies, the landscape and even concepts of time, giving them an apparently ontological force. Through these three effects, "kaffir" operated as a powerful discursive mechanism through which colonists secured a sense of belonging to the African landscape.

In addition to the emptying and reinscribing of the landscape through the term "kaffir," a second significant mechanism for generating a sense of belonging for settlers in South Africa was through an imagined relationship between colonists, slaves and indigenous people. In the colonial imagination, slaves were envisioned as an integral part of a triangular relationship, along with colonists and the indigenous Khoisan people, with the land. It was through this triangle that colonists asserted claims of ownership over and belonging to the land. In response to their anterior presence, colonists portrayed indigenous people as "idle", unreliable and unworthy of the land. In contrast, slaves working on behalf of the colonists were depicted as compliant, skilled and law-abiding. The opposition of "lazy" indigenous people with "industrious" slaves working on behalf of slave-owners facilitated a discourse through which colonists asserted a right to legitimate ownership over the land. To buttress this, colonists represented the system of slave-holding at the Cape as "mild" and picturesque (Keegan, 1996: 16).[12] The presence of slaves thus crucially shaped colonists' conceptions of identity and ownership over land, but, more importantly, their sense of *belonging to* it. In what follows, I show how this discursive mechanism functioned through the portrayal of the Cape landscape in visual art and fiction – a key site for "picturing" or presenting Muslims in the South African imagination.

The promise of the picturesque

If Africa was not a rediscovered Eden in which colonists could write a new beginning, white writing and art in South Africa reflected the desire to find a place of belonging in the landscape. J. M. Coetzee argues that this quest for "a dialogue with Africa" is the centripetal desire in white writing and art about landscape from the nineteenth century to the middle of the twentieth century (1988: 7). In light of the founding images of the menacing landscape of colonial South Africa, how were settlers to find a sense of belonging in it? The form that would solve their anxiety of belatedness was the picturesque, which was to become the dominant mode of representing the Cape landscape.

A picturesque landscape is composed in planes that recede from the foreground to a middle plane and finally to a "luminous distance" (Coetzee 1988: 39). Usually a shadow falls on the foreground, yet also throws it into relief. W. J. T. Mitchell reads the unconscious emotional tone built into the evident artifice of this form:

> The standard picturesque landscape is especially pleasing ... because it typically places the observer in a protected, shaded spot ... with screens on either side to dart behind or to entice curiosity, and an opening to provide deep access at the centre.
>
> ... the frame is always there as the guarantee that it is only a picture, only picturesque, and the observer is safe in another place – outside the frame, behind the binoculars, the camera, or the eyeball, in the dark refuge of the skull (1996: 16).

Mitchell shows that even in the metropolis, the picturesque landscape is a genre attended by anxiety. John Barrell writes in *The Dark Side of the Landscape* that although such landscapes strive to convey "an image ... of an English countryside innocent of division", nonetheless "it is possible to look beneath the surface of the painting, and to discover there evidence of the very conflict it seems to deny" (1980: 5). The picturesque perspective thus constructs the landscape as a visual correlate of the "dark refuge" sought in the mind. Paintings do not place a gloss of artifice on something that was originally true. Instead, nature itself has already been shaped and constructed to meet the gaze (Mitchell 1996: 14).

In the colonies, the formula of creating a "refuge" by reformulating the landscape was particularly appealing. Jessica Dubow notes "[t]he centrality and ubiquity of the picturesque within a colonial aesthetic" (2000: 98). To David Bunn, the psychological resolution promised by the picturesque mode offers the possibility of "locat[ing] the colonial self in its new context" (1996: 140). In South Africa, the picturesque seemed to offer a solution to the problem of the belated settlers finding a secure and *settled* place. It did so by "theatricalising" the landscape, as Bunn shows in an analysis of the frontispiece in Francois Le Vaillant's *Travels into the interior parts of Africa, by the way of the Cape of Good Hope* (1790). Here the African landscape is transformed into a "terrain … displayed as though already ordered to European conventions of taste", creating a space for European presence (2002: 129). This recreated landscape "helps to naturalise the settler subject" (Bunn 1996: 138).

However, as a counter to the anterior presence of indigenous people, this solution proved fragile. Dubow observes that in the colonies the picturesque "comes to be restated as a question and a problem", and that its failures are evidence of the partial, fissured and uncertain aspects of the colonial gaze (2000: 98). If anxiety is allayed through the artful arrangement of picturesque elements, there is as much significance in what is placed to the side as what is in the centre. Indeed, as Barrell observes above, the picturesque encodes in its form that which it excludes. The desiring colonial gaze required that the landscape be "emptied of rival human presences", yet this very emptiness indexed what was not there (Bunn 1996: 132). Therefore, the empty space and the silence of Africa had to be filled (Coetzee 1988: 177).

What would fill the emptiness of Africa?

In the project to construct the colonial landscape first as empty and wild and then domesticated by European settlement, the figure of the "Malay" would prove a useful discursive tool. Given the ubiquity of images of labouring "Malays" in the picturesque Cape landscape, it is striking that Coetzee, Bunn and Dubow do not consider the vast visual archive of "Malays" in their analyses. These figures are my focus. I argue that "Malays" played a crucial role in constituting the notion of landscape in South Africa.

Since the colonial period, the vantage point on Signal Hill above Cape Town has been a site from which many nineteenth-century landscapes of

Cape Town were painted (Murray 2001). It is also the location of the old-est slave graveyard in South Africa, named Tana Baru, the term for "New Place" in Behasa Melayu. The urbane and aesthetically pleasing colonial city represented in colonial-era paintings was therefore literally founded on slave bodies and their labour, but the picturesque landscape rendered the violence of enslavement invisible. Here too, the theme of charged beginnings asserts itself. I show not simply how Muslims are represented in landscape paintings, but that they are present in the *making* of a South African visuality. If the picturesque is as much about what is excluded as included, then the violence of slavery is a crucial "silence."[13] The very conception of landscape in the Cape has been shaped by the presence of enslaved Muslim bodies.

The visual archives in the South African National Library contain an ex-tensive collection of images under the category "Cape Malay" (though none under "Cape Muslim"). Among these are numerous paintings and studies of the Malay Quarter (the area in central Cape Town where former slaves settled) by Fred Page, Irma Stern, Gregoire Boonzaier and Constance Stuart Larrabee, among others. This, along with the seven-volume Kennedy Catalogues of the Africana Museum, the most comprehensive compilation of nineteenth-century South African prints and paintings,[14] Alfred Gordon-Brown's *Pictorial Africana* (1975) and George F. Angas' *The Kafirs Illustrated* (1849), is the source of some of the best-known images of "Malays" that ap-pear in later publications such as I. D. du Plessis's *The Cape Malays* (1944) and Achmat Davids' *The Afrikaans of the Cape Malays* (2011).

These visual archives typically show Muslims in two kinds of nineteenth-century landscapes: those of the "Malay Quarter", where former slaves settled, and those of the city of Cape Town as a whole. Since the Malay Quarter is an obvious association, I focus here on panoramas of Cape Town.

On studying the role of maps in establishing a sense of European domi-nance over colonial landscapes, the geographer J. B. Harley theorised that maps are rhetorical instruments that "redescribe the world" to reflect Euro-pean desires (2001: 35). He asserts that by focusing the gaze on a certain view of the world, maps render other sights invisible. He therefore argued for the importance of studying "cartographic silence[s]" (104) – those aspects left out of maps. To read a map in this way becomes "a search for silences" (45). Harley asks not only what maps emphasise, but also what they underplay and exclude. I read his description of a town plan or bird's-eye view as "a legible emblem ... of community" (48) as an invitation to seek the "cartographic silences" of panoramic landscapes of Cape Town.

Gazing at a number of eighteenth and nineteenth-century panoramas in sequence, a curiously consistent pattern reveals itself. The city is an ordered and domesticated place, distinguished by its iconic mountain and peopled by finely dressed colonists in the foreground. However, these views of the city almost always feature diminutive human figures standing to the sides, close to the edge of the frame, identifiable by their characteristically pointed ("toering") hats and colourful dress as "Malays", engaged in one of the identifiable forms of labour performed by slaves. The figures form a laconic visual gesture and barely draw the eye; the gaze glides easily over them. In tone, they are both mildly exotic and familiar, an ornamental motif that lends authenticity to the scene of colonial Cape Town. They are so common a feature in Cape landscapes that they form an immediately recognisable visual sign of the colonial period – both unremarkable and somehow necessary.

In these paintings, the "Malays" in their habitual postures and position – placed to the side, showing signs of labour – are *ambiguous* figures. While apparently marginal to the focus of the paintings, it is not possible to gaze at the centre without their presence. Through their characteristic position near the frame, these figures seem to mark the edge of the domesticated space of the city, revealing an intense investment in the idea of the boundary. The "Malay" figures mark the limits of the picturesque landscape.

Who are the "Malays" in the paintings? In *White Writing*, Coetzee argues that the taxonomic impetus at the height of empire meant that a tone of surveillance entered into writings about the indigenous inhabitants of the colonies. However, one can discern a narrative strategy embedded in patterns of classification and erasure that placed colonists at the centre of the occupied landscape and consigned "natives" to the margins. To the classificatory gaze, "the Hottentot,[15] on closer inspection, turns out to yield an extremely impoverished set of differences to inscribe in the table of categories" (Coetzee 1988: 23). Significantly, Coetzee reports that the ethnographer Gustav Fritsch, after travelling in the South African territories in the 1860s, remarked that "it would not be possible to use Boer life as material for stories because in Boer life nothing ever happens" (24). What material would fill the vacuum left by "Hottentot and Boer inactivity" (32)?

The "Malays" would provide a plenitude of content. A feast of detail –

clothes, activity, smell, texture of hair, colour of skin, sound of voices – was available for presentation. There is a clear tradition of typology in images of "Malays". Caricatures and cartoons kept in the South African National Library demonstrate the imperative toward classification. The "Malays" are shown in anthropological detail. Their clothing enjoys a particular degree of attention, especially the pointed or "toering" hat of the men and the long and often richly coloured dresses of the women. The occupations of both sexes are carefully documented: fishermen, fruit-sellers, tailors, washerwomen. As a result, the figure of the man with the "toering" hat and the brightly dressed woman with an elaborate hairstyle are identifiable by their apparel and labour as "Malay". They are the Cape Colony's slaves.

Labour presents a problem for the picturesque. As Raymond Williams notes, "a working country is hardly ever a landscape" (1975: 120). Yet labour is central to the representation of landscape in South Africa, and thus the colonial picturesque tradition had to accommodate the deep contradictions of the exploitative system through which the land was worked (Coetzee 1988: 3). South African landscapes have been haunted since the colonial period by a deep ambivalence about the representation of black labour, which stems from the Protestant belief in the necessity of work and the inherent sinfulness of being idle; yet to apply such a view in colonies dependent on slave labour had unsettling implications (Coetzee 1988: 5). As Coetzee points out, "if the work of hands on a particular path of earth, digging, plowing, planting, building, is what inscribes it as the property of its occupiers *by right*, then the hands of black serfs doing the work had better not be seen" (5). The visibility of black labour disturbed the colonists' claims to "occupation by right".

In light of these anxieties about the sight of labour, the compliant "Malay" figures in nineteenth-century landscapes of the Cape are striking because they are *labouring* figures. As water-carriers, fruit-sellers, fishermen and washer-women, their labour is highly visible. In fact, *it is by their labour that they are known to be "Malay"*. They contrast with the "natives", who are marked in colonial discourse by the absence of labour, and the leisured figures of the colonists.

Despite their labour, the "Malay" figures do not manifest the ambivalence to which Coetzee refers. The colour and sociality of the "Malays" in colonial writings and paintings signal keenly desired meanings to watching settlers, but it is their collusive, guilt-allaying visage that is most appealing. "Considering that these Malays were once all slaves, it is not to be wondered at that they enjoy their freedom, and have resolved to banish from their faces all trace of anxious servility" (Anonymous 1963: 25). A view of "Malay" slaves as passive and compliant therefore helps to resolve the contradiction between black labour and settler belonging by portraying a picturesque view of slave labour *in the service of white colonists*. This vision of the "Malay" as submissive and compliant secures a selfhood for colonists that resolves the question of place and labour.

Such picturesque colonial paintings thus perform a stark ideological labour. The portrayal of exotic and guilt-alleviating "Malay" slaves has shaped the conditions for speaking about the colonial period, helping to suppress discussion of its brutalities through a trivialising visual language that deflects attention from the systemic violence of slavery. The effect is to underplay the violence of slave-holding society and evidence of resistance by slaves, and to produce a picturesque view of a benign slave-holding society at the Cape that has persisted to the present day. This is despite the fact that, as Robert Ross notes in his ground-breaking 1983 study of Cape slavery, *Cape of Torments: Slavery and Resistance in South Africa*, "resistance, not acquiescence, is the heart of the history of human slavery" (3).

Picturesque landscapes allow slavery to hover on the edges of public visibility without being directly looked at. Through the image of the decorative slave, the remarkable impact of slavery in South Africa has been banished from serious public debate. The manner in which enslaved people have been portrayed has allowed the enslavement of Africans and Asians at the Cape to slide perpetually out of view. To accede to the picturesque discourse is to overlook the brutality of slavery, and accept the portrayal of slaves as complicit with the system that dehumanised them.

Oblique figures

"Oblique, ad. – Having a slanting direction or position
Oblique, v. – to turn in a sidelong direction. To slant at an angle.
Obliquity, n. 'The obliquity of the eye, which is proper to the Japanese and Chinese.' – Darwin [undated]
The obliquities of Eastern negotiation. 1818. Hence obliquatous, a. morally or mentally perverse." *Oxford Universal Dictionary* (1933)

There is another way to read these portrayals. The picturesque "Malays" in these paintings are "oblique" figures – simultaneously literal and figurative, they carry a profound ideological weight. The water-carriers, fruit-sellers, washerwomen and fish-sellers on the streets of the colonial city are figures of over-determined placidity whose task is to translate slavery into the unremarkable and the unremarked. Yet their loads are precariously balanced. The heightened sense of visibility and access created by these common portraits of "Malays" obscures the fact that they were also frequently suspected of eluding sight, as the Slave Code of 1754 intimates through its policing of visibility. This code compelled slaves to carry a torch at night in "an attempt to prevent plotting in dark corners" (Worden, Van Heyningen and Bickford-Smith 1998: 63).

Despite their reassuring surface, therefore, representations of the domesticated and picturesque landscape of the Cape are shadowed with hidden meaning and haunted by the contradictions at their core. In this way, the "Malays" in these paintings are doubled figures, both soothing and unsettling. Close to the picturesque surface is an unsettling underside – the "irrational Oriental" who runs amok.[16] Images of Muslims have oscillated between the poles of the picturesque and the menacing for at least two centuries.

This can be inferred from a panoramic scene of Cape Town called *Camp's Bay*, painted by George French Angas in 1849. Angas's *The Kafirs Illustrated* (1849) contains a series of detailed and highly romanticised landscapes and figure studies in southern Africa. The paintings contain no images of colonists, but they are implied in the perspective from which the landscape is beheld (Klopper 1989: 69). Angas's paintings have been treated as an authoritative source of information about their subjects, such as their clothing and social relationships. Yet there has been little critical discussion of Angas's paintings of "Malays", even though he devotes extensive attention to them both in his written texts and in the paintings. *The Kafirs Illustrated* was part of a market for illustrated books that brought the "exotica" of far-off lands to the metropole (Landau, 2002: 4). Sandra Klopper points out that in the process of transforming the watercolours into lithographs, "attempts were made to increase the picturesque quality of Angas's images through the addition of exotic details" (1989: 71). Therefore, the *addition* of imagined detail is precisely what makes the landscape alluringly picturesque.

The painting *Camp's Bay* gives a global view of Cape Town from a hill above the city. Distant mountains can be seen in the background behind

Table Bay. The city rests along the half-circle of the Bay, while the ships in the harbour indicate a busy traffic with the rest of the world. The even grid of the streets contrasts with the curve of the bay and the round hills. The city is regular and ordered, and the white buildings add visual interest through their varied shape and height. To the right, on a shadowed part of the road, are smaller houses, suggesting a spatial division in the city.

Moving up the hill, we approach the place from which the perspective of the painting issues. The abundant vegetation suggests a bountiful environment, verdant yet harmoniously structured. Overall, nature cossets the city, pleasingly rendered through the arrangement of flowers, trees, clouds and rocks. In the foreground on the left of the painting, stone steps and a wall decorated with columns and a gatepost appear. Amid the shrubbery and rocks, the wall recalls the straight lines of the town.

The wall marks a boundary, perhaps of a farm. Leaning against it, in shadow, are the only human figures in the painting. The two men are too small for their facial features to be distinct, yet by their pointed "toering" hats and the baskets set down next to the wall, they are identifiable as "Malay". Placed near the edge of the painting and thus the boundary of the panoramic prospect, they signal the limit of the Colony. The wall suggests a metaphorical boundary, hinting not only at what is kept in, but also what is kept out. In its orderly lines juxtaposed with the curve of the hill, the wall seems set against nature. The resting figures mark this ambiguous point.

The composition of the painting creates a play of the near and the distant, the bounded and open, the domesticated and the wild, and the light and the shadows of the mountains. The distant mountains beyond Table Bay speak of the space stretching beyond the boundary of the Colony. The two figures thus mark a point of balance between outside and inside. The "luminous distance" of this picturesque vista is the vast, uncontrolled space beyond the ordered outlines of the town, a space signalled by the two figures resting in the shadow of the wall, just as the shadows of the distant mountains unbalance the order and harmony of the city.

A careful logic governs the placement of the "Malay" figures. "Malays" *frame* the landscape and signal the edge of the knowable world. Placed near the edges of the landscape, they declare its boundaries and secure the territory over which authority is claimed. But beyond them lies the world outside the Colony. Herein lies the ambiguity of the figures. The paintings elicit the discursive collusion of the "Malays" by over-determining their meaning as compliant and reassuring; yet they also hint at something else, something beyond.

What lies beyond the figure of the picturesque "Malay"? Such portrayals suppress the violence of the Colony, and erase the runaway slaves who melted into the landscape and the communities established by runaway slaves, rebellious labourers and insurrectionary groups outside of the settler economy. Yet these repressed meanings remain a ghostly negative of the passive "Malay".

This insistently picturesque portrayal of Muslim figures in literature and art continued well into the twentieth century. By the end of the twentieth century, however, the doubled figure of the "Malay" was deconstructed by the images of Pagad, a crime-fighting group which drew on Islamic imagery as part of a rhetoric of potency, on the front pages of the South Africa's newspapers, and by new visions of Muslims in politics, visual art and literature.

Returning the gaze: *Colour Me*

In 1999, three years after the first appearance of Pagad in the news, two important works of art reverberated in the national culture, changing the way race, sexuality and slavery would be discussed in South Africa. In each, a pivotal moment occurs when a character gazes back. The two works are the visual installation *Colour Me*, by Berni Searle, and the novel *Disgrace* by J. M. Coetzee. I discuss the latter further in Chapter 4 and focus here on *Colour Me*.

Berni Searle is a South African visual artist based in Cape Town. Her 1999 installation *Colour Me* at the Mark Coetzee Fine Art Cabinet attracted widespread critical and popular acclaim. The installation consisted of digital prints of the prone, naked body of the artist covered in vividly coloured powdered chilli, cumin, turmeric, pepper and other spices. On the floor in front of the photographs, heaped mounds and small bottles of spices were arranged around the prints. The posture of Searle's body and the sensuous colours and textures of spices in *Colour Me* create works of arresting visual power that are also weighted with history.

The photograph *Untitled* is one of the most striking of the *Colour Me* series. It is a close-up of Searle's face and torso covered in red chilli powder. Her mouth, hair, nose and torso are layered with the spice, and she appears almost smothered by the colour red, but her gaze meets the camera directly. The straight line of Searle's gaze is contrasted with the abstract and sculptural shapes of her body – a series of curves and circles formed by her jaw, neck, shoulders and head resting on the ground, all covered by spices. The red of the chilli is startlingly vivid in the otherwise neutral composition, and evokes a sense of woundedness. Spice pools under Searle's head like blood. The chilli obscures her body, but also draws attention to its exposed outlines. The curve of her shoulder looks vulnerable and exposed, yet her gaze is quietly observant and questioning. The simultaneous sense of vulnerability and potency in Searle's persona creates an arresting ambiguity in the photograph.

This work was selected for the "Returning the Gaze" project of the 2001 Cape Town Festival (I discuss the history of this art festival in Chapter 5) and, as a result, was circulated widely in the city in the form of postcards and on billboards. In all these representations, Searle *literally* gazes back at the camera. However, the photograph also asks the viewer to think about ways in which the artist's body is made available to our gaze.

Colour Me uses spices – apparently familiar, domestic and innocuous – and inflects them with historically charged meanings. Spices drove the Indian Ocean slave trade, the plantation system of the West Indies and the trans-Atlantic slave trade (Morton 2000, 172). The trade in spices between Asia and Europe was the reason for the establishment of the Cape Colony, and slaves were transported to the Cape along the same routes as spices. Therefore the nutmeg, pepper, chilli and turmeric in *Colour Me* index a brutal history. The installation invokes vertiginous shifts of scale: the connection of domesticity with global histories of exploitation, and one body with thousands of others. The prone figure in the photograph seems to play the role of the compliant "Malay" figure familiar from nineteenth-century paintings, but in looking back, becomes a calmly noncompliant subject.

By layering "exotic" spices on "exotic" skin, *Colour Me* also recovers the theme of sexual exploitation from the erasures of the picturesque tradition. Searle's motionless, exposed body in the *Colour Me* photographs evokes the enforced sexual availability of slave women at the Cape. However, instead of offering untrammelled access to the spectator, the fact that she looks back creates an ambiguous and disquieting effect. In the photographs, she appears not so much adorned as almost stifled by the spices, which cover her mouth and eyes. Under the mesmerisingly rich colours, the unsettling availability of Searle's body invites the desire to look but also eludes the gaze. While her naked figure seems to offer unfettered access, *Untitled* creates a series of receding meanings. Her stillness suggests a withdrawal into an inaccessible space within the body. A desire for the receding subject becomes part of the experience of the artwork. The imperative form of the title suggests an active role by the subject: "[You/I/They/We] Colour Me". *Colour Me* stages the impossible promise that to look at the naked body will resolve all these unstable meanings. Instead, by being looked at, the artist presents viewers with the *act* of looking itself.

In this way, *Colour Me* engages with the legacy of a colonial gaze that rests on picturesque and exotic bodies. In the photographs, the prone body of the artist appears to re-enact all the conventions of availability that slavery and colonialism designated for bodies such as hers. However, as the silent object of the gaze, the artist enacts the role of being looked at so deliberately that the act of looking is itself made visible. In this way, her body "gazes back", insisting that the conventions that render black women's bodies available to the gaze are palpable. The viewer thus becomes aware of the act of looking while looking.

The *ambiguous visibility* of Muslim figures in South African visual art and fiction promises to resolve the anxieties that attend white belonging in the landscape. However, this strategy of using a marginal Muslim figure to secure a white subjectivity is haunted by the threat of irruption that hovers near the placid surface. The picturesque "Malay" is a doubled figure whose proximity can become unsettling and ominous, as Searle's *Colour Me* compellingly conveys.

CHAPTER 2

"Kitchen Language":
Muslims and the culture of food

Intimacy is never simple.
– Adrienne Rich (2009)

Ideology is externalised in food.
– Timothy Morton (2003: 108)

Unequal intimacies: The Ayah in the kitchen[1]

In his influential study of slavery, *Status and Respectability in the Cape Colony 1750–1870*, Robert Ross muses regretfully that "[b]ody language largely is outside the vision of historians", but notes that there are nonetheless ways to read the traces of social relations through the body, including through food (1999: 2). In this chapter, I read the gestures and desires of the body in relation to Muslim food at the Cape, which was crucially shaped by slavery. I do this by analysing the figure of the enslaved woman who crafts dishes that shape the tastes of slave-owners. This discussion continues the shift in scale from landscape to the intimate space of the household and the culture of domesticity evoked by Berni Searle's *Colour Me* series, and focuses on food as an important element of the history and representation of slavery.

For hundreds of years, images of Muslim food have been the primary vehicle for creating a South African vision of Islam. In 1849, George French Angas's *The Kafirs Illustrated* presented "Malay" food as colourful spectacle, highlighting the "table groaning beneath the weight [of] pots of preserved ginger and nutmeg", amid the sociality of "feasting" and "singing" (10), entrenching the connection between "Malay" cooking and spectacle. This convention continued well into the twentieth century, and eventually colourful images of Muslim food were seen as characteristic of the Cape itself. I. D. du Plessis's foreword to Hilda Gerber's *Traditional Cookery of the Cape Malays* (1954) proclaims that "[n]o aspect of Cape Malay life has been more closely interwoven with life at the Cape than Cape Malay cookery." I trace the role of this highly specific exoticism, which is echoed in other descriptions of "Malay" food in the formation of a more general South African identity. This formation gives an exotic version of "Malay" food a minor part in the construction of a broader South African culture – in which the brutal history of slavery is elided.

Despite the association of Muslim food with the picturesque, the cuisine is freighted with dissonant meanings. In the 1820s and 1830s, two-thirds of enslaved people at the Cape performed household work, and skill in cooking markedly increased the price of a slave (Mason 2003: 108). The food historian, doctor and poet C. Louis Leipoldt confirms that "slaves who had knowledge of this kind of cookery commanded a far higher price than other domestic chattels", citing an advertisement for the sale of five slaves after the death of their owner: "Malani, a good cook, exceptionally skilled and not wasteful in the kitchen", and an account (Leipoldt 1976: 18) of a slave auction where "there was spirited competition for Emerentia, who is an acknowledged artist of the pot".

Thus, it is not only the food, but also the figure of the skilled and usually unnamed Ayah in the kitchen (featured in South African recipe books by Hilda Gerber, Martin Versveld, C. Louis Leipoldt and Laurens van der Post), who carries echoes of slavery. Van der Post acknowledges that he gathered the recipes in his cookbooks from his "Malay" servants and cooks, revealing the required silence of the gifted but mute Muslim cook in the construction of dominant South African cuisine (Van der Post 1977: 129).

How can one speak differently about food? Scholars have coined the term "intimacy" to allude to the forms of charged proximity that were created by colonialism and apartheid, and which remain an under-discussed legacy today (Berlant 2000; Pratt and Posner 2012). In South Africa, the concepts of intimacy and entanglement have been proposed as ways to speak about the complex relations that emerged alongside and in response to the stark divisions of race.

In their introduction to the essay collection *Senses of Culture* (2000), the literary scholars Sarah Nuttall and Cheryl-Ann Michael suggest a hermeneutics of intimacy predicated on a set of continual if uneven exchanges since the colonial period, as a way of studying South African culture. They argue against "the over-determination of the political, the inflation of resistance and the fixation on race" that characterise previous approaches to South African history, which they contend has resulted in a sense of a South African exceptionalism (1).[2] As alternative models, they cite Tony Morphet's writing on the stylistic continuities between the architecture of Durban and other African port cities (Nuttall and Michael 2000: 4); also Jane Taylor and David Bunn's studies of poison in the colonial Cape, in which they point to the mutual influences and ideas about poison that circulated between the Khoisan and Dutch and British settlers. Bunn contends that, although intermittent and uneven, these exchanges "gesture toward the beginnings of an ambivalently shared knowledge of medicines and herbs" (Nuttall and Michael 2000: 8).

The most important precedent for Nuttall and Michael's theory is Robert Shell's ground-breaking historical study *Children of Bondage: A social history of the slave society at the Cape of Good Hope, 1652–1838* (1994), in which he wrote about the subtle and profound interactions between enslaved people and slave-owners at the Cape, a legacy he asserts is reflected in contemporary South African practices of food, language, architecture and music (see also Nuttall and Michael 2000: 5–8). In *Children of Bondage*, Shell observes that the paternalistic and often violent space of the slaveholding household was also a space of continual and intimate encounters between slaves and their owners that left a permanent imprint on South African culture. Using these instances of "intimacy" analysed by Bunn, Morphet and Shell, Nuttall and Michael propose an approach to South African culture that focuses not on "closure" and "borders" – tropes they claim have over-determined the country's intellectual and cultural production because of apartheid – but on "intimacies and connectivities" (2000: 8). Nuttall and Michael assert that previous approaches have overlooked that:

[a]longside the closure of South African imaginations there exist intimacies and connectivities, other ways of seeing. The recognition of such intimacies has tended to be end-stopped by invocations of segregation. Despite apartheid, a great many forms of continuity

and intimacy managed, if not to flourish, then at least to exist and develop (2000: 5).

What is the nature of the "intimacy" that Nuttall and Michael propose? The authors draw strongly from Shell's *Children of Bondage*, in which he identifies the dangerous physical proximity of domestic slavery as a site of cultural invention. Shell argues that

> slavery brought different people together, not across the sights of a gun, as on the frontier, but in the setting of a home. Each slave was exposed to each owner and each settler to each slave on a very intimate footing. There was, in fact, a common reciprocal legacy (quoted in Nuttall and Michael 2000: 5).

Under these conditions, he asserts:

> slave ancestors injected diversity and challenge into an oppressive settler culture, bending and finally changing it, creolising into a new … single domestic Creole culture, within the otherwise starkly stratified and bifurcated slave society of early South Africa … with its new cuisine, its new architecture, its new music, its melodious, forthright and poetic language, Afrikaans, first expressed in the Arabic script of the slaves' religion and written literature" (quoted in Nuttall and Michael 2000: 5).

Here Shell proposes that slaves "injected" new elements of "diversity and challenge" into the dominant slave-owning culture, eventually "bending," "changing" and "creolising" it, leading to a new "amalgamated" culture – whose legacy is central to South Africa today. This is a compelling vision. Little attention has been paid to the impact of enslaved people on contemporary culture, and a theory of "intimacies" opens a space for reading such legacies in a sensitive way.

However, does giving attention to "intimacies" introduce the danger of displacing the reality of the "blood, sweat and tears" (Gutierrez quoted in Stoler 2002: 14) of colonialism? Sean Jacobs (2002) argues that Nuttall and Michael's argument about foundational intimacies runs the risk of "hastily abandoning class and race, domination and resistance" in studies of South Africa. Thus the nature of intimacy is crucial in considering the legacies of the proximities of slavery. Rustum Kozain notes that "one still has to be cognisant of separation, of how segregation in fact structures 'intimacy'" (2002: interview).

While bearing in mind these necessary cautions, I accept Nuttall and Michael's larger point about the need for nuanced readings of the intersections, silences and complexities of South African history. Precisely because the exclusions in the archives mean that slaves' lives are absent except in highly constricted forms, if we read intimacy against the grain – as uncanny nearness, as charged silence and as coded trauma, following the model of Lisa Lowe's essay "The Intimacies of Four Continents" (2006: 192–3) on the effects of colonialism and slavery on the New World – we can productively engage the erasures of the historical archive. Such a reading of intimacy would allow us to address the silences in South African culture about the violence of slavery and its persistent contemporary impact.

Food is an exemplary terrain in which to explore this notion of intimacy. This chapter draws on insights from visual art, fiction, cookbooks, sociology and interviews with cooks that document narratives about food not available in written sources. From the period of slavery to apartheid, the South African kitchen has been a site of harrowing intimacy, power, knowledge and invisible ideological contest, with profound cultural effects. An amiable view of "Cape Malay" cooking has had the effect of domesticating images of slavery in South Africa, and has allowed dominant society to gesture to the presence of enslaved people while denying the brutality of slavery. Because food is central to the South African visual regime about slavery, images of the kitchen are weighted with repressed knowledge. Unsettling themes of secrets, magic and poison haunt the picturesque view of "Malay" cuisine as exotic and benign. In an article on views in the metropole about the use of poisons in the colonies, Jane Taylor notes that the "powerful organic toxins used in the colonies are associated with alternative systems of intelligence, unreadable representations ... and medical and cosmological practices that defy the English imagination" (Taylor 1996: 89). The stories and rumours that circulated at the Cape about the powers of slave cooks can therefore be read as an anxiety about an alternative epistemology that lay outside of colonial control.

The kitchen formed an unrelenting, perilous and transformative arena in which an uneven contest between slave-owner and enslaved was fought. Ultimately enslaved people came to shape South African cuisine in unexpectedly potent ways. Given the inequities of power in the colonial kitchen, how was this possible?

In *The Practice of Everyday Life* (1984), Michel de Certeau asserts that the powerless exert an unsuspected power that operates in the interstices of dominant culture by using objects of consumption in ways that elude the desires of dominant classes. De Certeau writes that the powerless invisibly subvert the culture of the powerful by making "innumerable and infinite decimal transformations within the dominant cultural economy in order to adapt it to their own interests and their own rules" (1984: xiv). In contrast to the "centralised, glamorous, and spectacular production" of the elites, consumption by the powerless can be:

> devious, it is dispersed, but it insinuates itself everywhere, silently and almost invisibly, because it does not manifest itself through its own products, but rather through its *ways of using* the products imposed by dominant economic order (1984: xii–xiii).

This is evident in the case of the Spanish conquest of the Americas, for instance, where indigenous people, despite their defeat, introduced into dominant practices an

> ambiguity that subverted from within the Spanish colonisers' "success" in imposing their own culture on the indigenous Indians.... Submissive, and even consenting to their subjection, the Indians ... often *made of* the rituals, representations, and laws imposed on them something quite different from what their conquerors had in mind; they subverted them, not by rejecting or altering them, but by using them with respect to events and references foreign to the system.... their use of the dominant social order deflected its power, which they lacked the means to challenge; they escaped it without leaving it (1984: xiv).

De Certeau's concepts of "[s]ubmissive[ness]" and "consent" as signs of a long-term and subtle process of transformation are illuminating tools through which to read the image of the docile "Malay". This allows us to read the work of desire in the food created in the slave kitchen, food that later became national dishes claimed by dominant culture.

In the case of South African food, the slave kitchen was the "ambiguous" space in which familiar objects were subverted in ways not immediately apparent as resistance to dominant parts of society. The historian John Mason terms this practice of resistance a deployment of "the weapons of the weak" by skilled slaves at the Cape (2003: 163). The separate practices and meanings given to Muslim food show how the powerless used instruments of domination for "events and references foreign" to dominant culture. Eventually, enslaved people's "ways of using" the ingredients of Dutch food reshaped the dominant cuisine.

The effect of this subtle legacy of the slave kitchen can be seen today in the similar dishes with different names in the cooking traditions of the descendants of enslaved people and slave-owners, such as the drink known in "Malay" cooking as "boeber" and in the Afrikaans tradition as "melkkos" (Abrahams 1995: 46). "Bobotie" is claimed as a national dish by Afrikaans-speaking people, yet is also a well-known "Cape Malay" dish. The familiar meeting among Muslims called a "merrang", which continues to be held today, arose out of occasions when slaves met while their masters were at church (Abrahams 1995: 69). A joke about "affal wat vleis geword het" ["offal that became meat"] refers to the fact that slaves made their food from the parts of animals discarded by the master (Abrahams 2002: interview). Because of the suppression of memories of slavery and the lingering effects of apartheid, the various food cultures in South Africa remain largely insulated from one another, and therefore these similarities and the reasons for them are mostly unexplored. In an essay that draws on Leipoldt's food anthropology, Riaan Oppelt argues that "Cape Malay" food can be seen as the original South African cuisine (2012: 51–68). This acknowledges that enslaved people made a fundamental contribution to the cuisine that would come to be called "South African cooking". Yet the interesting question is how the general came to be established through an erasure of slavery.

Perilous intimacies: Rayda Jacobs's *The Slave Book*

Rayda Jacobs's novel *The Slave Book* (1998) depicts the lives of slaves at the Cape in the 1830s and shows the multiple meanings encoded in Muslim food.[3] In the novel, the kitchen is the site of a brittle intimacy between slave-owners and slaves, where any encounter may turn suddenly perilous. Mason points out that the kitchen was not only the space of labour, but that "it was common for slaves ... to sleep in hallways and kitchens" (2003: 76). The language of domesticity provides an insight into the dangers of the slave household. At the Cape, the term "domestic correction" was given to the practice of "violent coercion and physical punishment that slave owners applied to their slaves" (Mason 2003: 73).

In *The Slave Book*, precisely because the kitchen is the location of precarious, if everyday exchanges, it is also the space of overheard information, a supply of extra food, and the sharing of secret knowledge such as healing potions among slaves – through these actions, the kitchen becomes the site of small resistances encoded into tastes, sound, touch, glances and smells. Here enslaved people learned not only how to survive, but gathered the resources for subversion. In the novel, Rachel, a slave who had been on Zoetewater farm for twenty-two years, comforts the newly arrived Somiela: "in the kitchen you hear many things" (1998: 30). The kitchen is where the slaves on the farm speak a language of tastes and flavours that eventually affects the entire household. Through food, Somiela silently speaks back to the masters in ways that the latter eventually come to desire. Soon after Somiela arrives at the farm, Andries, the slave-owner, consults his wife Marieta about arrangements for supper:

> "I told [Somiela] to make some of that food for tonight that she made the other day."
> "Someila can't cook."
> "She can. She's the one who made the – what's it called again?" he asked Somiela directly.
> "Cabbage bredie, Seur," Rachel spoke up for Somiela, sensing Marieta's hostility.
> "Well, whatever it is, we won't have it," Marieta said with finality.
> "... we'll serve what we usually serve – roast meat and potatoes and carrots". (Jacobs 1988: 65)

Though Marieta marks "with finality" a clear distinction between "what we usually serve" and "whatever it is" that Somiela makes, such boundaries between slaves and masters would eventually dissolve (Shell 1994: 415). Slaves and their descendants operated in the kitchen in ways that exceeded the control of dominant culture. Both "Malay" and Dutch, later Afrikaans, cooking would come to manifest the intertwined reality of the slave kitchen (Abrahams 2002: interview). By the time the German naturalist Henry Lichtenstein travelled through the country in the early nineteenth century, he found that cooking at the Cape echoed Batavian practices and dishes, including kerrie [curry], atjar and sambal (cited in Gerber 1954: 10).

The unsettling connotations suppressed by the picturesque remain close to the surface of "Malay" food. After the scene related above, Marieta whips Somiela in unprovoked fury, and in her pain, Somiela contemplates her response in the language of the kitchen:

> Tasting the saltiness of her own blood, she promised herself that she would make this monstrous woman pay. The first opportunity she had, she would pee in her coffee, poison her food (Jacobs 1998: 68–69).

This scene reveals that the image of the skilled and compliant cook has a double: the slave woman who exercises the dangerous power of the kitchen to "gool" or conjure by adding insidious, undetectable ingredients to food to form magic potions or, even more frighteningly, to poison the eater (Van der Post 1977: 146).[4] This fear, deriving from the proximity of slaves to their masters, circulated in the Cape both during and long after the end of slavery. In 1864, Lady Duff Gordon refers to the myth in her letters:

> [H]e compelled me to drink herb tea, compounded by a Malay doctor for my cough. I declined at first, and the poor old man looked hurt, gravely assured me that it was not true that Malays always poisoned Christians, and drank some himself. Thereupon I was obliged, of course, to drink up the rest; it certainly did me good, and I have drunk it since with good effect; it is intensely bitter and rather sticky. The white servants and the Dutch landlady where I lodge shake their heads ominously, and hope it mayn't poison me a year hence. "Them nasty Malays can make it work months after you take it" (1921: 37).

The trope of the closeness of medicine to poison and the fear of the hidden power of "Malay" potions convey a lingering anxiety about the knowledge produced in the slave kitchen. In his book *First Catch Your Eland* (1977), Laurens van der Post tells an innocuous version of this ability to heal that turns into a confession of his belief in the hidden powers of the "Malays":

> In my young days we also believed that the Malays could cure, with their own herbs and spices, diseases that our own doctors could not. The superstitious among us thought that the Malays were great magicians. There was a widespread conviction that they could "gool" – their word for the performance of magic deeds (146).

Van der Post's memory links spices to magic and secret powers in a vision that signals the power of the kitchen, and is the shadow side of the food conjured by the benign Ayah in the kitchen.

Representations of Muslims in cookbooks

In travellers' tales about the Cape published in the eighteenth and nineteenth centuries, "Malay" slaves were commonly associated with food, and nineteenth and twentieth century South African cookbooks form an important archive for images of Islam in South Africa. Muslim food appears in some of the earliest collections of recipes published in the country under the category of "East Indian", "Malay" and later, "Cape Malay" cooking. The first cookbooks published in South Africa were A. G. Hewitt's *Cape Cookery* (1889) and Hildagonda Duckitt's *Hilda's "Where Is It?"* (1891). Both books contain "Malay" and "East Indian" recipes such as "breedee" (stew) and "blatjang" (chutney). Such early cookbooks are a significant source of South African images of Muslims.

Cookbooks reveal shifts in conceptions of food, national identity and social relations. Arjun Appadurai's classic essay "How to make a national cuisine: Cookbooks in contemporary India" (1988) contends that cookbooks written in English and directed largely at a middle-class Anglophone audience helped to craft a national, postcolonial and post-industrial cuisine in India. The exchange of recipes across barriers of language, caste and ethnicity became a site for the "loosening" of old boundaries and the creation of a cultural space for the urban middle class, but also overwrote local and regional specificity (240). As in South Africa, the precise relation of the specific to the general – what is excluded and what is included in order to form a national cuisine – is a crucial matter.

In the South African context, disembodied versions of "Cape Malay" and indigenous Khoisan food, disarticulated from the people who made them, were used to craft a national cuisine. In the 1970s, popular books such as Laurens van der Post's *African Food*, Betsie Rood's *Maleier Kookkuns* [The Art of Malay Cooking] and Renata Coetzee's *The South African Culinary Tradition* extolled "Malay" dishes, but refer to slavery only as a passing detail. Cheryl-Ann Michael observes in her analysis of "Cape Malay" recipe books that in these texts, "[p]eople of Malay descent … are curiously vague figures, scarcely visible despite, or perhaps because of, their food" (Michael 2006: 261). This suggests that the visibility of "Malay" cooking in dominant food culture is paralleled by the invisibility of the people who make it. Furthermore, for the cuisine to serve as a part of national tradition requires a silence about enslaved beginnings. In contrast, the Muslim food historian Cass Abrahams, author of *Cass Abrahams Cooks Cape Malay*, insisted in an interview (Baderoon 2002) on observing the direct connection between slavery and cooking, noting that during the colonial period, when cargo ships entered Cape Town harbour, one could determine by smell whether they carried spices or slaves.

An example of Appadurai's theory of a national cuisine and its erasures can be found in Renata Coetzee's *The South African culinary tradition* (1977). In its version of a national cuisine, the book places "Malays" after successive European influences: *The Dutch Element, The German Contribution* and *A French Flair*, followed by *An Eastern Aroma* and then *Edible Wild Plants and Their Influence* and *Cape Edible Wild Plants*. In the course of the book, it becomes clear that Coetzee's definition of "South African" is *white Afrikaans-speaking South Africans*, who have absorbed these various influences to develop a "national" cuisine. Martin Hall critiques the self-erasures in Coetzee's elevated language, such as her references to "rissoles in vine leaves" and "watermelon preserve" to describe plain farm food (1992: 25). This genteel vision of a Cape past renders slavery invisible and turns Muslims into an *ingredient* in South African cooking. The book places "Malays" in a serene past, with slavery benignly alluded to in terms of the "skill" of the men as artisans and the "exotic oriental dishes" cooked by the women.

This characterises slaves as a piquant *flavour*: as if they, like their food, gave a pleasing tincture to a broader South African history. Indigenous people are not mentioned at all, but "edible wild plants" are listed. Ultimately, the colourful visibility of "Malays" in these books functions to give white, especially Afrikaans-speaking South Africans, a claim to a substantial and elaborated history. Coetzee's vision of a South African culinary tradition erases the history of slavery and colonialism.

The introductions, prefaces, forewords and illustrations of such cookbooks define a white South African national cuisine in which Muslim cooking plays a minor and exotic part. They locate Muslim food in a benign past, and their descriptions of recipes are tinged with a tone of loss and nostalgia, portraying Muslim cooks as holders of the secrets of a distinctive food tradition in danger of disappearing. This is the case even in the country's earliest cookbook, Hewitt's 1889 *Cape Cookery*, which refers to "really good old-fashioned recipes such as were almost traditional … in former times" (1889: 19). Muslim people themselves are either unnamed, as anonymous Ayahs in the kitchen, or named to secure the expertise of the author, where Arabic names are used as markers of authenticity, and by extension, of the writer's authority. In I. D. du Plessis' foreword to Gerber's book, he acknowledges "[t]he revision of some details by Sheikh A. Behardien, President of the Moslem Judicial Council". Most commonly, however, the authors refer not to their "Malay" informants, but to one another for authority. For instance, Betsie Rood's *Maleier Kookkuns* (Afrikaans for "The Art of Malay Cooking") reflects the success of Du Plessis's claims to expertise concerning "Malay" culture, since the author dedicates her book to "I. D. du Plessis and the Cape Malay community". Du Plessis' interest in "Cape Malay" cuisine is by implication part of his project of constituting the "Malays" as a body of knowledge over which he presided.

In contrast, Hilda Gerber's *Traditional Cookery of the Cape Malays* names the women from whom she received recipes, and even provides different versions of the same dish. Gerber's commendable approach has enabled descendants of these women to trace their contributions. Mrs Jorayda Salie told me in an interview that a relative of hers had provided Gerber with a recipe. On the other hand, the illustrations in Gerber's cookbook, drawn by Katrine Harries, convey an unvaryingly amiable, colourful and exotic image of Islam that neglects the complexity and shifts in the food, and contradicts the approach taken in the written text. As archival sources, cookbooks also reveal a history that subverts the placid reputation of the Cape Muslims. Cass Abrahams revealed that many of Betsie Rood's informants left out crucial ingredients in their recipes, rendering them unusable.

As the above examples show, cookbooks can be a way to erase and appropriate histories. However, there is another tradition of food history in South Africa, evident in Gerber and particularly in the writing of C. Louis Leipoldt, the most significant figure in the framing of public knowledge about Muslim cooking. Leipoldt collected an extensive archive of recipe manuscripts dating back to the seventeenth century, which are housed in the South African National Library. His *Cape Cookery*, published in 1976 (although the manuscript was completed in 1947), discusses the role of slavery in South African history and credits "Malay" cooks with inventing an original creole cooking tradition. Leipoldt is the source of enduring tropes about Muslim cooking in South Africa, including an almost unparalleled skill in the use of spices and being famously protective of food secrets. His description of their use of spices is the best-known South African verbal image of Muslim food:

> Malay cookery ['s] … outstanding characteristics are the *free, almost heroic*, use of spices and aromatic flavouring, the prolonged steady, but slow, application of moist heat to all meat dishes, and the skilful blending of many diverse constituents into a combination that still holds the essential goodness of each (1976: 11).

Leipoldt's evocative metaphor of the "free, almost heroic" use of spices, and his connection of spices with "freedom" and "mastery", suggests that the inventiveness of cooking allowed Muslims to claim a degree of control and power from dominant society even under conditions of slavery. Part of the resonance of Leipoldt's tropes of freedom and secrets comes from his insight into cooking as an assertion of mastery in a form that eluded the surveillance of slave-owners.

In my interview with her, Cass Abrahams recalled Leipoldt's quotation with even greater emphasis: "[spices] were readily available and [the slaves] added it to the food of the Dutch masters, as Leipoldt says, *with absolute free abandon*" (emphasis added). She noted further that when it comes to blending flavours, the "Cape Malays are masters, absolute masters, at doing that". This "free, almost heroic" gesture of an enslaved hand dispensing spices captured by Leipoldt's metaphor and the intensification of this in Abrahams's "absolute free abandon" powerfully convey the "body language" sought by Ross. The images articulate an assertion of "freedom" unreadable by the master and mistress, and a "mastery" they cannot equal (Ross 1999: 2).

Cookbooks by Muslim authors:
Food, gender and magic

Even at its most benign, there is always a secret in food, and good cooks appear to have an almost occult level of skill in the kitchen. Indeed, both during and after slavery, Muslim cooks were thought to have supernatural abilities, as the quotations above by Lady Duff Gordon and Van der Post show. The recurring theme of the skilled but silent woman in the kitchen was accompanied by an anxiety about the close relationship between skill and secrecy, cooking and magic, food and poison. Before emancipation, skill in cooking among slaves was both sought after and feared as an insidious and potentially dangerous power to "gool" or conjure. In its benign version, this is reflected in the image of a skilled but mute Ayah in the kitchen. However, this familiar feature of South African recipe collections was radically revised by the publication of cookbooks written by Muslim women.

Indian Delights (1961) was the first cookbook written by Muslim authors in South Africa. It was created by the Women's Cultural Group in Durban, led by Zuleikha Mayat, and became an unprecedented publishing success and an important cultural landmark (Vahed and Waetjen 2010). In her seminal analysis of Indian women's writing, *Sister Outsiders*, Devaraksha-nam Govinden (2008) showed that *Indian Delights* was not solely a book of recipes but, with its inclusion of advice and stories about the challenges faced by Indian indentured labourers in South Africa, it demonstrated that "[c]uisine was an important way of preserving cultural identity in a strange land" (102).

Govinden revealed that the initial impetus for the creation of the book was to refute the anthropologist Helen Kuper's dismissal of the Indian contribution to South African literature. In a passage quoted in the Women's

Cultural Group brochure of 1972, Kuper asserted that "despite the hundred years in South Africa, the Indians here had not achieved much in the field of literature" (quoted in Govinden 2008:102). The Women's Cultural Group at first intended to write a literary work in response to Kuper's comment, but later resolved to create a different intellectual and political project in the form of a communal cookbook. Because it was driven by a broader social aim, the authors did not obey the conventions of cookbooks and instead reinvented the genre, combining "recipes interspersed with numerous vignettes, nostalgic family anecdotes [and] convalescence remedies" to create a new genre that "has an invaluable intertextual and social character" and "projects a fascinating dimension of cultural history" (Govinden 2008:102). They refused the association of exoticism with Muslim food. The collection testified to the resourcefulness of the people from whom it drew its recipes, who had brought seeds from India and grew vegetables on "apron gardens" (102). The word "delights" in the title encompasses not only resilience, but inventiveness and pleasure. In the face of poverty, the women's ingenuity was also evident in handmade tablecloths cut out of old newspapers, which provided not only dignity but also beauty. By remaking the genre of the cookbook through *Indian Delights*, the Women's Cultural Group achieved an extraordinary degree of social, intellectual and financial influence. The combination in the book of social history, public and private narratives, and collectively formed knowledge has created an enduring resource for food history, education and women's leadership.

The next publication by a Muslim author was *The Cape Malay Cookbook* (1988) by Faldela Williams. My interviews with different generations of Muslim cooks suggests that on its first appearance, *The Cape Malay Cookbook* was addressed to an outside audience because the introduction refers to the use of "exotic" spices, whereas the use of spices is the most quotidian act in Muslim cooking. This reflects the requirement of exoticism that *Indian Delights* was able to subvert. The introduction also describes "Malays" in the third person, as "they", and many cooks I interviewed complained that the amounts given for spices in the recipes were woefully inadequate. Williams's strategy of including the names of cooks in recipe titles (such as "Mymoena's Almond Tart" and "Fawzia's Soetkoekies") gives credit to the women who provided the recipes while conveying her role as a scribe of circulating communal knowledge and simultaneously confirming her role as an expert who could draw on authentic sources (1993: 77). Ironically, because of changes in cooking practices in the decades after its publication, the book has become an important tool for passing recipes along between generations of Muslim cooks (Baderoon 2001).

Cass Abrahams Cooks Cape Malay is the next noteworthy publication in this genre. Interestingly bifurcated in its approach, it shows in an extensive introduction and foreword the author's awareness of an outside audience to whom the food would be seen as exotic; however, it also alludes thoughtfully to the history of Islam and slavery as part of her definition of "Malay" food. A former political activist and food historian, Abrahams emphasises the communal, pan-African character of the food. In contrast to Laurens van der Post, Abrahams asserts that its African location is crucial to "Cape Malay" cooking, and that indigenous Khoi and San people shared their knowledge of indigenous food resources with Muslims, thus contributing crucially to the cuisine. She contends that this combination of ingredients, histories and traditions makes "Cape Malay" dishes a "food from Africa." This contrasts strongly with the exoticising tone of Van der Post's writing on Muslim food in *African Cooking* (1970) and *First Catch Your Eland* (1977), which highlights its Asian origins and underplays its African and creole aspects. For instance, he describes an Eid plate of "brightly coloured cakes a la Javanese" (1977: 130), claiming that "on feast days, what is purely Malay in their cooking tends to assert itself" (132). In comparison, Abrahams's signal contribution to food writing in South Africa is to assert the "African" character of Muslim food, and to give due credit to its African, Asian and creole elements rather than simply foregrounding its Asian history.

The publication of books by Williams and Abrahams was an important development in the South African lexicon on Muslim cooking, but their transformative effect was limited by the genre of the cookbook, which relies on the persona of the skilled chef to establish its authority, and integrates Muslim cookbook authors into the commodification and exoticisation of food, ethnicity and culture. Despite this, the contemporary practice of the food retains its resistant and inventive origins in the methods of ordinary cooks. Abrahams's story about the Hertzoggie cookie, which I discuss at the end of this chapter, exemplifies the dissident practices within food production that exceed the frame of the commodified cookbook, and bring the subversive meanings of food into the foreground.

"Steal with the eye":
Taste, secret knowledge and hidden meanings

Such resistant elements are found in the practices of ordinary cooks, whose views I elicited in interviews. Abrahams revealed that in "the old Cape Malay books written by Betsie Roods [and Hilda Gerber], [the informants] purposefully left out three or four ingredients (2002: interview). This echoes Leipoldt's description of the secretiveness of Muslim cooks, and shows that with recipes, the rules of access are determined by those on the inside. While Muslim herself, Abrahams is not originally from Cape Town, and she encountered a determined secretiveness about recipes among Muslim cooks in Cape Town while writing her book. "I found I had to go and *steal with my eyes*; in a lot of instances I would chat and watch them surreptitiously" (2002: interview). She found it understandable that people who had been exploited and who knew that their knowledge of food had been commodified by others might be reluctant to share recipes: "You want to [hold onto] that [since] you have nothing else." To overcome this secretiveness, Abrahams revealed that one of the skills of good cooks is to be able to extract recipes even from people who do not want to share them. Two other cooks I spoke with used a similar metaphor for eliciting knowledge. Rose Fick told me that good cooks have the ability to "catch with the eye" (2002: interview), and Zainab Francis learned to make pizza bases when "I saw with the eye in a pizza shop one night" (2002: interview). This subtle use of "the eye" is one example of the hidden reversals described by De Certeau, and of the body language sought by Ross. What looks like compliance or submissiveness is actually an evasion of the classifying impulse, and the remaking of available knowledge through subtle and unexpected means.

I end this chapter with a coded history told in food. The Hertzoggie is a familiar "Cape Malay" cookie or biscuit that can typically be seen in photographs of Eid festivities in South Africa. It is a small, open tart made with two fillings of contrasting colours alongside each other. Unbeknown to many outside the Muslim community, this innocuous-looking confection also encodes an important political history. Cass Abrahams tells the story of how these meanings were translated into food by the less powerful. She takes us back to 1936 when General J. B. M. Hertzog:

was running for power. He made two promises ... He said that he would give the women a vote, *en hy sal die slawe dieselfde as die wittes maak*, he will make the Malays equal to the whites.[5] Achmat [Davids, the late linguist and historian] reckoned the Malays became terribly excited about this and they put this little short-crust pastry with apple jelly underneath and then had the egg white and coconut on top of it and baked it and called it a Hertzoggie in honour of General Hertzog. However, when he came into power he fulfilled one promise, he gave the vote to the women, but he didn't make the slaves the same as the whites. So the Malays became very upset and they took that very same Hertzoggie and covered it with brown icing, you know, this runny brown icing and pink icing and they call it a twee-gevreetjie [hypocrite] (Abrahams 2002).

This secret history recounting the memory of a political betrayal in a historically important set of bills is invisible to the unschooled eye. Not even the Muslim-authored cookbooks reveal the secret. Instead, the story circulates in oral form in the Muslim community.

Abrahams's account is revealingly and evocatively phrased. In the interview, she gives two versions of the promise made by J. B. M. Hertzog, who was Prime Minister of South Africa from 1935–42 one in Afrikaans and one in English: "*hy sal die slawe dieselfde as die wittes maak*, he will make the Malays equal to the whites". She translates Davids' phrase as "he will make the Malays equal to whites", but in fact the Afrikaans phrase she reports him using is that Hertzog promised to "make the *slaves* the same as the whites". Significantly, Davids did not use the words "Muslims", "Malays" or "Coloureds", but "slaves." The power of that phrasing and the insistent recollection of the broken promise is suggestive. The memory of slavery is encoded into the story and the practice of the recollection in the tart, and people still feel it viscerally. In fact, they can taste it.

However, the story also records an ambiguity, in which a nascent apartheid project sought to divide Black communities from one another. Hertzog's successive bills sought to dilute and ultimately remove the franchise from black people by entrenching the racial separation of voters' rolls into law. In several incarnations, the effect of the bills severely undermined the franchise of African and coloured voters by giving the vote to white (but not black) women in 1930; in another instance, they offered a deceptive enhancement of the Coloured franchise as part of the attempt to pass the bills through the parliamentary process. In effect, the bills laid the groundwork for apartheid (Worden 1994: 87). Hertzog brought the bills to parliament where they were rebuffed twice before being passed in 1936. Muslims were betrayed by Hertzog's predictably broken promise to "make the slaves the equals of whites", and those who voted for the deceptive Coloured enhancement betrayed their rights as part of a larger black collectivity. The Hertzoggie encodes these betrayals and also the ambiguities of history – the broken promise and the memory of a complicit act – and continues to be baked today, a familiar sight on plates of cookies and biscuits that are served at tea, weddings and Eid, conveying its oblique lessons of memory and betrayal.

The Hertzoggie is a complex sign. The word is a diminutive, potentially signalling familiarity and either affection or contempt. The cake is an invented and then changed ritual, a "delight" served at tea and special events like Eid and also a bitter memory. It speaks a secret language of keenly ironic and cutting critique. It is a way of remembering history through the body, and makes history by speaking to the body. But it is also a divided sign, multilayered, recalling the juxtaposition of the offer of commemoration, and why it was repealed. It speaks of a promise by the dominant society that would in some ways salve the lingering historical pain of slavery. The story of the Hertzoggie remembers that the terms "Malay" and "Coloured" are directly linked to slavery. By using the word "slawe", it speaks in the register of history and addresses 176 years of slavery, not only the prefiguration of apartheid. On the other hand, the terms of this offer, to *make the slaves the equals of whites*, were always constrained in the language of whiteness, of becoming closer and equal to whiteness. This was a poisoned bargain and inevitably, one of betrayal.

In contrast to its benignly picturesque image in popular cookbooks and media images, Muslim food thus carries the memory of enslavement and its long aftermath. During the colonial period, cooking was a way to marshal resources, presence and creativity under conditions of peril and poverty. In representation, food also signals dissonant meanings, as the discussion of *The Slave Book* shows. Enslaved people created a new language of food out of dominant traditions that eventually also influenced the tastes of slave-owners. One can trace the porous boundaries of the slave kitchen in contemporary South African food practices, with food thus constituting a powerful archive. This is evident in the story of the Hertzgoggie, whose coded meanings subvert the picturesque mode. The creation of new foods that fused African, Asian and European customs was the result of the reshaping of dominant food culture by the powerless. Instead of being exotic, "Cape Malay" food, with its local ingredients melded into a synthesis of African, Asian and European cooking traditions, is one of the ways in which Islam became indigenous in South Africa.

The publication of cookbooks written by Muslim women from 1961 meant that Muslim food would no longer be a realm presided over by white experts who drew from silent or apparently submissive black informants in their kitchens, and spoke on their behalf. The conception of *Indian Delights* as an intellectual project confirms the contribution that food makes to South African culture; and the word "delights" in the title reminds readers that the pleasures of the body remain insistently present in scholarship on food. The transformation of Muslim cooks from silent informants to spokespeople of tradition began to subvert the use of "Malay" food to solidify a "general" South African cuisine that marginalised Africans and centred a European-oriented whiteness. But it is in art and the daily, unremarked practices of cooking that some of the most radical possibilities of food as history can be seen.

CHAPTER 3

"The Sea Inside Us":
Parallel journeys in the African oceans

the sea is so heavy inside us
and i won't sleep tonight.
i have buckets of memory in a jar
that i keep for days and nights like these.

– Mxolisi Nyezwa, "Sea" (2000: 25)

Sunday 17 – We saw the coast of the Cape.
Tuesday 19 – Another slave died.

– Hendrik Frappe, *Journal of the Slave Ship Leijdsman Returning from Mozambique*,
November 1715, cited in Westra and Armstrong (2006)

At the vantage point at the end of Cape Point Nature Reserve, about an hour south of Cape Town, visitors are invited to gaze at the exact point where the Atlantic and Indian Oceans meet, where some say one can see waters of different hues of blue collide and merge. In truth, the actual southernmost point of the African continent is at Cape Agulhas, approximately four hours' drive east, and if oceanic waters could ever be distinguished, that is where the two would join. The indeterminacy of the dividing and the meeting points of the two African oceans is an apt metaphor for contemplating the theme of the sea as an archive of intricate meanings about Muslims and slavery. Recent South African poetry, memoir, fiction, art and accounts of pilgrimage present the sea as a protean theme that observes neither national nor temporal boundaries, combines public history with private and autobiographical narratives, and re-envisions the country's geography and temporality. The texts reveal "alternative modernities" alongside those of imperialism, including the temporality and geography of the hajj, and assert new affinities across spatial and historical boundaries (Hofmeyr 2007: 13). In the writings below, the sea is a metaphor for experiences that transcend conventional categories, the juxtaposition of multiple histories, the transformation of the self, and memories of slavery. They map the ocean through memory and ritual.

Despite the country's extensive coastline and long transoceanic history, South African literature has been strangely mute about the sea (Samuelson 2010: 543–57). Because land has been a great obsession for whites and a measure of anguished loss for the indigenous people of South Africa, the fraught theme of land is everywhere in the country's literature and art. As a consequence, it has been possible to turn away from the sea. But the oceans have had a profound impact on South Africa's history and present, so their absence is weighted and meaningful. If we turn back toward the sea, what might we perceive?

The two oceans: memory and history

In an analysis of the theme of the oceans in South African literature and culture, the literary scholar Isabel Hofmeyr observes that "the Atlantic seaboard [is] the site for the emergence of capitalist modernity as a transnational system" and "the Indian Ocean [is] the site par excellence of 'alternative modernities'" (2007: 13). In this chapter, I do not shift focus from the Atlantic to the Indian Ocean in South African narratives about slavery, but attend to both sites. In this view, both the Atlantic and the Indian Oceans are the oceans of middle passage, but also of cosmology, memory and desire, traced in the movement, language and culture of enslaved and dominated people. The descendants of enslaved and enserfed people in South Africa have made a "new place" where the two African oceans meet.[1]

A recent pattern of images in South African poetry, history and accounts of pilgrimage has re-imagined the sea through the themes of memory and history. In such works, the oceans represent complex visions of the self, retrieved pasts, and claims both of origin and alienation. This can be seen in Mxolisi Nyezwa's poem "Sea" in the epigraph to this chapter, in which the sea symbolises memory "heavy inside us". Nyezwa writes of the sea as a welling force that connects private memories with public history. In "Walking," the weight of the ocean orients the speaker's body and provides a personal compass, even as the roiling water and sky press on him with an almost irresistible force: "i see the unstable dark sea, furious / and on my back, my spine, the vertebral sky" (18).

In Yvette Christiansë's poetry, the sea is haunted by allusions to slavery and capture, but these are countered by a concurrent sense of origin and homecoming. This potent combination of trauma and belonging is also suggested in Nyezwa's "Walking", where the "furious" ocean maps itself onto the speaker's body with an immense and almost impersonal anger, yet the sea's vast turbulence also suggests a larger entity of which he is a part. For Nyezwa's speaker, the ocean, sky and body are intimate and continuous. The "vertebral" sky is as close as bone, and the sea's mutability and ceaseless movement symbolise the mystery of the speaker's sense of self and the world. In Nyezwa's vision, the sea conveys a voluminous and almost unknowable self, and also something beyond the speaker, a sense he can only intuit. This suggests that the intimate, bodily experience of the Indian Ocean is also a public one, weighted with history.

Imraan Coovadia's comic novel *The Wedding* (2001) is based on family stories about his grandparents' marriage. Its protagonists are a mismatched couple, Ismet and Khatega, who move from India to South Africa after their wedding, and whose long path to nuptial bliss takes place over the course of the entire novel. In *The Wedding*, the voyage across Kala Pani ("Black Water" in Hindi), the name given to the Indian Ocean, is an interregnum between two worlds. The sea is the dividing line "right at the edge of the world". For the protagonists, both the point of disembarkation and arrival are heavy with history, the ineluctable expectations of family and society and their own complicated relationship. Yet for three weeks, the sea creates its own singular unhurried space and time.

While most of the novel consists of dialogue showing the comic conflict between Ismail and Khatega, with almost every conversation leading to misunderstanding, during the voyage there is little talk. Instead, the narrator is riveted by the strange and protean beauty of the ocean. "By early afternoon the horizon was nothing but a line of dark orange; light streamed out over the ocean, making angry bright smudges here and there on the infinite surface. Right at the edge of the world was a single, clean white band, marking the point where the sky swept upward from the ocean" (133–34). The sight of the ocean interrupts the pattern of failed exchanges between the protagonists and instead unites them in silent fascination during the ship's slow voyage. "The sea divided into great watery slabs that crashed over one another, surged against the ship's plate, growled in the middle of the night ...The wind beat on [the ship], whistled across the decks, raised up by the sea. Now and then lights showed through the gloom, but mostly the ship was alone, water-battered" (134). The unpredictable but unerring beauty of the sea also prefigures the ultimate resolution of the story, which recalls the welling and wordless allure of the ocean: "then, a slow fluting, a gentle needling, a silence, a pause, a junction, a sliding in and a sliding out, a tunnelling, a burrowing, a shunting and a shuffling, a downing, a muffling and a diving ... My grand-parents made love" (256–57).

Yvette Christiansë's private oceans

Because of the history of slavery in South Africa, the country's view of the Atlantic Ocean includes loss – slaves were transported via the Cape from Asia and East Africa to the Americas – but also homecoming, exemplified by the return of Sarah Baartman's body from France in 2002 to be buried in South Africa (Abrahams 2000). This dual vision of the Atlantic is reflected in the poetry collections *Castaway* (1999) and *Imprendehora* (2009) by the South African poet Yvette Christiansë.

Castaway portrays the island of St Helena in the south Atlantic off the south-west coast of Africa through fractured narratives about its famous exiles Napoleon and Fernao Lopez (the disgraced Portuguese soldier who in 1515 became the first denizen of the previously uninhabited island), but also by tracing the life of the poet's grandmother Fin, a grandchild of slaves, to whom St Helena was a beloved homeland. Christiansë's St Helena is thus portrayed in two registers: the public history of exile and enslavement; and the "private" language of poetic memoir. The collection crafts a vision of the island in fragments of "lost" texts by speakers who lived on the island in dif-ferent eras – Lopez, Napoleon and an unnamed woman in the contemporary era embarking on a search for origins. Revealed in episodic and intersecting narratives, the poems suggest that the island can never be fully known. Frequently, the poems end with questions. "Is this real?" a speaker asks (17).

In *Castaway*, St Helena is a place of wind, mist and constant change. Surrounded by the immensity of the Atlantic, the small island emphasises the power of the sea, audible even when shrouded in mist. The tides, birds and ships that cross the vast stretch of ocean are metaphors of indeterminacy and change in *Castaway*. On the approach to the island, neither ships nor island are fully visible to one another. Decks dip beneath the waves and the horizon is enfolded in fog. History layers St Helena like its perpetual mists and wind, and nature aids the island's resistance to being known. "There are things I know nothing of / things that go on in the island's sharp dark" (14), a speaker acknowledges. On the approach, the island appears and then recedes behind a wave, seen only in a shifting form. The unknowability of the island is also part of the European view of St Helena as irretrievably distant from civilisation, and the denial of the role of slavery in that concept of civilisation.

Once on the island, we find the speakers in *Castaway* desiring to be elsewhere. To its exiled speakers Napoleon and Lopez, the island is so far from Europe that it seems to be at the end of the world, a lost place, "married to the losses" (2). By virtue of this distance, simply to be on St Helena was a form of punishment for Europeans. Its most famous inhabitant, Napoleon, was exiled to the island in 1815 until his death in 1821. In *Castaway*, the general, who was once "the measure of all things", spends every day feeling his distance from the centre of power. Lopez, the exile who was the first inhabitant of the island, names St Helena "the worst place" (1), lamenting that by being here, he has been "taught about distance and desire" (16).

In the collection's alternative imagining of the island, St Helena is the place where Christiansë's family originates, and where Fin, the speaker's grandmother, was born, so *Castaway* also contains an intimate view of the island, in which the sea is the route to certainty and belonging. Fin's recurring desire to return to the island conveys *Castaway*'s private vision of St Helena as a place of homecoming rather than exile: "She longed / for the sea. Not any sea, / but that green sea / she knew" (7). In poems about Fin, the sea is certitude, when "[t]he fin of a sleek dark fish […] finds a current and slips clean into its long sweep all the way around the world without moving a muscle" (8). Poems about Fin speak of the island with longing, as the locus of origin. In "The Island Sings Its Name", "a circle / of elders ... replenish themselves / like waves in a slate-green sea" (6). However, Christiansë's grandmother was the grandchild of slaves, so the sea also symbolises cruelty and loss. In returning

Fin to St Helena, *Castaway* does not attempt to redeem the losses of slavery, and the poems do not claim to trace the truth that has eluded family memory. When the speaker asks about her grandmother's date of birth, the answer is 1898 – with the caveat "we think".

Thus the poems refuse an innocent approach to St Helena. The island was part of the Atlantic slave trade, and in *Castaway*, ships leave with loaded holds. In several poems, the sea therefore signals capture and entrapment. Some of the most powerful lines in *Castaway* evoke the experiences of slaves transported from St Helena to the Americas. In these poems, the waters between Africa, Europe and the Americas have a cruel breadth that cannot be tracked with the eye. The poems take readers into the airless space of the ship's hold, where slaves are trapped in the dark without water. In "Eclipse", the speaker testifies that "I saw the great silver- / backed, shark-tipped ocean open / and those men and women – yes / there were children too – opened / their eyes and their lips were silver with waiting …/ I heard them. I heard them" (77). The island's darkness resembles the dark of a ship's hold, where the cries of slaves reveal that the trade in human beings was central to European notions of progress and expansion. In the poem "The Enlightenment sees its face in a different light", the slaves hidden beneath the surface or deck of the ship become a "rigid silence / that threatens the deck" (66). Their presence discloses the violence that the Enlightenment keeps hidden.

Yet, even unacknowledged and invisible, the presence of the slaves also sustains the ship. In the colonies, Europeans defined themselves in opposition to the people they encountered, but in this poem, the presence of the slaves is a "howl, those / sounds [...] grow into the hull's own song" (67). Listening to the hidden sounds within the "hull's own song," the speaker turns the barely audible voices of the slaves into a sign of presence in the poem, breaking the silence required about the contradictions of slavery within the Enlightenment.

Christiansë's second poetry collection *Imprendehora* links the Atlantic and Indian Oceans in poems about the eponymous slaving ship (the name is a version of the Spanish word for "enterprise"), which plied its trade around the Cape. The collection is divided into two sections: "Atlantic", the longer of the two, and "Indian". In the poem "Abundance" in the "Atlantic" section, the epigraph quotes an item from the island newspaper, the *St Helena Register*, about seven slaves who "in a fit of despair" escaped the island in a small boat (15). Despite its brevity, the news article is given depth and poignancy by its observation of the "despair" of the escaping slaves. In recounting the interior lives of the enslaved people, "Abundance" crafts a fuller portrait of them than the brief notice in the newspaper.

The poem imagines their journey after the escape – precisely what cannot be known from official records. The tasks of sailing, but also quieting the world to enable escape, are divided among the seven people: "Two to hold the water still / Two to leap, two to climb, / One to put his face to sea." "The length of waves" and "stern" water evoke the scale of the task they have undertaken. The poem envisions the posture of their bodies engaged in the pursuit of survival: "One man calls, wind to shore. / One man waves, a crane's wing" (15). The scale of the challenge of surviving their flight from slavery is suggested by the contrast between the small vessel in which they are pursuing their freedom, and the cold and vast ocean. In the poem, we hear the shocked breath of its protagonists immersed in the immeasurable Atlantic: "One to gasp, one to tread." To name the man's call the "wind", and to envision the gesture of waving as a "crane's wing" gives these small, hopeful gestures a larger weight, and offers the possibility that they will continue and return, like the wind and birds. Combining an attentiveness to the physical as well as the metaphysical, the poem ends with a description of one of the escaped slaves "[s]inging to slake his thirst" (15). By concluding with an image of physical suffering transformed into song, these last words allow the song to resound and continue, creating a memorial to the unnamed slaves, of whom there are no further traces. Through song, the poem defers an ending.

The collection as a whole becomes an act of memory, explicitly so in the last section on the Indian Ocean. Here, the poem "Ship's Register" rewrites official records. At first, the poem relays only the functional details in a ship's register, details that constitute an archive of loss and pain. Yet, as in "Abundance", the records sometimes offer glimpses of lives that would otherwise be almost impossible to retrieve. Inscribed alongside utilitarian details are multiple, phonetic attempts to spell an African name – "345 Male Samuel Age 4, Stature 3.3 / Mother Neammhoo? Neammorhoo?" (93), which may be as close as we come to the sound of that name spoken by the boy or his mother. The poem therefore acts as a calling-out of such names, but also expands the functional, dehumanising list of the ship's register in an attempt to speak in the voices of the enslaved people themselves.

Returning to the trope of poem as song and to the silenced memories that the poems convey, the speaker in "Ship's Register" urges her daughter to "Sing, sing these words – / they are alive." "[D]o not forget," she commands in the last stanza (93). The last lines of the collection exhort readers to remember, echoing the speaker's vision that memory will create a new history: "Make a dawn for them / in the reds and yellows / of remembrance" (93).

Pilgrimage as sacred geography and temporality

As Christiansë shows in *Castaway*, the register of autobiographical and family memories can open a path to history. Such narratives can deliver a "homemade cosmopolitanism" that recovers new spatialities and temporal connections in the multidimensional resonances of the sea (Hofmeyr, quoted in Samuelson 2007:81). The cyclic nature of tides and the borderlessness of the oceans are suggestive of what escapes boundaries of time and space. In this vein, I explore narratives of pilgrimage as an archive about Islam in South Africa.

The oceans hold a particular meaning for Muslim pilgrimage in South Africa because most Muslims in South Africa arrived via the Indian Ocean into lives of slavery and indenture. The reclamation of the same ocean for pilgrimage is an assertion of a new and sacred geography away from these traumatic histories. Even during slavery, the Indian and Atlantic Oceans became a path to pilgrimage for Muslims in the Cape Colony. Can this history of pilgrimage offer new meanings about the two African oceans, vast and seemingly featureless bodies of water that border the continent, but seem nothing in themselves?

In an illuminating article written in 1999, Tony Morphet contested the stubborn exceptionalism of South African architecture by asserting the then-unprecedented connection of Durban with ports on the East African coast. Morphet wrote that "[i]n topographical and climatic terms the city has more in common with port cities to the north – Maputo, Zanzibar, Mombasa – than it does with highveld Johannesburg or the Mediterranean Cape" (1999: 5). For more than a century and a half, Muslim pilgrims had established the connection between these South African cities and their African counterparts further north along the East African coast through the infrastructure and sacred geography of the hajj. Through pilgrimage, Muslims have thus mapped alternative spatialities and temporalities.

Pilgrimage to Mecca is one of the five requirements of faith for observant Muslims. By performing the hajj, pilgrims are absolved of their sins and are symbolically renamed "Hajji". Importantly, pilgrimage produces a specific relation to place, belonging and return. Pilgrims travel to the centre of Islamic practice and circumambulate the Ka'aba, the orienting point toward which Muslims all over the world pray. As Barbara Cooper notes, "[t]o go to Mecca is to go home" (1999: 100). South African accounts of the hajj, from the earliest published memoir (that of Hedley Mahmoud Mobarek Churchward, who performed the hajj in 1910), to oral testimonies about pilgrimage by ship in the 1950s and recently published accounts, reveal the hajj to be an important historical archive about relations between South Africa and other parts of Muslim Africa, and with the polities pilgrims encountered en route to Mecca.

Considering the difficult circumstances in which Muslims practised their religion during the colonial period, there is a remarkably long history of pilgrimage to Mecca by South African Muslims. Sheikh Yusuf, who was exiled to the Cape in 1694, had already completed the pilgrimage by the time of his banishment. Ebrahim reports that the earliest known pilgrimage by a Cape Muslim was by Carel Pilgrim (Hajji Gassonnodien) in 1834–1837, immediately after the end of slavery, although Imam Frans van Bengal had attempted the hajj in 1806, while Imam Abdulgamiet completed the hajj in 1811, but did not return to the Cape (2009: 17). The introduction of a steamship to Zanzibar enabled broader access to pilgrimage, and the arrival from the 1860s onwards of Muslim teachers from Arabia, India and Turkey helped cement a sense of connectedness to the rest of the Muslim world (Worden et al. 1998: 187). Michael Wolfe's compendium of ten centuries of hajj narratives includes an account by the Englishman John Keane during his pilgrimage in 1877 of meeting

a Cape of Good Hope Malay, one of an English-speaking Muhamedan community, who yearly send their half-dozen pilgrims to Mecca. He had been living some years in Mecca ... the Cape Malays have now outlived all prejudice, and my new friend told me that he was very comfortable in Mecca (Wolfe 1998: 269).

In the post-emancipation period, the ability to go on hajj also became a way to negotiate status and authority within the South African Muslim community and during leadership struggles in mosques (Tayob 1999: 33–34). Indeed, for South Africans and other Africans who live at a distance from Mecca, the ability to go on pilgrimage to Mecca grants an important power to assert religious authenticity and authority, an effect that is of particular significance for women, converts and ethnic minorities in Islam (Hermansen 1999: 65).

For South African Muslims, pilgrimage and other practices of Islam such as communal prayer, the ritual visiting of shrines and burial practices redrew the colonial map and reoriented the land- and seascape toward a new sacred space and temporality. For instance, South Africans lay their prayer mats north-north-east to face Mecca. This posture of the praying body oriented at an angle precisely aligned to the spiritual centre of Mecca thousands of miles away is reflected in the poem "Brother, Who Will Bury Me?" by Rustum Kozain, which is set in Paarl, near Cape Town, where the "trees bend north-north-east in witness. / Close to God" (Kozain 2005: 58). In the poem, not only the human body but nature itself reflects a sacred map.

Other sites of religious importance also redefine the meaning of the urban and peri-urban South African landscape. For instance, the kramat (burial place) of Sheikh Yusuf has become central to local cultures of the hajj in South Africa. Mogamat Hoosain Ebrahim reports that pilgrims visit the kramat when they state their intention to go on pilgrimage to Mecca. In *Mecca Diaries* (2005), Rayda Jacobs recounts that when she made the intention to go on hajj, "we met with hundreds of other hujaj (pilgrims) at the shrine of Sheikh Yusuf in Faure" (2005: 17). Reflecting the histories encoded in place names, Faure is also known locally as Makassah, after Sheikh Yusuf's birthplace in Indonesia. In addition to its religious meanings, this kramat has also acted as a beacon of colonial memory and slave resistance, and aided the development of an indigenous Sufist Muslim identity in South Africa.

The map drawn by pilgrimage is evident in recent published accounts of pilgrimage. In their collaboratively written account, the South African anti-apartheid and gender activists Na'eem Jeenah and Shamiema Shaikh describe the hajj as a "journey of discovery" in which they experienced an oscillation between memory and discovery that began even before they left South Africa; they ask, "isn't all discovery an exercise in remembering"

(2000: 36). If to arrive in Mecca is to arrive home, the pilgrimage begins in one's place of origin. This assertion connects South Africa and Mecca in a profound way. The connection is confirmed in a story about Table Mountain and Mecca told by Hajji Churchward, which I recount later.

The sea is an apt theme through which to approach pilgrimage since, in several chapters in the Qur'an, the image of the bountiful and powerful ocean conveys the omniscience of God. In *A Hundred Horizons: The Indian Ocean in the Age of Global Empire*, the historian Sugata Bose cites Surah Luqman from the Qur'an at the beginning of his chapter on pilgrimage: "the ships sail through / The Ocean by the Grace / Of Allah". This use of the sea as a metaphor for an untroubled life reminds sailors that they are kept safe through the mercy of God (Bose 2006: 193). Such verses evoke for believers the knowledge that both the punishing power and the compassion of God are as infinite as the sea.

Bose draws on this double meaning of the ocean in his discussion of pilgrimage across the Indian Ocean, which he argues is a powerful unifying factor in a region seemingly separated by distance, imperial divisions and national boundaries. Bose contends that hundreds of years of pilgrimage across the ocean have created a crucial form of continuity instead: "The hajj had been a key integrative element in the economy, religion, and culture of the Indian Ocean in the precolonial era" (2006: 195). During the period of British imperial control, the hajj was the site of a complex interplay between pilgrims and colonial authority, tradition and modernity, spirituality and rationality, the colonial and the pre-colonial, and the national and the transnational. The movement of people in such a complex and ritualised manner was inevitably also political. Bose observes the competing influence of the parallel orders of religion and empire. "Religion, even more so than the idea of nation, proved adept at crossing seas", he points out (195). In fact, he contends, "Muslim colonial subjects who undertook the pilgrimage could never be wholly subjected to the discipline of states. The hajj turned out to be a crucial Indian Ocean activity that was a vehicle for an anticolonial current that state boundaries could not contain" (195).

To read the Indian Ocean through pilgrimage is therefore to uncover parallel modernities. Bose sees the hajj as a form of universalism that rivalled that of imperial modernity. This was particularly evident in the late fifteenth century, at the start of the European era of exploration, when the ascendancy of the Muslim world was a source of competition, envy and fear in Europe. The expulsion of Muslims and Jews from Spain occurred in 1492, the same year as Columbus's westward voyage and Vasco da Gama's rounding of the Cape en route to India. Europeans at the time had a fraught relationship with Islam. At the same time, however, they relied on Muslim interlocutors in their encounters with Africans along the African coast, where Arabic was a language of contact, and, even more crucially, for their navigational expertise at sea. Nonetheless, they also saw the Muslim polities they encountered as their competitors and enemies. In accounts of the Portuguese empire in Asia, "[t]he constant foe for Portugal was Islam" (Johnson 2012: 15). This complicated combination of competition with and reliance on Muslims is revealed in *One Thousand Roads to Mecca: Ten Centuries of Travellers Writing about Muslim Pilgrimage*, where Michael Wolfe points out that

> Vasco da Gama, on his first great eastward voyage, was guided across the Indian Ocean from East Africa by an Arab pilot named Ibn Majid, who happened to be the author of *Nautical Directory* (1490), a popular Arabic compendium of contemporary nautical science, including all the information then available for sailing the Red Sea and the Indian Ocean (1997: 76).

The oceans therefore carry crucial histories in several registers.

Growing up, I experienced pilgrimage stories almost exclusively as oral narratives recounted by family members who were embarking on or had returned from hajj. In these stories, the narrator, whose account is often echoed or supplemented by other hajjis, conveys a narrative of quest and transformation in which physical challenges of travel, heat, health, food and accommodation are transcended by spiritual renewal. Typically, in the pilgrim's narration of the hajj, accounts of travel are preliminary to the focus on actually being in Mecca. While prefatory to the hajj itself, the elements of intention and preparation are very important, particularly because the hajj usually requires several years of saving, studying and spiritual orientation. With my interest in the journey and the map drawn by pilgrimage, I was an unusual listener, drawn by details that seemed to the hajjis to be of passing interest only. However, I was following Bose's model in noting that the passage itself was a component of the pilgrimage: "We circle around the centre of the pilgrims' ultimate destination, Mecca, before reaching it" (Bose 2006: 195).

Auntie Galiema and the parallel maps of pilgrimage and empire

In 2008 I interviewed an eighty-year-old family friend, whom I will call Auntie Galiema, about her pilgrimage to Mecca by ship in 1951. In doing so, I participated in the genre of oral hajj narratives, but also stretched it by asking her to reflect on the details of her journey to Mecca as much as her time in the Holy City itself. Auntie Galiema was able to perform the hajj at a young age because an uncle and aunt in Zimbabwe invited her to accompany them in gratitude to her father for his kindness to them several decades before. This demonstrates the collective nature of the hajj, and the networks of family and friendship that form part of an informal and formal infrastructure of pilgrimage. After consulting with her parents, Auntie Galiema said her niyaat, or intention, to go on pilgrimage. Her uncle then invited an imam from South Africa to Zimbabwe for four months to teach the future pilgrims the necessary lessons to perform the hajj. Hajj education is also part of the institutional infrastructure of pilgrimage developed by Muslim communities in southern Africa. Auntie Galiema showed me the handwritten pages of the fragile fifty-seven-year-old book (known as a koples, or memorisation book) in which she recorded lessons about preparation, prayers, clothing and spiritual orientation for the hajj. After the lessons had been concluded, the pilgrims left for hajj in April 1951. They returned in November of that year.

The ship to Mecca departed from Durban, so Auntie Galiema and her relations took a train from Salisbury (now Harare) to the port. From there, they embarked on a boat for Mombasa, where she and her uncle and aunt stayed for a few days. In Kenya, they changed modes of transport and flew to Mogadishu and Khartoum and then to Jeddah on small planes. She recalled the "unbearable heat" of Khartoum as she showed me her passport, which was as old as her koples book. On yellowed pages, I saw the stamps of the different empires whose lines she crossed in order to go on hajj: the Brit-

ish stamp in Mombasa for the "Kenya Colony" on 14 July 1951, which has
a handwritten entry "In Transit to Mecca". Two days later, the page shows
a stamp from the "Eritrea Police Force" at Asmara Airport on 16 July 1951;
and the return journey is indicated by a stamp for the "Aden Colony", where
she was in transit on 4 October 1951. The parallel institutions represented
by the immigration officers' stamps in this South African passport, marking the imperial possessions en route to Mecca, was stored in the same box
of treasured memories as Auntie Galiema's koples book. These juxtaposed
books exemplify the parallel universalisms to which Bose refers. In Auntie
Galiema's memory of the hajj, a private map of family, friendship, hajj lessons,
prayer books and communal ties of spirituality connects Cape Town, Harare,
Durban, Mombasa, Khartoum, Aden, Jeddah and Mecca.

In a separate interview with another family friend in her eighties, her
grandson showed me photographs of what he calls the "ship hajjis", in which
men and women sit together on wooden decks, leaning against crates and
railings, lightly dressed in what seems to be great heat. This is contrasted with
a second set of images, of the hajjis once they have arrived back in South
Africa. The hajjis in the latter photographs are dressed in formal and beauti-
ful clothing, the women in white dresses and burkas, and the men in long
robes and typically Arabian head coverings. In one photograph, which the
grandson titled "Hujajj-Ladies", a woman wears a robe embroidered in white
lace and formal Arab headwear that leaves only her eyes visible. Such photographs, displaying the comportment and resplendent dress of hajjis in their
new roles as respected pilgrims, are precious mementoes of Mecca, and are
often displayed prominently in Muslim homes. A local photographic studio
called Van Kalker in Woodstock, Cape Town, specialised in producing hajj
photos with backdrops of the Great Mosque and the Ka'aba.

Hedley Churchward and the connection of the Cape to Mecca

The earliest published account of Muslim pilgrimage in South Africa is that
of an Englishman named Hedley Mahmoud Mobarek Churchward, who
went on hajj in 1910, and whose memoir was published in 1931. Born in the
1860s, Churchward was an English stage designer who became entranced by

the architecture of mosques in Andalusia in the 1880s, and subsequently converted to Islam (the precise dates are not specified in his memoir). He travelled extensively in Morocco before moving to Egypt shortly after the turn of the century, where he married the daughter of an imam and took classes in Islamic education at Al Azhar University in Cairo. In 1908 at Al Azhar, in anticipation of later going on hajj, Churchward took a rigorous ex-amination conducted by the Qadi of Egypt. After passing, Churchward was granted a passport by the Qadi that "authorised me, not merely to visit Mecca, but any sacred shrine or building in the whole of Islam", guaranteeing him untrammelled passage through the Muslim world (Rosenthal 1981[1931]: 50). Churchward soon moved to South Africa, where he helped to establish the first mosque in the Transvaal (present-day Gauteng Province), and then to Cape Town in 1909, from where he commenced his pilgrimage in 1910. Just as Hajji Galiema's South African passport mapped her route of pilgrim-age across several imperial borders from South Africa to Saudi Arabia in 1951, so Hajji Churchward's "Islamic" passport enabled him to cross both imperial and racial boundaries in 1910. Crucially, it helped to save his life when a fellow pilgrim accused him of being a non-Muslim imposter. Drawing on both his Islamic knowledge and the Qadi's passport, Churchward convinced the Meccan authorities of his credentials, and completed the hajj. He returned to Cape Town and lived there until his death in 1929.

The story of Churchward's pilgrimage by ship in 1910 flourished as oral history in the Muslim community before being recounted in the memoir *From Drury Lane to Mecca* (1981[1931]), written by the South African his-torian Eric Rosenthal, based on extensive interviews with Churchward. The power of Churchward's story of the hajj is due in part to the ways in which his narrative ties Cape Town to Mecca. During his time in Mecca, Churchward heard a story of a magic ring given to a man named Abdul Malik from Cape Town, who returned home and presented the ring to his wife, a loving and deserving recipient of the gift. Unfortunately, one day while washing laun-dry on the slopes of Table Mountain, she discovered that the ring had gone missing. This story demonstrates again the capacity of pilgrimage to remake geography by tying the spiritual power of Mecca directly to the iconic moun-tain in Cape Town, remaking it as a Muslim site. The story of the magic ring lost on Table Mountain means that a fortunate person, one as loving and deserving as Abdul Malik's unnamed wife, may yet receive the promise of abundance offered by the lost magic ring. A self-deprecating joke told to me during an interview takes up this theme of a connection between Cape Town and Mecca: "[T]hese Muslims from the Cape think that the Ka'aba is in the shadow of Table Mountain". Both commenting on the staunch devoutness of Cape Muslims, and reflecting a confident humour about the depth of Muslim belonging to the landscape, the joke cements the relationship between the southernmost part of Africa and the centre of Muslim observance.

Churchward's journey from Egypt down the East African coast to South Africa in 1909 creates a map of the Indian Ocean region that is retold in reverse when he goes on pilgrimage the next year. His memories connect Durban to a highly specific path across the Indian Ocean that includes waiting for the monsoon, and joining both British and Muslim-owned shipping lines. After the ship departs from Muscat, Churchward notices that Halley's comet is passing overheard. The Muslims on board read this as a sign of divine approval for Churchward's pilgrimage, and he finds that "Halley's comet added a good deal to my prestige" (86). Days later, the ship learns from another steamer that King Edward has died, bringing the two timetables of pilgrimage and imperial rule together. *From Drury Lane to Mecca* is illustrated with a photograph of Churchward in the flowing robes of Arab Muslims. Such photographs of returned hajjis, usually displayed in pride of place in Muslim homes, further cement the linking of the Cape and the Ka'aba.

In 1993, Na'eem Jeenah reflected on the South African political transformation and wrote that "Allah smiled on South Africa" (38). In 2005, in a jointly written memoir of pilgrimage with the late Shamiema Shaikh, the two writers see in the tide of humanity in the Great Mosque of Mecca "the complete equality of all people before the creator of all things" (33), and note with pleasure that "there was absolutely [no gender separation]. And God smiled" (39). In these accounts, the metaphor of "God's smile" connects the equality of South Africa's new dispensation with the racial and gender equality of prayer in Mecca.

As the narratives by Na'eem Jeenah and Shamiema Shaikh, Auntie Galiema and Hajji Churchward suggest, the culture of the hajj, conveyed in a powerful indigenous tradition of storytelling, has long reclaimed the South African landscape and the Indian and Atlantic Oceans from traumatic memories of slavery, indenture and apartheid, creating instead a parallel set of geographies and temporalities imbued with spiritual possession. Private narratives of pilgrimage therefore offer an archive of alternative modernities that have connected South Africa, East Africa, the Indian Ocean world and Mecca for hundreds of years across national and imperial boundaries.

Stories of pilgrimage reveal a map of belief laid over the South African landscape that is circulated in oral narrative. Rituals of the hajj place Shaikh Yusuf's kramat outside Cape Town on the route of pilgrimage to Mecca, and anticipate the connections between Cape Town, Durban and other African coastal cities later traced in studies of architecture. The hajj itself has a circular beginning that makes Mecca a "home" to which one travels in a "circumambulation of return", yet pilgrimage begins with the intention, which is stated at home. As a result, a visit to the kramat of Sheikh Yusuf, who had already gone on pilgrimage by the time he was exiled to the Cape, has become an integral part of the ritual of going on pilgrimage by South African Muslims. The sacralisation of home through pilgrimage is also reflected in Hajji Churchward's story of the lost magical ring on Table Mountain. Parallel modernities are found in passports that enable travel across both imperial and confessional borders, and in the sight of Halley's comet as a marking of the transitions of pilgrimage and empire. Tracing the metaphor of the sea in South African literature and art subverts the exclusions of the picturesque, and evokes a different vision of the land and sea, including memories of slavery and the sacred geography and temporality of Muslim pilgrimage.

CHAPTER 4

"Sexual Geographies of the Cape":
Slavery, race and sexual violence

History is what hurts.

– Fredric Jameson (1981: 102)

*Tell me that old story, the one about
the girl in the schoolyard. The Coloured
girl who was surrounded by boys ...
... Do you
remember that story? It has been
running between my legs like blood
for years.*

– Yvette Christiansë, "Sunday School" (1999: 47)

*So I guess
the P is not for poetry.*

– *Reclaiming the P... Word* (2006)

Silence, slavery and sexual violence

What is the relationship of slavery to sexuality? For almost two hundred years, the system of slavery ensured that systemic sexual violence was built into the colonies that would eventually form South Africa. Due to a gender imbalance in the Cape Colony, enslaved as well as free black women were a source of marriage partners for settlers throughout the slave-holding period, while the Slave Lodge, which housed

VOC-owned slaves, was "Cape Town's main brothel" (Keegan 1996: 20). By 1830, domestic labour in paternalistic slave-holding households was the primary role carried out by two-thirds of enslaved people in the Cape, a system that exposed them to serial violence and sexual abuse (Mason 2003: 108). John Mason's research into the records of the Office of the Protector of Slaves revealed numerous cases of sexual abuse brought against slave-owners by slave women. Indeed, as the feminist historian Gerda Lerner points out, "for women, sexual exploitation marked the very definition of enslavement, as it did *not* for men" (quoted in Mason 2003: 101). Gender and sexuality were therefore crucial factors in South African slavery.

At the Cape, colonial discourses about the licentious and animalistic sexuality of colonised people normalised the violation of black women's bodies (Hendricks 2001: 37). Enslaved and Khoisan women's bodies were designated as available for sexual access with impunity. Robert Ross notes that the "authorities at the Cape did not question the right of an unmarried or widowed slave-owner to the body of his female slaves" (1983: 114). During the entire period of slavery at the Cape, not a single free or enslaved man was convicted of the rape of an enslaved woman, Ross shows. Sexual violence was therefore fundamental to colonisation at the Cape, and the scale of such violence under the founding social system of slavery in South Africa demands sustained scholarly attention.

While the picturesque tradition has generally diverted attention from the violence of colonialism, the topic of sexual aggression under slavery suffers particularly from "the problem of silence" (Wrathall 1992: 165). However, in the past fifteen years, scholarship and art about South African slavery have countered the erasure of sexual violence from the history of slavery through radical experiments in form and theme. In this chapter, I examine the traces of slavery's violence and sexual subjection left in language, historical scholarship and recent visual art and fiction that have recovered these repressed topics. The texts illustrate that the legacy of slavery affects all South Africans, not only the descendants of enslaved people.

The first source of evidence of the systemic nature of sexual exploitation in the Cape Colony is in the name of the city of Cape Town itself. Etymology reveals the hidden geography of sexual subjection in the Cape. The phrase "van den Kaap" (Dutch for "of the Cape") was used as the last name for Cape-born slaves (Bradlow 1981: 14) and indicated mixed-race parentage, often as a result of the impregnation of slave women by their owners or the men to whom they were forcibly prostituted. The very name of the city thus encodes the stark forms of sexual violence in the colony.

Representation is a crucial register for analysing the relation of slavery to sexuality, and the symbolic meanings and perceptions of enslaved people's sexuality by dominant classes allow us to discern how they were treated. A comparison of representations of enslaved women shows the commonalities in different imperial territories. Martha Abreu's study of representations of "mulatto" women in Brazil cites consistent references to their lush and available sexuality (2005: 267–88). In the records of the British colonies in Southeast Asia, Ann Stoler shows that "Asian women are centrefolds for the imperial voyeur" (2002: 44). At the Cape, John Mason points out that "the erotic allure of young slave women was explicit in the accounts of the Cape that white men composed … [This] depended as much on taboo … as on the exotic beauty of the women" (2003: 93). When I did archival research into the nineteenth- and early twentieth-century newspaper archives in the Cape, the attractiveness of "Malay girls" was a frequent theme (Baderoon 2005). As Mason notes, there was a subtext to the constant testimony about the allure of the "Malay" women:

> Commentators on the Cape stereotyped slave women as sensual and abandoned, in much the same way that slave women were described in the Caribbean and the American South. As in the New World, these stereotypes served to legitimate sexual exploitation (2003: 95).

The image of the physically alluring Muslim woman thus served both to rationalise and obscure sexual violence.

The colonial period is thus the primal scene for understanding racial and sexual codes in South Africa. In colonial settings, sex was central to the making of race, rather than acting upon already stable, raced identities. At the Cape, both under Dutch and British rule, control over sex was fundamental to imperial definitions of race. In her study of Dutch imperialism in Indonesia, Stoler points out that "the very categories 'coloniser' and 'colonised' were secured through forms of sexual control" (2002: 42). This is evident in the way white colonists were granted sexual license to black women's bodies, while black men's access to white women's bodies was violently policed.

At the same time, European beliefs about the perverse sexuality of colonised people were used to justify imperialism. According to Philippa Levine, the perception of the "naturalised prostitution, promiscuity, and homosexuality claimed to be central to Chinese, Indian, Arabic, 'Oriental', and Aboriginal societies were definitive of what made these places ripe for colonial governance, unworthy of self-rule, and inferior to their colonial masters" (2003: 325). She notes that practices that regulated sex in British colonies led to "the merging of blacks and prostitutes as a category" (2003: 182). The theory that "all 'native' women [had the potential] to be prostitutes" in effect granted sexual control over the bodies of enslaved and indigenous women to European colonists (Levine 2003: 182).

Precisely because colonists' sexual license to indigenous and enslaved bodies was fundamental to colonialism and slavery, the racial implications of sexual transgression haunted the colonies.[1] Permitted sexual relations between Europeans, enslaved and indigenous people ranged from marriage to concubinage and sexual slavery; yet, as Levine points out, "sex out of place" defined colonial culture (2003: 179). Sexual relations with enslaved and indigenous people posed an intolerable threat not only to the class but also the *racial* status of whites; consequently, Stoler notes, "obsession with white prestige was a basic feature of colonial thinking" (2002: 54). In her study of prostitution and race in the British Empire, Levine points out that in the colonies "fears around racial difference ... were often represented in sexual terms" (2003: 324). Stoler contends that it was "through the policing of sex ... [that] racial boundaries were maintained" (2002: 54). Given this history, it is unsurprising that black bodies in South Africa have been imbued with unsettling sexualised meanings since colonial times.

Systemic sexual violence was driven by a strong discourse about the threatening sexuality of both male and female slaves. Wendy Woodward writes that "slave bodies constituted a particularly threatening group in their symbolic figuring because ... they lived in the same domestic space as the slaveholders. [And] slaves' corporeality, especially their sexuality, was perceived as both powerful and dangerous" (2002b: 55–84). Just as the image of sensual slave women justified sexual exploitation, the large numbers of enslaved men relative to male colonists fuelled intense anxieties about black male sexuality. Fears about the insidious threat of black men drove public sentiment and policy in the colonies.

In fact, we can track the creation of gendered white identities in the colonies through heightened public panics about "black peril" and the corresponding need to protect white women from the perceived threat of the predatory sexuality of enslaved and indigenous men. In 1823, when the British took steps to moderate the power of slave-owners at the Cape, slave-owners in Stellenbosch framed their response as a need to defend white women and children from the twin dangers of insurrection and sexual violence by male slaves. In a letter to local officials, the slave-owners assert that amelioration would result in a threat "from the dagger of incited slaves. Not alone our Wives and Daughters, but also yours, will in a libidinous manner be prosecuted by our Slaves with rape and defloration" (cited by Mason 2003: 72). The threat of rape and miscegenation was also used to police the sexuality of white women and lower-class white men in the colonies. Yet even while colonists expressed panic about the sexual vulnerability of white women, black women were labelled brazen and animalistic, rendering invisible the systemic sexual violence to which they were subjected. The "panic" about the potential for sexual violence by slaves obscured the systemic sexual violation of enslaved people.

An old story: "Sunday School"

The ongoing consequences for women and men in South Africa, both black and white, of widespread sexual license to enslaved and indigenous women's bodies during slavery, are shatteringly conveyed in the poem "Sunday School" by Yvette Christiansë, cited in an epigraph to this chapter. The poem suggests that the commonplace sexual violation of black women today is directly linked to the shockingly "old story" of sexual violence that lay at the core of the slave-holding society at the Cape. The present-day epidemic of sexual violence, and the combination of silence and denigration that greets sexual violence towards black women in South Africa, are direct legacies of slavery. It is necessary therefore to seek the founding moments in which this system of sexual violence entered South African culture.

The extent and scale of sexual violence during slavery has had a critical impact on black identities in South Africa. This legacy is found not only in the historical record, but also in the self-representation of descendants of enslaved people, who were given the name "Coloured" after emancipation. In an essay titled "Shame and Identity: The Case of the Coloured in South Africa", the novelist and feminist literary scholar Zoë Wicomb argues that for the descendants of enslaved people, the memory of surviving slavery is burdened by an almost ontological shame – because of the accusation that black women were complicit with their own sexual violation. Sarah Baartman, the woman taken from South Africa in 1810 to London and Paris, where she was exhibited in public as the "Hottentot Venus", is best known for figuring sexual and racial difference in European discourses of science and medicine. Wicomb, however, places her in a feminist history of South African slavery by arguing that Baartman came to epitomise the association of black women with sexual shame: "The display of her spectacular steatopygia and its generation of medical discourse on the Khoi genitalia established the iconographic link between the black woman and sexual lasciviousness" (1998: 91). Baartman, in fact, "exemplified the body as site of shame" (1998: 82). As a consequence, black women's bodies symbolise *both violation and culpability*, or, as Wicomb phrases it, "the shame of having had our bodies stared at, but also the shame invested in those (females) who mated with the coloniser" (1998: 92).

In a painful reversal, therefore, black women's bodies have been made the bearers of the marks of sexual violence during slavery, making them responsible for their own violation and rendering invisible the *systemic sexual violence* of slavery. The intense, internalised shame associated with sexual violence and miscegenation has led to a powerful form of forgetting among the descendants of enslaved people in South Africa – in fact, "the total erasure of slavery from folk memory" (Wicomb 1998: 100). Such erasure has an obverse side, however: South African popular language is strewn with oaths and vulgar phrases based on derogatory terms for black women's bodies. These familiar and ubiquitous curses summon black women's bodies peremptorily into public visibility – evoking slavery's legacy of sexual violence without mentioning slavery. As "Sunday School" demonstrates, the consequence is that "Coloured" women's bodies symbolise an "old story" of centuries of sexual violence, but the accusation that they are responsible for their own violation licences extraordinary violence against them.

This heritage is starkly drawn in the poem "Sunday School", which was published in *Castaway*, Christianse's collection of poems that recalls the history of slavery in South Africa (discussed in Chapter 3). It asserts a direct link between that past and sexual violence in the present. The poem shows how the legacy of sexual violence under slavery transforms "Coloured" women's bodies into disposable and meaningless objects. For the men who rape the girl, race and Christianity prove no impediment to murderous violation. Whether the men are "Coloured or white" does not matter. Their ideas of manhood are inherited across generations and racial boundaries through "stories /of Coloured girls' bodies" that confirm that such women are available for violent abuse. In order to become "just men", they have learned to despise the kind of body labelled "Coloured girl"; that such a body is available for violation with impunity; that there are no boundaries to the degradation that can be visited on it; and that a schoolyard and religion can be spaces in which such violence can be practiced.

The speaker shows how the language of "a good preaching" and the location of a schoolyard prove no impediment to sexual torture. In fact, the violation of "Coloured" girls is so familiar that it has become an "old story" and almost "a joke". The poem subverts the "old story" which turns the "Coloured" girl into a "hunted" object and therefore creates a counter-history, a protective education she offers to other women. In the "old story", the woman is "hunted" by the men in the "schoolyard where she ran", emptying her fate of meaning and her life of any other details. Yet the speaker "think[s] of her" differently, constantly asking the reader to "remember," asking if she has heard *this* story, the story of a particular woman, a story not obscured by the tired familiarity of violation. In this version, the woman gives birth to a different kind of story. While it is born of "broken things," it is not solely written by violence. The speaker insists that the rape of this young woman in a schoolyard on a Sunday by men who had probably just listened to a "good preaching" will not be forgotten as a commonplace event, inevitable and barely noticeable. Instead, the speaker in the poem writes a hidden history of the woman and in the process creates a form of solace and protection for her and the many others like her.

The "old story" that threatens to turn black women's bodies into the occasion for violence likewise turns men's bodies into the instruments of women's torture. Such sexual violence rebounds on men too, as can be seen in the novel *The Quiet Violence of Dreams* by K. Sello Duiker, which shows how men can also be feminised and made subject to sexual abuse. The violence of the nameless woman's fate in "Sunday School" is thus also a story of men trapped in a pattern of normative violence. According to a script inherited from the colonial period, they are caught in a cycle of hunting some women and retreating to others[2] – "go[ing] softly / back to their mothers and sisters / wives and daughters".

These reverberating effects of sexual violence for both women and men make the nexus of slavery and sexuality a crucial area of scholarship and activism.

Like Christiansë, other writers have moved away from realist forms in representing slavery and sexual violence. Proposing that an emphasis on violence can unwittingly re-inscribe invasive acts and representations, the texts below show that poetic registers can be used to write women's bodies into alternative modes of visibility. In *Remembering the Nation, Dismembering Women? Stories of the South African transition* (2007), the feminist literary scholar Meg Samuelson contends that since 1994, women have been brought symbolically into the public space of the post-apartheid nation in highly constricted ways, either as silent but enabling mother-symbols in nationalist discourse, or as dissident figures who unsettlingly dare to speak in public space, and therefore need to be reined in and disciplined. This creates an opposition between the womb and the tongue that is subverted by recent texts, which represent black women's bodies in non-realist and non-nationalist forms. As "Sunday School" illustrates, poetic language provides a powerful means to register and name ubiquitous and normalised violence. Such language can also offer regenerative ways of configuring the resilience, authority and even pleasures of those usually seen as violated bodies. Through a complex interplay of silence and reclamation, the texts unflinchingly confront the legacies and meanings of slavery and sexual violence.

In a striking line in "Sunday School" that recounts the way the nameless girl is seen by the men who violate her, the speaker in the poem herself feels the threat of impending violence, which causes her to "keep [her brown legs] covered". Blood runs between the legs of the speaker in empathy with the girl, suggesting that the way one looks at "Coloured" girls' bodies is critical to whether they are subjected to violence or not. This attention to the way black women are looked at allows me to return to the question of the colonial gaze raised in the discussion of Berni Searle's *Colour Me* in Chapter 1.

Sexual geographies of the Cape: *Disgrace*

The visual marking of certain bodies as available for violation has a "long history", which is also evoked in the novel *Disgrace* by J. M. Coetzee, published five years after the first free elections in 1994 (1999: 53).

Then one Saturday morning everything changes. He is in the city on business; he is walking in St George's Street ...

For an instant, through the glass, Soraya's eyes meet his. He has always been a man of the city, at home amid the flux of bodies where eros stalks and glances flash like arrows. But this glance between himself and Soraya he regrets at once (1999: 6).

In its narrative of the fall into disgrace of David Lurie, a disaffected white professor of English at a university in Cape Town, the novel *Disgrace* directly addresses themes of racial and sexual violence. Set in the 1990s in post-transition South Africa, *Disgrace* has elicited praise for its lucid prose and unswerving attention to the impact of South Africa's history of racial and sexual exploitation. However, it has also generated intense opprobrium for its bleak tone concerning post-apartheid South Africa, and for a scene in which a white woman is raped by three black men. In an interview, Coetzee called this theme "the *ne plus ultra* of colonial horror-fantasies" (quoted in Attwell 2002: 336). The novel shows an intense interest in the history of sexual violence in South Africa, and the sense of sexual entitlement this has given both white and black men. In the course of its narrative about Lurie's sexual relationship with a young black student, *Disgrace* draws attention, in the words of the character Farodia Rassool, to "the long history of exploitation" exemplified by Lurie's actions (Coetzee 1999: 53), referring to the record of sexual exploitation of black women by white men in South Africa since the colonial period.

This history is also suggested by the opening pages of *Disgrace*, which describe a series of sexual encounters in Cape Town between a woman named Soraya and the protagonist Lurie. In these scenes, *Disgrace* maps the geography of Cape Town as a sexual space through Lurie's eyes. Walking through the city, Lurie is at ease, "at home amid the flux of bodies where eros stalks and glances flash like arrows" (1999: 6). Cape Town conceals its trade in sex amid the bustle of the city streets and in quiet suburbs. "On Thursday afternoons he drives to Green Point" (1999: 1). This suburb just outside the centre of Cape Town was notorious for prostitution and for transgressing the strict demarcation of neighbourhoods along racial lines during apartheid. Like Hillbrow in Johannesburg, Green Point resisted the Group Areas Act and remained a place where black and white people interacted with one another, and even continued secretly to live with one another. Such "grey areas" were seen as spaces of both racial and sexual transgression and gave an association of sexual ambiguity to Green Point. Interracial sex was forbidden by the Immorality Act during apartheid, and bodies like Soraya's were the focus of both revulsion and attraction because they indexed the history of forbidden sex between whites and blacks.

Graham Pechey suggests that even with those Coetzee novels that are "realistically and topically located ... we are made ... to see obliquely and prismatically" (2002: 375). I take Pechey's point to mean attending to the heightened sense of pattern and alertness to history demonstrated in the novel. *Disgrace* displays a keen awareness of the legacy of colonial discourses of sexuality and their long record of exploitation and violence. This includes the ways in which white sexual trauma is highlighted, as Coetzee's comment on "colonial horror-fantasies" shows, while violence against black bodies, particularly those of black women, is normalised. In his essay "Race in *Disgrace*", David Attwell notes that few markers of race appear in the novel. However, among those that *are* given, "[i]n the novel's very first paragraph we are told unmistakably that the prostitute, Soraya, is coloured" (2002: 337). In fact, Attwell mis-states Coetzee's wording, since we are *not* told in the novel that Soraya is "coloured" but that she is "Muslim" (Coetzee 1999: 3). The distinction is important, for Lurie's confusion about where Soraya lives, in "Rylands or Athlone", reveals his privileged distance from and lack of knowledge about these suburbs, whose inhabitants were regarded as racially distinct under apartheid: Rylands was for Indians and Athlone for "Coloureds".

Soraya appears in the familiar language of the picturesque in the novel: "She was on their books under 'exotic'" (7). Lurie describes her "honey-brown body", "lustrous hair and dark eyes" (6). Sex between them is figured as a form of instruction and obedience. He finds that "[h]er temperament is in fact rather quiet, quiet and docile" (1), and notes approvingly that she is "a ready learner, compliant, pliant" (5). Referring to the owners of the flat in which he meets Soraya every week, Lurie muses, "in a sense they own Soraya too, this part of her, this function" (2). She is a possessable figure, "owned" and pliable to Lurie's desires. Soraya's availability to Lurie's commands and her "ownership" by the people who run the brothel foreshadow Farodia Rassool's later comment about the "long history of exploitation" of black women by white men. The novel thus recalls colonial discourses about sexuality, just as Coetzee's earlier fiction "The narrative of Jacobus Coetzee" in *Dusklands* (1982) recalled settler narratives about land. Soraya can be seen as a postmodern literary summoning of the placid, picturesque "Malay" figure and perhaps even the submissive "Malay" slave who unquestioningly complied with the commands of those who owned her.

Through the possessable body of Soraya, Lurie sees the city as explicable, "contented" and "lull[ing]" (8). However, when they encounter each other in the city streets and Soraya *looks back* at Lurie, "everything changes". The instant the body that holds the explicable landscape in place returns the gaze, the careful edifice of Lurie's grasp on Cape Town collapses. This returned gaze inaugurates the disruptions of the rest of the novel.

The novel alerts us that "the strangeness" starts in Cape Town (6). This is evident in the doublings and circlings in the novel, such as the "worm" and the "snake" totem through which Lurie envisions sex with Soraya, and the animal images through which later sexual encounters are described. Lurie's watchful, abstracted description of his assignations with Soraya as "living ... within his emotional means" (2) is frighteningly echoed by the rationality and calculation of the sexual assault on Lucy that follows later in the novel. The opening pages of the novel, therefore, far from being a prelude to its real substance, prefigure the "strangeness" that follows. Read in this way, Soraya can be seen as a postmodern instance of the marginal Muslim figure who holds in place a white self. Coetzee's novel invokes and subverts the fraught desire of white subjects to find a place of belonging in the South African landscape through the body of a compliant Muslim figure, and evokes the long history of exploitation behind the image of the exotic Muslim woman.

As I have shown in my discussion of the *Colour Me* images (in Chapter 1), "Sunday School" and *Disgrace*, non-realist forms offer a powerful means of contesting the erasure of sexual violence and slavery. The novel *Unconfessed* (2007) by Yvette Christiansë and the play *Reclaiming the P... Word* (2006), which was collaboratively written and performed by students and staff at the Gender Equity Unit of the University of the Western Cape, give insightful and moving attention to the sexual violence suffered by black women since the colonial period. Both also insist on a holistic exploration of black women's pleasure and power. While the texts differ in genre, period and subject matter, they are connected by a productive attention to poetic language and form. As the title of a South African essay collection proclaims, such textual worlds have powerfully generative effects and hold the potential to create "the country we want to live in" (Mkhize et al. 2010).

Poetic form as map and memory: *Unconfessed*

Unconfessed, a novel about slavery in South Africa written by Yvette Christiansë, is set in 1826 in the Cape Colony, and recounts the life of an enslaved Mozambican woman named Sila. In telling the story of a woman who had been kidnapped as a child and brought to the Cape where she experiences relentless injustice and abuse, the novel demonstrates that sexual violence was at the core of the world made by slavery at the Cape.

The character Sila is based on a real woman whose life Christiansë researched for twenty years in the Cape archives before writing her novel. The woman entered the archives because of her conviction for the murder of her child, and through the single word she uttered during the proceedings in the courtroom: "hartseer" (heartsore) (Christiansë 2007: 321). This resonant word, which testified to the inner life of an otherwise invisible woman, is transformed by Christiansë into a three-hundred-page testimony by the protagonist. In contrast to her archival silence, *Unconfessed* allows Sila to recount her life, from her childhood in Mozambique to her forced enslavement and the unspeakable fate of giving birth to several children sold into bondage at the Cape.

This harrowing narrative is made remarkably affecting by the poetic language, indicated in italicised prose, in which Sila speaks. *Unconfessed* employs poetic language to invoke trauma while avoiding realistic descriptions of the violating acts, and also to allow the protagonist to communicate with people whom it is literally impossible for her to reach, such as those who have died or been sold to owners in distant parts of the country. The novel therefore suggests that an "impossible" connection across time and space is made possible through elliptical and lyrical language. Sila's communication with the dead and the lost is presented as a form of psychic resilience and resistance to a violent system that called itself rational.

In the course of her life as a slave, the protagonist was renamed: from Sila van Mosbiek (Sila of Mozambique) to Sila van den Kaap (Sila of the Cape), a shift that recalls the enslaved woman's birthplace in her name and then records the mis-naming by an owner to hide his illegal sale of Sila. Her renaming allows us to reread the landscape of the Cape, conventionally celebrated for the aesthetic appeal of Table Mountain and the sea, for traces of slavery.

When the novel opens, Sila has been imprisoned by the colonial authorities for the murder of her son Baro, and is known to the authorities as "Sila van den Kaap, slave woman of Jacobus Stephanus Van der Wat of Plettenberg Bay in the District of George. A woman moved from master to master, farm to farm, from the district's prison, to the big town's prison. A woman fit for a hanging. Child murderer" (12). The fact that Sila has killed her child seems to consign her to the trope of the monstrous black mother. However, while she refuses to "confess" at the trial, as the title of the novel conveys, the long interior monologue of the novel recounts that Sila chose to end Baro's life after he had been grievously injured by her owner, rather than suffering him to continue to live as a slave. We also learn that Sila had been granted her freedom by a former owner, Hendrina Jansen, but that the will in which this was stipulated was stolen by Jansen's son. Instead of being freed, Sila was sold from farm to farm until she arrived in Cape Town.

Unconfessed reveals the stark reality of the sexual abuse of women slaves. Sila's children are the result of rape by her owners and by prison guards and men who pay the guards for sex with imprisoned female slaves. When an official arrives to hear her evidence for commuting her sentence, Sila thinks at first that he has paid to have sex with her before realising that he believes her story: "This time would be different from all the other times, all the other visitors … There would be no quick counting of coins, or the rough laugh he gave as the visitor ran to wash himself" (Christiansë 2006: 19). This recounting of sexual slavery refuses to counter the stereotype of black female dissoluteness by creating a virginal heroine; rather, it testifies to the brutality of repeated sexual abuse to which enslaved and indigenous women were subjected.

Rayda Jacobs's novel *The Slave Book* also displays the brutal logic that blamed slave women for sexual exploitation by their owners. Because *The Slave Book*'s light-skinned protagonist Somiela is the visible result of interracial sex between her mother and a slave-owner, she is judged guilty of the sexual violence that led to her birth and accused of sexual immorality. The slave-owner's wife Marieta uses a crude sexual jibe to insult Somiela: "We can see alright what she is. A naai-mandje" (1998: 25). "Naai" is a crude word for sexual intercourse in South Africa, which literally means "to sew" in Dutch and Afrikaans. "Mandje" means basket in Dutch, and it insinuates that their use as sexual objects is the only function that defines slave-women. As noted above, Wicomb pointed out that all enslaved women were assumed to be guilty of sexual deviance by virtue of slavery itself. Both *The Slave Book* and *Unconfessed* make it clear that this claim is utterly unjust, but do so in different ways. Because of the formulation "woman-native-prostitute", a heightened sensitivity to sexual shame in communities descended from slaves has led to an insistent valuing of respectability and propriety. The result, in novels like *The Slave Book*, has been an emphasis on sexual virtuousness in Muslim women characters. In fiction, as in etymology, the legacy of slavery can be read in the meanings of women's bodies. *Unconfessed* takes a different approach by unflinchingly revealing the sexual violation to which enslaved women were subjected.

During her life as a slave and a prisoner, Sila is subjected to continual sexual violence. In a revealing scene soon after the novel opens, a new warden visits her cell:

> "What have you to say for yourself?" he demanded ... "Ek se, wat het hjy vir jouself te se?" His accent was so stupid. She lay back and laughed, drawing her skirt up. This was how they liked it, filthy and stinking ... The naaimeidjie was here. Yes he should know who and what this place had made of her in all these years (Christiansë 2007: 8).

Since she assumes that the warden is there for the same reason as the guards, Sila lifts her skirts. This abrupt physical gesture reveals the incontrovertible truth of sexual violence, and testifies to what it means for a woman to be a slave at the Cape:

> they took her when she was old enough to cry for a life that already had full memories, and ... she had to work ... on a farm for a man who had no wife, and it does not matter that she knows what it is like to be ridden like a horse or milked like a cow ... We are women who are horses. We are poese up to our chins (320).

The word "poes," the Afrikaans term for vagina, has migrated into South African English as a curse word, and marks a subsumed trace of slavery that cannot be spoken of otherwise. As Sila testifies, through slavery, black women became "poese up to our chins." Her life since childhood has taught her that slavery makes women available for constant sexual violence.

In contemporary South Africa, the word "poes" occurs ubiquitously in public as a swear word. As a character in the play *Reclaiming the P…Word* (discussed below) enumerates, it is "scrawled on toilet doors, station walls and schoolboys' desks." In fact, the word "poes" is the despised entry point of black women's bodies into public discourse, illustrated by the display of Baartman's genitals at the Musee De l'Homme for 159 years. "Poes" evolved through the transformation of the Dutch word for cat into the Afrikaans word for "vagina", and then into a translingual derogatory term for a woman or weak person. The dual absence of public discussion of slavery and the ubiquitous presence of terms of public denigration for women makes continuing sexual violence possible, as both *Unconfessed* and *Reclaiming the P… Word* suggest.

The centrality of sexual violence to the slave narrative in *Unconfessed* is path-breaking in South African literature. Yet there are other avenues for writing about enslaved women, sexuality and the bodies of black women. As the etymology of "poes" indicates, the history of painful words offers such an avenue through a subtle interrogation of history.[3] This is because to look unflinchingly at the language of bodily contempt – literally through common South African swear words such as "poes", "naai" and "moer" (womb) that translate the names of intimate parts of women's bodies into terms of denigration and implicit violence – allows us to deconstruct the formulation that makes black women's bodies the basis of a language of violence and brutal exclusion.

This approach does not seek to speak back to the litany of curses, but to draw attention to a level of meanings not evident in the formal languages of power and national visibility. Hearing these words spoken in another register also allows us to see how formal language disregards or overlooks the ubiquity of curse words based on women's bodies, which are most commonly used against women, but can also be used by men to assert their dominance over other men (Raditlhalo 2005). These words always evoke women's bodies to project weakness and contempt onto others. To examine how such language operates may offer the possibility of reversing the implied culpability for sexual violence that the use of these words implicitly holds for women.

In the light of pervasive sexual violence, the bodies of slave women in *Unconfessed* speak in languages other than those imposed on them by their owners. An allusive and poetic form signals in a different register the brutality of slavery as well as the impossible desire of the protagonist to speak to her dead children, to recall her past life before slavery, to envision a time in which she is free and to sentence her slave-owners to a cursed future. *Unconfessed* is notable for giving its protagonist a memory of her life before slavery. Sila remembers her childhood in Mozambique before the slave raiders arrived: "I remember my mother – my mother from whom I was born – and her dancing when the day had grown late" (Christiansë 2006: 67). When her case is reviewed and the inspectors hear evidence of the sexual violence Sila has experienced in prison, her death sentence is commuted to fourteen years on Robben Island. In a scene in which she crosses the water from Cape Town to the prison island, Sila narrates that "sometimes I set myself the task of staring at the ships … And some days I make my eyes reach far, further still, and I tell you I see the anchors splash into the water off that coast, there, that Cape of Tears, Cape of Death, Cape of Struggles" (66).

This passage subverts the obscuring of slavery behind the image of the Cape as a place of leisure and beauty. The novel notes the cruelty of this aestheticising discourse through the words of a visitor to the prison on Robben Island: "it is such a shame that such wretched creatures should be in such a place of beauty" (73). From this prison island just off the coast of Cape Town, a forbidding sight to the city's inhabitants, Sila watches the Colony from within the two institutions of incarceration on which the Cape relied – Robben Island and slavery – and testifies silently to their brutality.

Just as poetry can be a language of incantation and enchantment, it can also be wielded as a curse. Because she sees how slave-owners use language against slaves, Sila curses her slave-masters with "liv[ing] with what they have seen", envisioning their fate in a future in which she and her children have achieved some justice:

And all they will be left with is a wounded house…. And their hands will have been stripped of all skin and flesh, right to the bone, for having beaten us. Their hands will be the sign of all they have done. Yes. And of what will come for them. That is what the sight of me and my right hand, come for my children, will do to them (326).

Slavery makes communication between slaves and slave-owners impossible, and this impossibility is an important theme of the novel. None of Sila's story is heard by the dominant slave-holding society. The title *Unconfessed* refers to the fact that Sila refuses to speak during her trial and declines to make a confession. Her mocking laughter at the start of the novel in response to the warden's question "[W]hat do you have to say for yourself?" shows her rejection of the terms in which slave-owning society demands that she speak. Sila refuses to defend herself before the courts, having concluded that the colonial language of justice and religion has in fact made slavery possible. She therefore rejects the basis for recognition she is offered by the slave-owning society: which is to accept that she is a slave and to acknowledge her guilt.

Instead, her "confession," consisting of the thoughts she conveys to invisible interlocutors like her dead son Baro and a fellow slave called Johannes, is heard only by the reader, and these thoughts constitute the anguished but ultimately triumphant words of the novel. Sila's elliptical, non-realist language creates an original and resolutely iconoclastic perspective on the Cape. The terms in which she testifies to her experience register as dissidence and madness to slave-owning society. To the novel's readers, however, Sila's poetic words express a complex subjectivity and an acute reading of the social mechanisms of the Colony. By refusing to engage with the dominant society, her response transcends straightforward resistance, and the text conveys a powerful resilience, intimacy and wholeness.

In acts that constitute a secret and unreadable form of resistance by the least powerful, the enslaved characters in *Unconfessed* use languages unknown to those in power, call each other by their original names and take pleasure in one another's bodies. The characters rename the landscape and name places even with their deaths. The death of the slave woman Hester, who tries to drown herself and her children, is narrated twice and is therefore deferred. In the first telling of the story, unvarnished in the cruelty it recounts, we learn from the narrator that:

> A woman named Hester threw her children, then herself, into the water of Table Bay. Dragged out, she found herself, and one child saved. And then they tied a leather strap around her neck. One man took one end, another the other end and they pulled and pulled. That was how she was punished. And then they threw her into the sea (40).

However, later Sila tells the story again:

I am a small boat bobbing just there off Cape Town ... I have come to pick up Hester and her babies. She walked into the water with her children so that they would escape this country. But cruelty of cruelties, she and one child were pulled free of the water ... Kom, Hester. I am your boat ... We are bound for the place where sun and sky hide a gate that only we will be let through. Come, Hester (76).

By retelling this story, Sila rescues Hester and her children through her memory of them. She recovers them from death and remakes Table Bay into a poetic memorial for an otherwise unremembered injustice.

Toward the end of the novel, Sila and an indigenous woman and fellow prisoner named Lys make a sanctuary for each other through a relationship that cannot be recognised by the guards: "Lys. Lys is the one who brings me warmth. We reach out and we are there. Being woman is enough here. Ja. That is the relief of how it is. A relief ... That is how it is. And Lys finds everything good in me" (334). As this description shows, Sila's sanctuary is created in language, in which the name "Lys" is repeated like an incantation. Sila repeats the phrase "That is the relief of how it is. A relief ... That is how it is," and the circular, reciprocal paragraph starts with Sila's observation that Lys "brings me warmth", and ends when she says: "And Lys finds everything good in me."

In *Unconfessed*, Sila's watchful gaze strips Cape Town of its feigned innocence about slavery and testifies to the constant violence that the Colony's founding system visited upon enslaved people. Through the novel, Christiansë reframes South African discourses on slavery and sexuality by drawing on material in the archives, and also by conveying the interiority of her protagonist. The novel replaces the relentless prettiness of conventional portrayals of the Cape by showing its aesthetics from the site of the prison on Robben Island, where these aesthetics have a different meaning. Portrayed through the cruelties of sexual slavery and physical abuse, the city of beauty is renamed "Cape of Tears, Cape of Death, Cape of Struggles". To the slave-holding society at the Cape, the protagonist Sila gives only her silence, but to the readers of the novel she is transformed into speech at the moment when she seems most silenced. When Lys dies, Sila envisages Robben Island in a new way: seeded with the names of everyone she has lost. Sila becomes language itself, "scatter[ed like names] all over this island"

(346). The novel's strands of resilience in poetry, memory and the sanctuary created by female bodies for one another form a subterranean legacy taken up in the text I discuss below.

The history of a painful term: *Reclaiming the P…Word*

As *Unconfessed* reminds us, history can be recovered through proscribed words, a possibility also explored in radical forms of theatre. *Reclaiming the P… Word* is a collaboratively written and performed play in eight scenes by staff and students from the University of the Western Cape in South Africa. Simultaneously attentive to history and intensely personal, the play's themes include the impact of colonial settlement at the Cape, the seventeenth-century figure of Krotoa, the life of Sarah Baartman, the high levels of sexual violence in contemporary South Africa and assertions of sexual pleasure by black women. The final scene reclaims the word symbolised by the ellipsis in its title. *Reclaiming the P…Word* employs theatrical performance to present women's voices in a range of registers to call attention to the damaging effects of misogynistic terms. The play's supple and radiant use of language also re-shapes the violent meanings of words.

In its themes, conception, writing and mode of performance, *Reclaiming the P… Word* forms part of a tradition of radical theatre-making in South Africa. The play was first performed in 2006 in response to the prevalence of sexual violence encountered by students and staff (Hames 2007). Even more than this physical context, the play addresses the mental universe for black women created by the constant pressure of sexualisation and sexual violence, as a result of which "sexual assault stalks the imagination of many South African women" (Mkhize et al. 2010: 4). In responding to the high levels of gender-based violence in the country, *Reclaiming the P… Word* draws on collaborative, non-realist modes of performance and "the use of private de-tails as a means of public resistance" (Dolan 2010: 34) to challenge the norms that sustain violence.

What can the "p-word" tell us about ways of representing the black female body in South Africa? As Mary Hames, the director of the play, writes in her essay "*Reclaiming the P…Word*: A reflection on an original feminist drama production at the University of the Western Cape" (2007), the use of the "p…

word" in the title alludes to the use of the word in South Africa to regulate women's access to public space through its connotations of violence and threat. The word carries such derogatory connotations that it is unsayable in polite society. As a term of abuse and contempt, it is used against men as well as women as a means to disempower them. The play takes this common practice and makes it the basis of a powerful reclamation of the word, which ultimately comes to include pleasurable meanings.

Already in its title, the play signals the strategic way it engages with women's bodies. Like the futurity implied in the curse of future justice that Sila casts on her owners in *Unconfessed*, in *Reclaiming the P…Word* tense is important; in this case, the sustained immediacy of the present continuous tense. Why, then, does the title of the play use the ellipsis in "p…word" instead of "poes", the word it stands for? Partly because this opens up a productive ambiguity, for instance, by posing the question: does the "p…word" stand for "poes"? We know from the rest of the play that the answer is mostly yes, but as one of the characters says, "I guess the P doesn't stand for poetry." "And why not 'poes' poetry?" asks the next line. However, the larger answer is that the word "poes" is already in the public sphere, and the play wishes to bring it to visibility in a different way. It seeks to reclaim the space that is already occupied by several uses of the word "poes", almost all of them damaging to women. The title signals the ongoing nature of its attempt.

As the play shows, the word "poes" has a remarkable degree of semantic dexterity; although it is a swear word, it can act as a noun ("poes"), adjective ("poeslik") and diminutive ("poesie"). Its meanings include the denotative "vagina", but it is most often used as a curse, as in "Jy is 'n poes" (You are a 'poes'). Thus, to look at "poes" in this way offers the possibility of seeing the body differently, not by directly countering its negative stereotypes, but by attending to its strange and powerful currency, and listening carefully for meanings that hover in it.

The common South African swear words "naai" (both "to sew" and a crude term meaning "to have sex"), "moer" (matrix or womb), "poes" and "doos" (literally "bag" but also a vulgar word for vagina) are ubiquitous on the streets of Cape Town, and, through the association with slavery above, are associated with the very name of the city. When I look up the word "poes" in the multi-volume *Oxford English Dictionary*, I find nothing under that term, although there are several entries for "puss". And indeed, in Dutch, the word "poes" means "cat". English retains this sense in "puss" and "pussy". So where does the expletive force of "poes" come from, its abrupt intimacy, the intake of breath at the taboo of saying it? Like "moer", the word asserts rage, disgust, rejection and violence. The *Dictionary of South African English on Historical Principles* (*DSAE*) shows that "moer" is slang for mother but "not in polite use". To say "jou [your] moer" and "jou ma se moer" (your mother's 'moer') is always an obscene and abusive mode of address. As with "poes", when used as an expletive, the word "moer" expresses rage, disgust or aggression. Indicating the close association of the word with violence, to "moer" someone is to beat or even kill them. While this information is included in the entry in *DSAE* for "moer", there is nothing on "poes".

In engaging with the latter word, *Reclaiming the P…Word* enters a long-standing debate about how to respond to abusive but widely used terms for women and sexual minorities. Reclaiming the power of proscribed words is a venerable political strategy, but it continues to be a sensitive one. By eliding the word to which it refers in the title, the play signals that the project to reclaim a familiar term for a woman's vagina is subversive, and yet also potentially hurtful. The reclamation of words such as "poes" is aimed at encouraging "those who have been insulted and abused to proudly reclaim their voice and bodies" (Hames 2007). This act of reclamation is exemplified in a startling moment in the climactic last scene of *Reclaiming the P…Word*. In the performance I attended in Observatory in August 2010, "Jou ma se poes" was shouted loudly and slowly from behind the audience. At first, I could not see who was speaking, and it was unclear if this was part of the play or if someone had walked in from the street and was shouting this far-from-uncommon interjection at the audience. Then I saw the speaker as she entered from behind the audience and wound her way to the front of the room that acted as the stage, continuing to shout the phrase several times, in various registers.

Does it grab your attention?
Or are you one of those that pretend that you did not hear it.
JOU MA SE POES!
On the street, in the township. Oh and let's not forget the taxi!
Parow, Elsies, Cape Town!
Hallo girl, ga jy saam! What, are coming? No? Your Poes!

103

Women, men, children, some can't even speak yet. They all use it.
Your Poes,
You are a Poes. You look like a Poes. You act like a Poes.
I mean really, come on listen to it. Poes. Women, men, children,
some can't even speak yet. They all use it. Your Poes!
One of the UWC managers said, when told about the name of this
production, "So I guess
the P is not for poetry."
And why not Poes poetry?

(*Reclaiming the P… Word* 2006: Scene 8)

In her performance, the woman intones the many inflections that the phrase
can hold, from incipient violence to derisory laughter, part of its humour
coming from its very familiarity. What if we took the word away from its
usual associations, the play asks? What if the audience of women and (some
men) were given mirrors and female condoms at the beginning of the performance and invited to look differently at themselves, to visit, to touch, to think
and speak with pleasure about their bodies? The last scene, which commences
with the repeated use of "Jou ma se poes!" ends with the poetry of "poes".

The movement in the play from pain to pleasure is as difficult and formally challenging as is the task of highlighting the topic of violence and invisibility. To reclaim the wholeness of black female sexuality presents a profound
political and artistic test. Desirée Lewis notes that within a broader history
of visual representation, "black women's bodies have often been the subject
of voyeuristic consumption, the consumption not only of black women's
sexuality, but also of black women's trauma and pain" (2005: 15). A repeated
focus on violation and trauma becomes a dangerous formula that entraps
people in narratives of violence, rendering them vulnerable to further violation and distancing them from the possibility of empathy and exchange with
others. *Reclaiming the P… Word* is acutely aware of this danger and interrupts
a voyeuristic focus on trauma through humour and word-play; for instance,
through puns like "My vagina is *gatvol*" (meaning "fed-up" but also literally
my "arsehole is full"). This section of the play, titled "Vagina Dialogues", refers
to the precursor play by Eve Ensor, and to the multiple ways in which women
view their own bodies. Even to say the list of transgressive words used to

denote vagina – "doos", cunt, "poes" – is to enunciate a litany of forbidden words that becomes funny when said in the usually polite space of the theatre.

To counter this list of insults, the speaker in this scene remembers a term for vagina learnt from her mother: "Thank god I grew up with my mother telling me I had a honeypot … a honeypot mind you." She reminds the audience that we have been *trained* into using certain words for the body, from her home (where she learned that she had a "honeypot") to the reversal of tone at school, where her mother's language was overwritten and a new code for black women's bodies was scrawled on the "toilet doors, station walls [and] schoolboys' desks" of the broader world. Clearly, the denotative meaning of "jou ma se poes" (your mother's vagina), is only part of the effect of this phrase. What does this powerful and intimate insult connote? The second person address hails the person in a direct call to engagement. It invites reciprocity, followed by an open-ended, incomplete sentence, an eternal beginning. The rest of the sentence proclaims access to "your mother's vagina", everyone's entry point into the world, and the history that it holds. *Jou ma se poes.*

"The Vagina Dialogues" ends with a list that becomes a tool of reclamation. The speaker intones a series of words, renaming and reclaiming the vagina, and recasting it in the first person possessive, "My pussy, my cunt, my poes, my doos". And with this list, the speaker makes a call for "[p]leasure, my sisters". With soft sequential alliterative plosives, the speaker arrives at a climactic reclamation, "[m]y vagina … my honeypot … has reached a stage where she's into pure, pristine, pussylike pleasure". To say these various incarnations of the word "poes" out loud also means that, briefly, the vagina issues from the mouth. This recalls the division between the tongue and the womb charted by Samuelson (2007), who showed that women could be domesticated by the womb (and the role of motherhood) and directed away from the tongue (and the promise of speech). The connection between the vagina and the mouth shows what happens when the black female body occupies a space hitherto unimagined, and owns power and pleasure: the body becomes the site of desire, of words, of mouth, of vagina.

In the plasticity and constant inventiveness of its language, *Reclaiming the P…Word* fashions new meanings for words that have been used to exclude women violently from public space. Like *Unconfessed*, the play draws both on silence, suggested by the ellipsis in the title, and on words spoken too often and with violent intent. *Reclaiming the P…Word* excavates a history buried beneath the plethora of South African curse words based on women's bodies, and gives them a complex set of meanings in the present.

The paucity of public discussion about sexuality and slavery in South Africa is countered in recent fiction and art, as well as alternative ways of reading language itself to reveal the ongoing salience of slavery for contemporary attitudes about race and sexuality. The novel *Disgrace* recalls the history subsumed behind images of exotic Muslim bodies in portrayals of the Cape. In their innovative and dissident use of language, "Sunday School", *Disgrace*, *Unconfessed* and *Reclaiming the P... Word* craft powerful ways of representing erased histories. They employ poetic language to envision black female bodies in ways that neither replicate the violating hyper-visibility of earlier representations, nor ignore the legacy of slavery's sexual violence. Through poetic language they craft a necessary and haunting silence, and then write into that fertile space a history and future that could not otherwise be envisioned.

In doing so, they form part of a provocative shift in recent South African literature, one that rewrites the official record on slavery and claims alternative modes of visibility for black subjectivities. They look unerringly at sexual violence, but do not confine themselves solely to themes of suffering. They also portray their characters' resilience, wholeness and sexual pleasure. Using poetic form and performance, these works show the profound impact of slavery on contemporary discourses of race and sexuality in South Africa and stake a powerful new claim on public space by black women.

CHAPTER 5

Regarding Muslims:
Pagad, masked men and veiled women

*Photography is worse than eloquence: it asserts that
nothing is beyond penetration, nothing is beyond confusion,
and nothing is veiled.*

– Paul Morand quoted in Alloula (1986: 37)

*In this whole history of Pagad in South Africa, what stands out
for me is not a media moment but a real event which has the
colourings of a media event … There was a [funeral] procession
just down my street. There were probably three thousand people.
To me, growing up Muslim, it's not an oddity. But suddenly it
brings to my attention that [to my neighbours] it's like a CNN
report coming to life in some vague Arabic country.*

– Rustum Kozain (2000: interview)

The front page of the *Cape Times* on Monday 5 August 1996 was called
"the most dramatic front page in the long history of the [newspaper]"
(Spencer-Smith, quoted in Vongai 1996: 2).[1] The emergence of Pagad into
national and international prominence through images of masking, violence and militancy interrupted the longstanding picturesque tradition and
changed the way Muslims would be portrayed in South Africa. Media coverage on that day and in succeeding weeks struck me not only as a story about
the group called Pagad, but as a new idiom for representing Islam in South
Africa. This chapter returns to the "recursive beginning" of images of Pagad
in the mid-1990s and places them in the context of the growing force of
menacing images of Muslims, an effect resulting both from local dynamics

in South Africa and the power of a *global* imaginary about Islam. The unique local trajectory of images of Islam I have traced in the preceding chapters has nevertheless had moments of strong cross-fertilisation with transnational debates. This was particularly true in the period after the end of South Africa's cultural isolation in 1994, when the South African media became interpelated into international discourses about democracy, "freedom", "terror" and Islam.

My interest in Pagad was prompted by the set of highly gendered photographs of the group that appeared in the media, tilting the oscillating pattern of images of Islam in South Africa from the picturesque in the direction of violence and alienation. The central image in these narratives was the masked man – an image that soon became indispensable to telling the Pagad story, and which required the erasure of the significant female leadership and membership of the group. The image of the masked face in portrayals of Islam evokes a longstanding Western fascination with the hiddenness of the East. This suggests that the masked man in the Pagad stories was a mechanism through which a story about Muslims in South Africa intersected with a global idiom for representing Islam. The history of colonial photography provides a useful context for understanding the powerful impact of news photographs about the group.

Photography relies on the metaphor of scientific veracity to anchor its claims to truth. Anne McClintock argues that in the colonial period, this belief drove an intensified quest for the truth of the Orient through the body of the veiled woman:

Colonial photography, framed as it was by metaphors of scientific knowledge as penetration, promised to seek out the secret interiors of the feminised Orient and to capture, in the image of the harem woman's body, the truth of the world (1995: 124).

The belief in photography's ability to uncover "the truth of the world" intensified the drive to secure access for the dominant gaze to the hidden sights of the East. The gendered effects of this quest are made clear in a study by Linda Steet, who reveals that photographs of Arab cultures published in *National Geographic* were in some cases made by the same studio that produced the pornographic French postcards analysed by Malek Alloula in his well-known study, *The Colonial Harem*. In fact, some of the *same photographs* sold as

***D'Almeida and his men killed by Hottentots on the shore of Table Bay
in 1510* by P. Van de Aa (1707)** (discussed in Chapter 1):
One of the earliest drawings produced at the Cape after the beginning of settlement, the
image depicts a battle at the Cape almost two hundred years earlier. In a battle with Khoisan
warriors, provoked when Portuguese sailors kidnapped Khoi children and stole cattle, the
feared Portuguese general Francisco D'Almeida was killed, along with sixty-four of his
sailors. In many ways, this image inaugurates a European conception of the South African
landscape as perilous and threatening.

Hertzoggies (discussed in Chapter 2):
Arranged innocuously amidst an array of other biscuits, Hertzoggies
in fact bear a coded message of political betrayal.

***Cape Town from the Camps Bay Road* by George French Angas (1849)**
(discussed in Chapter 1):
This print of Cape Town seen from the road to Camps Bay shows the neat grid of the city
cosseted by a domesticated nature; yet the two "Malay" figures resting by the wall suggest
the play of opposites and boundaries in the painting – city and mountain, colonist and
slave, ordered and wild, bounded and infinite.

Three people in front of the backdrop of the Kaa'ba (undated) (discussed in Chapter 3): This precious, well-worn photograph of three Hajjis in front of the backdrop of the Kaa'ba brings the meaning of pilgrimage directly into the home. Such photographs are often displayed in pride of place in Muslim homes, and convey the renewal of spiritual identities through the dress, comportment and name ("Hajji") of those who have returned from Mecca.

Pilgrimage to Mecca across empire (discussed in Chapter 3): The stamps in the passport of "Auntie Galiema" on her way to Mecca in 1951 shows how the "parallel modernities" of the Hajj and empire articulate with one another in the course of her carefully marked passage through European imperial territories.

On the voyage to Mecca (undated) (discussed in Chapter 3): This image on the deck of the ship from Durban to Mecca shows the different levels of accommodation on the ships that took pilgrims to Aden en route to Mecca. On their return, they would be photographed in more formal clothing, signalling their status as Hajjis.

**Imam and other pilgrims on the ship
(undated)** (discussed in Chapter 3):
Imam Abdullah Haron (1924–1969)
on his first pilgrimage by ship from
Durban to Mecca, accompanied by
other pilgrims.

Woman in black veil on the ship (undated)
(discussed in Chapter 3):
The woman in this photograph wears a black
veil, suggesting the role of dress in signalling
the spiritual meaning of pilgrimage. Her use
of formal dress distinguishes her from the men
who stand near her.

Gatesville mosque with Casspir (1996) (discussed in Chapter 5):
Gatesville Masjid is a mosque in a suburb of Cape Town. This image, showing an
armoured police vehicle in front of the mosque, recalls a trope of the apartheid era,
when the state brought its force to bear against the anti-apartheid movement, here
translated into the complex post-apartheid terrain in which Pagad's claim to fight
crime seemed at times to shade into resistance against the state.

WEDNESDAY AUGUST 7 1996 — **NORTHERN EDITION** — **R1,60– Country R1,90 incl VAT**

Mandela accepts Nigerian envoy's credentials

Mass action on gangs

Pagad gives drug merchants till Sunday to quit dealing – or be 'taken out'

Steady decline in number of Cape bankruptcy orders

ARMED WITH A PRAYER: A Pagad member reads the Quran while a shotgun lies within grabbing distance during the protest against gangsterism.

BIG SUPPORT: A large crowd of marchers listens to a speaker.

● More reports, pictures on page 3

"Mass Action on Gangs", *The Argus*, 7 August 1996 (discussed in Chapter 5):
The figure of the masked Pagad man recurs in this photograph. The juxtaposition of the shotgun and the man reading a Qur'an along with the caption "Armed with a Prayer" demonstrates that the complex and uneven use of iconography associated with Islam by Pagad members is read as giving a religious tone to the organisation's activities.

Single masked man (1996) (discussed in Chapter 5):
The photograph of the masked man became the primary visual image for articulating stories about Pagad in the news. This telephoto image of a man at the Vygieskraal meeting of Pagad members wearing a "Makka doek" and holding a gun overshadows the fact that the many of the people at the meeting were unarmed women.

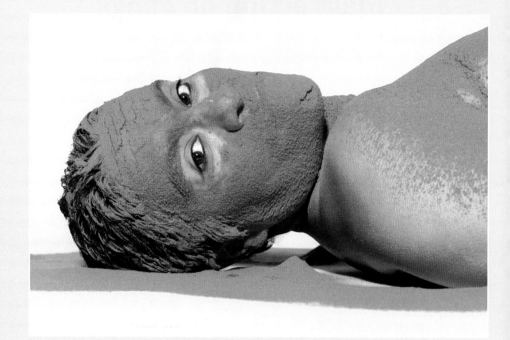

Berni Searle (discussed in Chapter 1):
Berni Searle's *Untitled* (1999) appears to give untrammelled access to the body of the
artist, yet it also shows her thoughtful, questioning gaze looking back. The dual action
in the photograph encapsulates "to be looked-at-ness" so self-consciously that the act
of looking itself becomes the subject of the artwork. The image "returns the gaze" in
more than a literal sense.

pornographic postcards were included in *National Geographic* under the rubric of "*absolute accuracy*" about Arab culture (2000: 42; 17, latter emphasis in original). The transferability of pornographic and ethnographic photographs like these suggests that dominant fantasies strongly inform the global history of images of Islam. The South African experience of a local Orientalist tradition, as well as the opening of the South African media to international investment and media idioms after 1994, led to a complex and flawed set of responses to the representational challenge posed by Pagad. I explore this convergence below.

People against Gangsterism and Drugs (Pagad) is an anti-crime coalition in Cape Town that emerged in the mid-1990s. Initially, it appealed to a broad membership, but by 1996 had increasingly come to use Muslim prayers and symbols in its rhetoric and activities. On Sunday 4 August 1996, hundreds of Pagad members marched to the house of Rashaad Staggie, the alleged co-leader of the Hard Livings gang, in Salt River, a working-class neighbourhood near the centre of the city. Staggie, who was shot and then set alight, died in a particularly brutal manner in the presence of the police and the media. The consequences of this act would dominate newspaper headlines in Cape Town and prove a major preoccupation of much public policy and scholarship during the rest of the 1990s.

In South Africa, representations of Muslims perennially shift from the margins to the centre and from the picturesque to the menacing. Islam has intermittently come to national public attention in moments of crisis, for example, the "cemetery riots" in 1886, the "skollie problem" in the 1940s, "international terrorism" in the 1970s, the anti-apartheid struggle in the 1980s, and the Pagad story in the 1990s. This echoes the general pattern of obscurity and crisis that has shaped coverage of Islam in the West. In his study of US media representations of the 1991 Gulf War, Mahmut Mutman shows that little attention was paid to Islam until the oil crisis of 1973 (1994: 6). With the rise in oil prices, a vertiginous shift occurred from obscurity to constant presence: "Muslims suddenly became the news" (6). Olfat Hassan Agha identifies the Iranian revolution in 1979 as another crisis that intensified attention to Islam in the West (2002: 222). Similarly, in Britain, Elizabeth Poole (2002) notes the heightened visibility of Islam following the crisis about the *Satanic Verses*,[2] in which British media coverage featured tropes such as the enraged Muslim crowd. In crisis, Muslims become explicable through stereotype – Muslim women through the veil and Muslim men through militancy.

From the mid- to late-1990s, developments associated with Pagad changed the South African political landscape concerning media, culture, law and religion. For the media, these developments presented formidable challenges, in which journalists faced hostility and physical danger. The Pagad stories also raised complex questions about the political economy of the media, the post-apartheid judicial system and the place of Islam in South Africa. During the trial following the murder of Rashaad Staggie, the prosecutor in the Western Cape, Frank Kahn, subpoenaed journalists under Section 205 of the Criminal Procedures Act in an attempt to secure access to their notes and photographs (Botes 1996: online). Section 205 was infamous for its use during the apartheid era to coerce the media to reveal the identities of people at anti-apartheid marches (Fisher 1999: online). After protests by the editor of the *Cape Times*, journalists' organisations and South Africa's Freedom of Expression Institute, the government modulated (although did not withdraw) its use of Section 205, and withdrew some of its subpoenas (Botes 1996: online).

Also in the legal arena, the events associated with Pagad precipitated the revision of the South African Anti-Terrorism Bill of 2002. Pagad's actions also had international ramifications when the United States State Department declared that the group was an "emerging terrorist organisation" (Pillay 2003: 292). In August 2004, Pagad was the subject of speculation about plans for acts of international terrorism in South Africa, a theory that was rejected by the South African government (SAPA 2004: online). The rise, methods and initial popular support for Pagad spurred studies of crime, gangs and vigilantism, which had already been stimulated by the widening evidence of vigilantism in post-apartheid South Africa seen, for instance, in the growth of Mapogo a Mathamaga, a group in Alexandria near Johannesburg that at one point claimed fifty thousand members.[3] Pagad has also been the subject of extensive debate in the disciplines of criminology, security studies, religious studies and history.[4] Therefore the group compels attention for several reasons. In this chapter, I do not address the dynamics, politics and evolution of the group, but focus on the *representation* of Pagad and its impact on South African depictions of Muslims more generally.

The media was the arena in which the Pagad events had their greatest impact.[5] The *Cape Times* sold out on 5 August and its sales increased markedly in the weeks that followed (Fisher 1999: online).[6] According to the journalists whom I interviewed, attention to Islam in the local media expanded to unprecedented levels and newsroom discussions and journalistic practices were dramatically influenced by the Pagad events. For his photographs of the murder of Rashaad Staggie, the *Cape Times* news photographer Benny Gool won the Fuji Press Award and, with Roger Friedman, received the 1997 South African Award for Courageous Journalism from the Ruth First Memorial Trust for their series of stories on Pagad (Samie 2003: online). However, Gool also received death threats as a result of the photographs, and was the subject of six government subpoenas between 1996 and 2003 in attempts to secure his negatives for use in prosecuting Staggie's death (Samie 2003: online).[7] In interviews, journalists confirm that these stories were among the most important and difficult they covered. The *Cape Times* coverage was also severely criticised by its own readers and Pagad called for a boycott of the newspaper (Anonymous 3, 2003: interview). As a result of such criticism, threats against its journalists, heightened tensions in the city, and the phenomenon of "urban terror" in the late 1990s, in 1999 the *Cape Times* initiated the "One City, Many Cultures" project, in which it attempted to craft a new way of talking about political, religious and cultural difference in Cape Town.

While images of Islam in the South African media generally form part of a picturesque tradition, during apartheid, another discourse around Islam appeared as Muslims became visible in the anti-apartheid struggle: the association of Islam with violence (Bangstad 2005: 188). In his essay "Experts, Terrorists, Gangsters: Problematising public discourse on a post-apartheid showdown" (2003), Suren Pillay demonstrates that the Pagad stories were characterised by a conservative and limited South African discourse on gangs and Islam (291). In an analysis of media coverage and academic articles about Pagad in criminology and political science journals, Pillay finds that much of this material characterises Pagad "as representative of a homogeneous Islam and as the local incarnation of a global 'Islamic threat'" (283). This perception of homogeneity obscured the fact that the group was highly distinctive in relation to Islam in South Africa. Shamil Jeppie (1998) and Ebrahim Moosa (1996) both note the lack of consensus about Pagad within the country's Muslim community. Moreover, the organisation itself is extremely heterogeneous and its disparate parts were often in tension and fluctuated in influence internally. Pillay analysed the way that the shifting components within Pagad deployed signs associated with Islam, observing that:

[t]he organisation is made up of a diverse range of competing elements. Among these elements are contested meanings of Islam, its role in a plural society, party-political legitimacy, a normative disdain for drug abuse and gangsterism, and elements of gung-ho machismo. It is also one narrative within a wider range of Islamic narratives, which are being constructed using global and local symbols, which produce specific and hybridised Muslim identities … It presents us with an assemblage of tensions which are intensely internal and local, while at the same time being external and global (2003: 304).

Pillay shows that the "competing elements" of the group shaped the way they used Islamic iconography in their rhetoric. This resulted in a vision of Islam assembled from diverse signs and deployed in often contradictory ways. The media did not comment on this complex engagement with symbols of potency drawn from several international arenas.

Unlike the anti-apartheid resistance movements of the 1980s, Pagad produced relatively few material artefacts such as handouts, posters and pamphlets (Jeppie 1998: online). Aside from its meetings and mass marches by its supporters, Pagad's communicative repertoire occurred almost exclusively at the level of image and rhetoric in the media. Jeppie argued that the group benefitted particularly from access to the audience of the Muslim community radio station, Radio 786 (1998: online). He terms the complex presentation of Islam that Pagad delivered a "bricolage" of Islamic iconography (Jeppie 2000: interview). This consisted of Afghan caps, checked red or black Makka scarves[8] and headbands marked by calligraphy, items drawn from "the distant and disparate worlds of Middle Eastern conflicts" (Jeppie quoted in Pillay 2003: 300).

Pagad employed such "fragments from the global" in a gendered public image that created an impression of local potency, and also conveyed a sense of solidarity with a global community of Muslims (Pillay 2003: 300). Out of an "assemblage" of Islamic symbols supplemented by their actions, the group constructed a highly specific local identity. To Jeppie, while the media coverage was unequal to these complexities, Pagad's rhetoric was itself reductive. In its bricolage of Islamic images, "[t]he complex tribal, civil and political contradictions of Afghanistan, Palestine, south Lebanon, and Iran are reduced to a single issue" (quoted in Pillay 2003: 300). The relation of the international to the local was therefore central to the construction of Pagad's image, and in the process, a distinctively new, local vision of Islam arose in the South African media. The challenge of understanding this complex choreography of symbols and politics and discerning between Muslims, Islam and Pagad fell to a South African media schooled in a tradition of constricted and stereotypical reporting on Islam.

The relationship between Pagad and the media was one of intense and often hostile interaction. In some ways, the group itself was a creature of the media, partly because it learned the advantages of playing to the stereotypes that drew the most attention. On the other hand, as noted by Jeppie, the media both consciously and unconsciously colluded with Pagad's strategy by giving extensive coverage to some of the group's actions while underplaying others, such as the participation of women in the group. Media attention to Pagad, which drove up sales, was at times marked by "sensationalist language" that conveyed "a more extreme picture that the reality prevailing on the ground" (Jeppie 1998: online). This was combined with inadequate analysis of its "assemblage" of Islamic symbols (Pillay 2003: 304).

The Pagad story occurred at a time during which newspapers were attempting to adjust to the post-apartheid political context. During apartheid and to some extent since, media ownership, audience profiles and the political sympathies of the press in South Africa were highly racialised. During the transition from apartheid, the media had to undergo its own transformational shift away from this history; newspapers with historically white readerships and staff had to address previously neglected black audiences. The new government led by the African National Congress welcomed international investment in the previously insulated South African media in an attempt to shift the entrenched pattern of racialised media ownership, newsroom culture and audiences. The entry of global capital into the South African media, including through the sale of local media companies and titles, inserted the country into the dynamics of globalised media, with its emphasis on the market and increased commercial pressure on the way journalists worked (Webster 2002: 120). The impact of such market pressures significantly influenced the pace of transformation in the South African media, contradictorily giving the impression of changing modes of operation established during apartheid, while in fact reinforcing the tendency towards conservative practices because of a reduction in the amount of money spent on gathering news and the emphasis on drawing a high-income audience. Therefore, at exactly the time that the new Constitution gave the South African media an unprecedented freedom to report the complex stories of the transition, they faced intensified commercial pressure to draw an affluent audience in order to attract advertisers.

The entry into a globalised media market had an impact not only on content and newsroom structures, but the *culture* of news in South Africa. Stories in the international media are characterised by certain cultural idioms. In this context, the Pagad images, characterised by masking, violence and militancy, posed a steep challenge for analysts. Because of the pressures created by the reduction of newsroom resources, as well as a history of inadequate attention to Muslims, it became easier for a reductionist international idiom to take hold in the media's reporting on Pagad's complex allusions to Islam.

The *Cape Times*

On Monday 5 August 1996, the entire front page of the *Cape Times*, aside from one advertisement, was devoted to the Staggie murder under the headline "Night of bloody execution". The page was dominated by four sequential photographs taken by Benny Gool of the last moments of Rashaad Staggie's life. The photographs are explicit, detailed and evoke shock at the public nature of the murder. They show Staggie being shot multiple times, set on fire, and his body being jumped upon by angry members of the crowd. The lines of perspective and foreshortening within the photographs indicate that Gool was within close range of the events. Gool described moving into the line of fire to take "the picture of him in flames with his eyes looking straight at me" (quoted in Gondwe, 2001: online). Given the documentation of gunfire from multiple directions, the photographs testify to a notable focus and presence of mind in pressured circumstances, and are an extraordinary achievement by the photographer.

The article written by Roger Friedman supplements the sequence of photographs with a minute-by-minute account of the rapidly unfolding events that culminated in the murder. Friedman reports an eyewitness account of the gunfire exchanged between the crowd and people inside the house in London Road, the immediacy of the events conveyed in both the past perfect and the past tense. During this gun-battle, Rashaad Staggie arrived in his car. When he was recognised, "[members of the crowd] surrounded the van and jostled with each other to pull Staggie from his driver's seat. At this point a man pulled out his firearm and shot Staggie in the side of the head. He slumped in his seat, then fell into the street."

The violence captured in this account confirms the content of the photographs. Friedman's point of view is reported from the immediate proximity of Staggie and the crowd. He also documents that the violence took place in full view of the police, the emergency services and the media, a fact that would be revisited in subsequent investigations of the murder. The article provides a context by observing that the events of that Sunday night were preceded by two weeks of increasingly visible activity by Pagad. In the following days, Friedman's reports would provide additional context, covering as they did issues such as weaknesses in the criminal justice system and perceptions of the police as ineffective and corrupt. During the week of coverage that followed, Gool and Friedman provided compelling and multi-layered perspectives on the story.

Page two of the *Cape Times* on 5 August continued the coverage of the Pagad story and featured three sequential photographs of Rashaad Staggie: one sitting in his car holding up his hands as though indicating he was unarmed, the second a moment later after he had been shot, blood streaming from his ear, and the third of him lying in the street with someone jumping on his body. A fourth photo showed a group of men crouching behind a car. Significantly, many had hidden their faces with the chequered scarves known in Cape Town as Arafat or Makka doeke. Photographs of men with their faces covered in red-and-white chequered scarves would become indispensable to the newspaper stories about Pagad in succeeding days.

The photographs intensify the sense of chaos of the night's events, including the extended death of Staggie (estimated by Friedman to have taken twenty-five minutes), and the extreme violence members of the crowd showed in their treatment of Staggie's body. An accompanying article by Lindiz van Zilla, with a headline "Hushed silence broken by cries of why, why", shows the complex views about criminal gangs in poor neighbourhoods. He points out that reaction among the crowd to the killing was extremely mixed, and that several Salt River residents later expressed sadness at Staggie's killing. "Rashaad was a good man," one elderly woman pronounced. "He helped anyone who came to him."

Echoing the *Cape Times*, the extensive coverage of the murder in the afternoon daily *The Argus* on the same day confirms the scale of the events. The top half of page three of *The Argus* contains four photographs under the headline "Staggie died as he lived." While the largest image is placed in the centre of the page with the caption "Drug War: Police surround a mortally wounded Rashaad Staggie after he was shot and petrol-bombed in a street in Salt River last night", a smaller photograph of a masked man appears to the side with the caption: "Masked: One of the anti-drug vigilantes conceals a firearm under his jacket". This was the first appearance of the figure of a masked man in *The Argus*. In the coverage of this story in the days that followed, this figure would move from the margins to the centre of most photographs in the newspaper. In both visual and verbal images, the figure of the masked man became a primary marker of the Pagad stories.

During the course of the week, Roger Friedman presented an increasingly complex and nuanced series of articles in the *Cape Times*. However, on Tuesday 6 August, the front page of the newspaper conveyed a tone of panic, fear and intensifying threat. The article above the fold, written by Friedman, had the headline "Pagad leader warns of suicide bombs". The piece conveys a sense of the escalating rhetoric surrounding the story, reporting that the Pagad military leader Ali "Phantom" Parker had given notice that "the city should brace itself for a new phenomenon of suicide bombers". This shocking assertion was unprecedented in Cape Town. The article also stated that "the city [was] bracing itself for a 'holy war'" between Pagad and gangsters: "The underworld has threatened to destroy mosques and Muslim small businesses. Some schools have closed in case they are targeted by the gangsters." This acceleration of mutual threats between Pagad and the gangs, along with reports that soldiers were being flown in from other provinces in response to a request by the police for military support, indicated the tension and seriousness of the story.

The article, using terms such as "fundamentalist", "holy war" and "suicide bombers" in an atmosphere of extreme tension, suggests that an international media idiom about Islam had embedded itself in the coverage of the story. While the article itself includes a sophisticated level of detail and discussion, the headline (written by a sub-editor rather than Friedman) undermines the overall impact of the discussion. The journalist and former deputy-editor of the *Cape Times*, Yazeed Fakier, cites this headline as the moment at which the Cape media "lost control of the story" (2000: interview). To Fakier, the headline symbolised the sacrifice of context to sensationalism. One immediate result was that relations between Pagad and the media deteriorated badly, as Friedman's article on Wednesday 7 August indicated. Here he reported Pagad's warnings to the media to stop describing the organisation as "vigilantes", "extremists" and "fundamentalists", "on pain of death." Pagad indicated its awareness of the reverberating connotations of such terminology, but couched its objections in a dangerous and self-defeating way.

A report on the deployment of government resources seems to confirm Islam, rather than Pagad, as being implicated in these stories. On page three of the *Cape Times* on 6 August, a photograph shows a Casspir (an armoured police vehicle) parked outside Gatesville Mosque, the site of many Pagad meetings. Historically, Casspirs were used by the apartheid state to enact visible and militarised policing of black areas during periods of heightened resistance. They became powerful signs of the oppressive state apparatus operating against ordinary people, as well as those involved in the anti-apartheid struggle. The *Cape Times* reported on 8 August that the-then Minister of Safety and Security, Sydney Mufamadi, had ordered the deployment of army units to protect mosques. However, in the context of the recently ended apartheid era, the sight of heavily armoured military vehicles outside mosques carried unsettling associations of the weight of the state being brought to bear against a subversive force.

On Monday 12 August, a week after the first articles on Rashaad Staggie's murder, the *Cape Times* reported on a mass meeting held on Sunday at Vygies-kraal Stadium, attended by an estimated ten thousand people. The photograph used to illustrate this meeting offered an exemplary image of the masked man. It appeared on page three under the heading "Shotgun Sentinel", and with the caption "On guard: a member of Pagad, his face masked and a shotgun at the ready, stands guard during the Pagad rally at Vygieskraal Stadium yesterday afternoon". The composition and structure of this photograph compel attention. The photograph, by Thembinkosi Dwayisa, was taken with a telephoto lens, and its subject is the figure of a man in medium shot holding a shotgun, and wearing a red Makka scarf and a ski mask that completely obscure his face.

He is strongly foregrounded and in sharp focus, while the crowd of people in the background are barely in focus. Revealingly, in a compelling article on "The Women of Pagad" originally published in the South African version of *Cosmopolitan* magazine, by Alex Dodd, Fatima Zahra, a female member of Pagad, claims that "[at] the Vygieskraal mass meeting … there were more women than men there without a doubt" (1996: 66). The absence of an active female presence in images of Pagad reflects the gender politics of the international idiom of Islam, which is characterised by images of dangerous men and vulnerable women. The prominent female members of Pagad had no place in this discourse.

During the week of 5 to 12 August 1996, the *Cape Times'* coverage of the Pagad story demonstrated a notable effort to grapple with a complex story in which the media itself became a part of the content, not least because of increasing levels of personal danger faced by journalists reporting the events. The *Cape Times* coverage showed a grasp of South African politics and incorporated diverse perspectives and angles, drawing on interviews with national political leaders, the views of academics studying gangsterism and vigilantism, and a broad array of eyewitness accounts. The sustained approach by the journalist Roger Friedman lent consistency and depth to the coverage of the *Cape Times*. Friedman provided not only comprehensive coverage, but also opinion and comment on the context surrounding the events. In his comment on page two of *Cape Times* on Friday 9 August 1996, under the headline "Government must shoulder the blame for the bloody drug violence", Friedman provided an assessment of the context of ongoing crime, frustrated prosecutions and allegations of corruption. He tracked the promises and commitment on the part of the regional and national governments, and also the failure to meet these promises, as part of the context in which the public lynching of Rashaad Staggie occurred. Headlines in the *Cape Times* were detailed and attention-catching and generally not sensationalistic. They included quotations, and drew on experts' comments and reflections by journalists themselves.

The Argus

The tone in *The Argus* was considerably different.[9] The headline in *The Argus* on Monday 5 August 1986 was "Vigilante war." The article has a heightened tone not evident in the *Cape Times*. Terms such as "full-scale war", "militant Muslim lynching", "slaying", "gangsters threatened to burn down mosques" and "heavily armed Muslim anti-drug extremists" convey a highly pressured atmosphere. The newspaper's idiom echoed the swelling rhetoric of threats and retribution exchanged between gangs and Pagad members.

On 7 August, *The Argus* reported the alleged connection of Pagad to international Muslim terrorists, following allegations reported by Agence France Presse (AFP). AFP quoted a senior government source on the existence of "secret cells" and "foreign training" for Muslim militants in the Western Cape and in Durban. Libya was alleged to be the main funder of the training. In her article "The spy report that got it all wrong" in the *Mail and Guardian* on 30 August 1996, Ann Eveleth investigated the source quoted by AFP and demonstrated it to be an extremely flawed discussion document drawn up by the South African police. Eveleth conveyed anti-apartheid activist Maulana Farid Esack's scrupulous analysis and comprehensive rebuttal of the flawed premise and conclusions of the document. Esack listed the report's stereotypes, lack of basic research and confusion about the distinction between international Islamic movements and South African Muslims.

The document, which was disavowed by the African National Congress, drew on an international discourse on "terrorist" Islam, and also appeared to reflect apartheid-era views lingering in the country's intelligence services after the political transformation of 1994. The reliance on this global view of Islam by some within the conservative provincial government was revealed in the assertion by Hernus Kriel, the National Party Premier of the Western Cape, that Pagad posed a "fundamentalist threat" (Jeenah 1996: 18). The complex political situation of South Africa at the time in which the African National Congress had formed an uneasy Government of National Unity with the former apartheid ruling regime, intersected with an idiom about extremist Islam that circulated in the Western media and became a factor in the escalating tone around Islamic terrorism in the wake of the Pagad events.

One of the most thoughtful pieces on the Pagad phenomenon in *The Argus* was written by Professor Ebrahim Moosa, at that time the director of the Centre for Contemporary Islam at the University of Cape Town. In an article titled "Islam against the world, flawed radicalism will hurt the Muslim faith", Moosa pointed out the dangers for a well-meaning public anti-crime initiative in adopting a militaristic ethos combined with anti-state elements.

The target of Pagad's intentions seemed to shift from addressing gangsterism and criminality in the face of law enforcement failures to questioning the legitimacy of the Mandela government. Moosa also noted the ambivalence among Muslims about the activities of Pagad. He revealed the range of perceptions of Pagad within the Muslim community, including people intimidated into silence or quiescence. Moosa concluded by noting the regrettable abuse of religious rhetoric for the purposes of spectacle and demagoguery. Significantly, even this complex and layered analysis was accompanied by a picture of a masked man. In *The Star* (the sister newspaper to *The Argus*, published in Johannesburg) on 12 November 1996, the same article (published as "Groups Like Pagad Hurt Islam") was also accompanied by a drawing of a masked man. This image had become indispensable to the telling of the Pagad story.

The photograph on page three of *The Argus* on 12 August exemplifies the problem of attaching a simplistic and anachronistic visual vocabulary to images of Islam in South Africa. The caption to this photograph reads "On the march. Manenberg residents marched yesterday in protest over ongoing wars between Pagad and the Hard Living gang." A closer examination of the photograph shows that the majority of people in this public gathering *against violence*, who appear in the background to the photograph, are not wearing coverings on their heads, nor masking their faces. However, the photograph has been taken with a telephoto lens, and the two women who are in focus in the foreground are wearing scarves. The woman on the left is wearing a Makka scarf, a familiar item of clothing. The woman to her right is using an ordinary scarf to obscure her face. The photograph demonstrates the problem in interpreting commonplace details (such as scarves) as having solely religious meanings.

The media did to an extent reflect a range of views on this story. However, there was a further order of meaning operating through a symbol that superseded discussions on the visible level. As I have shown, the figure of the masked man rapidly became the iconic image in stories about Pagad from 5 to 12 August 1996. This was partly due to Pagad's contradictory attempts to widen its support base by drawing on Islamic iconography and discourse, such as prayers and the familiar chequered scarves, while simultaneously proclaiming its appeal to a broad range of people beyond the Muslim community. Pagad's other explanation for using these scarves as masks was that its members needed to protect their identities after a Pagad member named

Faizel Ryklief was murdered, allegedly after gang members identified him from media reports. There were parallel orders of signification in the image of the mask, one operating at a functional level (the Ryklief explanation), and another at the level of symbolism.

The allure of the mask is proven by the numerous articles that dealt with unmasking or revealing secrets; for example, "Pagad unmasked – Aslam Toefy", which appeared in the *Saturday Weekend Argus* of 16/17 November 1996. The article provides the name of the-then leader of Pagad, who had agreed to an exclusive interview with the newspaper "to try to break down misconceptions about the organisation". This pattern can also be seen in articles such as "Murdered Pagad Leader was informer" by Marianne Merten in the *Mail & Guardian* on 23 July 1999. Pagad, with its public image of hiddenness, combined with its eagerness to attract media coverage, appeared to invite a series of revelations.

Gender and masking

Gender is central to the theme of masking and unmasking. The recurring image of masked men also invokes the trope of veiled women. The association of the veil with Islam developed during colonialism and is so familiar as an icon of the religion in the West that its meanings operate at an almost intuitive level. According to Helen Watson, the image of the veil remains one of the most common methods in the West of portraying the "problem of Islam" (1994: 153). Yet there is an important ambivalence in the image: it signals both the oppression and the eroticism of Muslim women. In fact, there is an obsessive "association between the veil and the Western man's sexual fantasies" (Mutman 1994: 13). In the imperial imagination from the sixteenth century, the projected vulnerability and availability of Eastern women sustained a strong Orientalist fantasy: the desire of the European coloniser to enlighten the Islamic world, and to deliver its women from oppression.

The fantasy of Orientalism is thus predicated on sexual difference. The veiled woman of the East signals allure and exoticism, but she also symbolises that the Orient itself is feminine, "always veiled, seductive, and dangerous" (Yegenoglu, 11). Part of the appeal of the Orient was that it "remains incomprehensible" (Kabbani 1986: 122). To the imperial Western gaze, whatever was revealed about the East paradoxically remained a sign of mystery. The exemplary exposed-yet-mysterious object is the veiled woman. The Turkish feminist scholar Meyda Yegenoglu argues that gendered fantasies organise co-lonial relations (1998: 2). The imperial gaze obsessively studies the scene of its potential failure – an object that refuses to be looked at (Yegenoglu, 1998: 39). Because a gendered Orient is not only differentiated into men and women, but is itself a feminised space, Yegenoglu consequently reads the visibility, or unveiling, of the Orient as a crucial imperial imperative. She writes that:

> the colonial feminist discourse to unveil Muslim women in the name of liberation was linked not only to the discourse of En-lightenment but also to the scopic regime of modernity which is characterised by a desire to master, control, and reshape the body of the subjects by making them visible. Since the veil prevents the colonial gaze from attaining such a visibility and hence mastery, its lifting becomes essential. I argue that the desire to unveil women should not be seen simply as an uncovering of the bodies, but as a re-inscription, for the discourse of unveiling is no less incorporated in the existential or embodied being of Oriental women than the discourse of veiling (12).

The imperative to "re-inscribe" the Muslim woman's body into the script of visibility means that, for Yegenoglu, the veil becomes intolerable to the "scopic regime" of modernity. In South Africa, this "scopic regime" would encounter a tradition of highly visible images of Muslims suddenly obscured by masks and veils.

However, it is not only the veiled Muslim woman who had become the focus of the Western gaze. In an analysis of Western media coverage of the First Gulf War in 1991, Mahmut Mutman found that there was an evolu-tion in the meaning of the Eastern man. The image of the veiled woman re-mained – indeed, "during the war, the woman was everywhere, as the veil, as the metaphor of truth, and as the truth" (21) – but the masked Eastern man shifted from irredeemable extremism toward a more ambiguous sexual and political meaning. During the Gulf War, "the media kept asking one question every night in the news, in every single TV program: 'what is in Saddam's mind?'" We are of course reminded of the question which Freud articulated:

what does woman want?" (1994: 21). In this formulation, Saddam Hussein is placed in the position of the "native" or woman who is both lacking and excessive, and withholds a secret. Mutman argued that through portrayals of an ambiguous sexuality, men like Saddam Hussein came to occupy the fetishised role classically held by women, which both affirms and unsettles the Western subject. It is in this light that we can read the riveting images of the masked men of Pagad. The Pagad story intersected with the international discourse at a time when the latter was developing greater interest in images of the men of the East.

The shifting meanings of Islam and gender in the global imaginary are therefore also relevant to the Pagad story. Three months after Pagad's sudden rise to visibility, the writer Alex Dodd deliberated on the gendered dynamics of media representations of the group. In her *Cosmopolitan* article on "The Women of Pagad", Dodd confesses that due to infrequent contact with Muslims, she held "manufactured notions about Muslim women", that they were "silent", "submissive" and "oppressed" (2001: 65). She noted that media coverage about Pagad confirmed the absence of women:

> When the pictures hit the articles they're, more often than not, images of men. Men with scarves. Men with guns. Men talking. Men shaking their fists and holding their banners. The position of women is glaringly absent from the reports and images of PAGAD (1996: 64).

This gendered absence caught Dodd's attention when she discovered that women played a prominent role in the organisation's founding, membership and activities. Men's visual appeal is evident in the repetition of "*Men* with scarves. *Men* with guns. *Men* talking. *Men* shaking their fists." The short sentences also suggest the solipsism of such images. The men appear unconnected to other elements, self-generated, lacking reciprocity, and unanchored to context or moderation.

Dodd finds that the female members of Pagad whom she interviews are wary of the stereotype that Muslim women are "voiceless and oppressed" (65–66). She is careful to show that they did not convey a one-dimensional message. In fact, their views are not only varied, but sometimes in tension with one another. Significantly, the women historicise their use of the veil in their accounts. They assert that "many of the movement's women who are veiled are not veiled normally, but 'because of the gangsters. They veil themselves because of the fear of exposure'" (66). Dodd asks the women why media reports never refer to the women in the movement, and why the complexity of their motivations as female members of the group is not shown. They reply that this is "the fault of the journalists who never show them" (66). As Bangstad's review of the Pagad stories also showed, gender is present even when the stories focus only on men and machismo, but the underplaying of women's complex roles within Pagad is particularly notable in the media coverage.

Media reflections: Journalistic practice in the wake of reporting on Pagad

Between 2000 and 2007, I conducted interviews with several journalists from Capetonian and national newspapers, television and community radio stations who covered the Pagad stories. They agreed that the Pagad stories were a defining moment for the media and for coverage of Islam. "In the last ten years, Pagad has been the biggest story on Islam" (Anonymous 3, 2003: interview). Before the Pagad story, Islam registered very little in the local media. Anonymous 3, who wrote on the Pagad story for the *Cape Times*, reflected that before the events of August 1996, "in mainstream media Islam certainly never received anywhere near the attention". Mahmood Sanglay, the editor of *Muslim Views*, a Cape Town newspaper addressed to a Muslim audience, noted that before the advent of Pagad, the most common theme in stories about Islam was the Muslim contribution to the anti-apartheid struggle. Sanglay observed that there were "watershed moments when Muslims and Muslim names [such as prominent activists Ahmad Kathrada, Ebrahim Rassool and Imam Haron] became visible". However, as Anonymous 3 points out, these figures were often seen as "activists first, and maybe Muslim later."

The importance of the story was clear in the journalists' accounts. Anonymous 2, then an editor at the *Cape Times*, at the time reported centrally on the Pagad story. He confirms that "as a journalist, it was probably the most exciting time of my life". For the newspapers, the story guaranteed huge sales. Anonymous 3 notes that "when those pictures appeared that Monday morning, sales shot through the roof". Anonymous 2 also recalls the dangers of reporting the story: "It was probably the time I was most scared, and I've been in dangerous situations in my … life. A lot of my coverage … was not popular. I was caught in the crossfire, literally." Sanglay himself received threats against his life. Anonymous 3 recounts that "it could take one sentence to set off … a massive reaction. The police, the gangs, Pagad – there were attacks from all sides." Anonymous 3 notes that for South African newsrooms, these challenges were unprecedented: "A lot of us had never encountered that before."

In Sanglay's assessment, the Pagad coverage in the media contained "unfair representations of Muslims, unfair in that the mainstream media did not differentiate [among Muslims], or show the contradictions, dichotomy, polarities and ambivalence" about Pagad in the Muslim community. As a result, according to Sanglay, "Muslims became tainted with the image that Islam represented violence". The main reason for this, he contends, is "because of a lack of understanding of the community". He acknowledges that "there are some militant and violent voices, but by far in the minority". However, elements of the Muslim community contributed to the media "frenzy" of attention to violence and sensation: "Muslims need to concede that the conduct of Muslim themselves … contributed to that misperception" (2003: interview).

Reflecting on the coverage of the Pagad stories, Anonymous 3 concedes that "there is some merit to the criticism [of the media]". He concurs that "there was not a distinction made between Islam and Pagad". He explains that "that was difficult, because they were almost exclusively Muslim.… The rhetoric that went out, with one or two exceptions, was from Muslim or Islamic scholars.… It was very difficult to distinguish, if you take it at face value". In addition to the requirement to attend to such distinctions, for Anonymous 3, reporting on the story "you were treading a fine line. There were threats. In that environment, it was very difficult to write any stories. Half the time the police didn't know" (2003: interview).

Anonymous 3 noted that complexity battled with newsworthiness in the Pagad stories. "The thing is, something has to be newsworthy.… I think complexity only came out much later. Maybe if it had been spotted earlier, one could have gone to ordinary Muslim people and asked them [their views]." However, instead of such perspectives, Anonymous 3 says, "a lot of time the media got caught up in it [the story]. It was happening all the time all over the place. It was so big, so fast. The sales went through the roof." Assessing the trajectory of the Pagad stories, Anonymous 3 reflects that, with hindsight, "there were moments when the media overplayed the story. Maybe the story called for introspection. [But] what are you supposed to do? Ali and Toefy [Pagad leaders] almost appeared larger-than-life figures due to the media effect. They had fiery rhetoric. You can't turn a blind eye. You can't ignore the story" (2003: interview).

On the question of the complexity of media reporting of the stories, Anonymous 2 concludes that "given the nature of the newspaper, I don't think we probably did on a day-to-day [basis give sufficient complexity]. We're not going to find out the definitive piece on the complexities of what was being played out, especially in encompassing the Muslim community ... I don't think we did justice to anyone. Over a long time it was an attempt to take the readership along [to show] why and how that developed ... How successful we were is for people like yourself to judge" (2003: interview).

The relationship between Pagad and the media was famously contentious, even hostile. Anonymous 3 notes that "at one stage, there was a boycott against the *Cape Times*. I think it was a Pagad call saying the *Cape Times* was biased against Pagad and the Muslim community." Anonymous 2 confirms this announcement of a boycott: "At the time Moegsien Williams was the editor. [As a Muslim,] it was expected for him to be much more [understanding of Pagad]." Yet behind this well-known contentiousness, the journalists reveal another dimension. Anonymous 2 points out the complexity behind such apparent hostility: "They [Pagad] bought the newspaper themselves. Whenever there's trouble, they will call for meetings. When they weren't happy, they came to us. When I needed something, I went to them. They were playing the media, getting maximum exposure" (2003: interview).

For journalists, the Pagad story "left an indelible mark" on the South African media (Sanglay 2003: interview). Anonymous 2 notes that "a lot of debates – morality, ethics, sensationalism, the outcome, the long-term effect on people and sensitivities of people in the field – these are not really debates that we have in the newsroom. We have them one-on-one, but not necessarily as a collective. With the Pagad issue, we were forced to sit down and have these discussions. We became a lot more aware of the realities. In the letters pages there was a lot of feedback. It forced people and communities to discuss and come to some sort of insight on issues" (2003: interview). Sanglay notes that relations among media organisations subsequently improved, with more interaction between the major media companies and independent and alternative media such as *Muslim Views*.

While denying that it was solely a Muslim group, Pagad conveyed mixed signals about Islam, for instance, by holdings its meetings in a mosque and using prayers and religious rhetoric in its communications. Pagad also used icons associated with Islam to project a sense of potency. In contrast to the images of "Malay" men as placid, law-abiding and domesticated, Pagad projected machismo through combative rhetoric and the deliberate flaunting of weapons. Such machismo resulted from the dynamics of Pagad's competition with gangs for media space, in which both performed reckless masculinity through transgressions of the law, such as posing with weapons or smoking marijuana. This contradictory and shifting performance of symbols from various international Muslim experiences was interpreted as an assertive and uncontested local declaration of membership in a global Islamic alliance. The largely uncritical way in which the South African media reported Pagad's complex performance was due to the paucity of its resources in dealing with the subject of Muslims. "What is this Islam thing?" – this question, posed by a South African journalist to the scholar Shamil Jeppie, suggests not just an illuminating bewilderment but also perhaps a perception of the performativity of the "thing" called Islam – revealed in the constructedness of Pagad's evocation of the religion (Jeppie 2000: interview). The performativity of Pagad's self-image suggests that local identities were starting to be self-consciously shaped in relation to global politics.

Significant efforts to provide context about longstanding non-vigilante anti-crime initiatives within black communities, the use of drugs and gangs as political instruments by the apartheid regime in the 1980s, and complex responses within Muslim communities toward Pagad, were made by reporters such as Ann Evelyth in the *Mail & Guardian*, Marianne Merten and Roger Friedman, and by academics like Farid Esack and Ebrahim Moosa. Such articles articulated historically informed analyses. However, the perception that Pagad represented Islam was determined not solely by individual articles, but by the *combination* of articles and the cultural idiom surrounding Islam in the local and international media.

If the mainstream media has conventionally seen Muslims as "cultural curiosities" (Anonymous 1: interview), the Muslim media has also tended to be relegated to the arena of edification rather than news. In July 2007, I interviewed Muslim journalists who worked in Muslim and mainstream South

African media about the ways in which Islam is portrayed in South Africa, as well as the role of Muslim media organisations in the country. Many of the journalists worked both in the mainstream and Muslim media.[10]

Most of the journalists from the Muslim media whom I interviewed regarded the coverage of Pagad in the mainstream media during the 1990s as "sensationalised" (Ayesha Mall 2007: online interview). Yazeed Kamaldien noted that "Pagad sold newspapers. News editors realised this." The kind of coverage that resulted "has led to distrust in the Muslim community of mainstream press" (2007: online interview). In contrast, he argued, "the Muslim media … reported more responsibly" because they showed that "the Muslim community itself is not united on the Pagad issue". An anonymous journalist confirmed that the effect of the Pagad stories was to "paint a picture of South African Muslims as part of a global idea that all or most Muslims are militant and aggressive terrorists". Within the Muslim community there was a defensive response toward the media. In her view, this mutually constricting set of responses limited the range of possibilities for both South African Muslims and their fellow citizens: "It … created polar opposites between Muslims and the rest of South Africans and … this is especially problematic if you do not fit into either category or feel that you fit into both." The journalist Ayesha Mall pointed out that "while [the story] was sensationalised by mainstream media", another critical failing was that "key Muslim voices [and] publications were silent – [they] did not condemn Pagad". Kamaldien also found "one doesn't find a sense of investigative journalism or interrogation in the Muslim media's news pages". The anonymous journalist felt that "Muslim media should play the role that all other media should, to uphold justice and to be the watchdogs of society". For her, this meant "maintaining freedom and equality for all citizens in light of the country's political past". She concluded that "there is a serious need for a liberal Muslim media that challenges injustices" (Anonymous 1 2007: online interview).

The media faced a defining test in reporting the Pagad stories, which raised complex questions about how to represent violence, the rise of vigilantism, the strains seen in the post-apartheid judicial system, and the relation of South Africa to its Muslim minority. The Pagad stories, according to the journalists I interviewed, led to unprecedented levels of attention to Islam in the local media; newsroom discussions and practices were also dramatically changed by these events (Anonymous 2 2003: interview).

Post-Pagad: The persistence of the new idioms

The new idiom for speaking about Islam has survived the historical events that gave rise to the first wave of reporting on Pagad. What were the long-term consequences for representations of Islam of the Pagad stories? After the controversy of the Pagad coverage and the tensions it raised in Cape Town, the *Cape Times* launched its "One City Many Cultures" initiative on 1 February 1999, in which it attempted to find a new way of talking about social differences. The project took the form of a double page each week on matters of identity and culture (such as births and weddings), viewed through the lens of the "many cultures" of the city. Articles on such themes written by well-known writers such as Marianne Thamm, Mike Nicol and Rayda Jacobs attempted to move away from crisis and discuss culture in an indigenous vocabulary. "Ordinary" people were interviewed in the side-section called "Street Talk", which complemented the feature-length articles in the centre of the pages. The panorama of cultures was made concrete by a rendition of accounts of pregnancy in the three different languages of the province, Xhosa, Afrikaans and English, and this trilingual section became a feature of the initiative.

The "One City, Many Cultures" project gained a substantial public profile and gave visibility and sensitive attention to aspects of city life that had not been widely discussed before. Mahmood Sanglay called the "One City" initiative "an important and admirable attempt" (2003: interview). Anonymous 2 observed that "[a]t that time, the city was quite divided, almost at war with itself. It was an initiative of the *Cape Times*. The idea was to bring the city back together. In as far as what a newspaper like the *Cape Times* [could] achieve it was probably an important aspect of getting their target audience ... to understand the city" (2003: interview).

However, the idea that a panoply of distinctive cultures can be brought together in a public space and introduced to one another is at once utopian and static. It assumes that visibility is by itself a virtue, and that difference can easily be made available to the gaze. Because of the value given to what is observable, the project tended to focus on the most visible aspects of cultures, and in some ways the coverage resembled the picturesque approach through which Muslim food, dress and customs had been staged in the past. The approach also failed to engage with the question of whose gaze was at the centre of the cultures that were being introduced to one another.

The initiative also presented a conceptual problem: if multiplicity is reserved for a special section of the newspaper, it can also be limited to that part. Anonymous 2 confirmed that "[the marketing aspect] never reached the other end of the newspaper [the newsroom]" (2003: interview). Mohamed Shaikh at *Die Burger* also reflected on the relation between marketing and outreach in the project: "Sometimes I wonder [if it was] social responsibility or a marketing exercise" (Pillay 1999: 18). Anonymous 2 articulated a concern about the reach of the initiative beyond a privileged minority to a broad audience: "That whole media and marketing campaign was a shortcoming. The broader Cape Town community was largely uninformed. The actual events attracted largely the same people. In a city of three million people, only ten thousand attended. It became an arty-farty, elitist, artists-around-the-city thing" (2003: interview).

To Suren Pillay, the problem of the "One City Many Cultures" initiative lay in its conception of culture (1999: 15). To him, there was something disturbingly familiar in the view of culture as separate, static and given. "Has culture become a synonym for race and/or religion?" he asked. Instead of encountering one another's distinctive practices and behaviours, Pillay asserts that such occasions *generate* and *solidify* differences. The static and commodified presentation of differences undercuts the way we are always many things at once, and fails to recognise that we are constantly changing. Pillay therefore found the project a regressive one that evaded the real problems of spatial division in the city and "normalise[d]" what were, in effect, "racialised differences" that recalled apartheid. For an anonymous journalist, the problems presented by the initiative were still more serious. "It was a plaster [band-aid]. Look at the little Xhosa performance group, look at the jazz bands for the coloureds, and then you get a brass band military sound thing to appease the whities" (Anonymous 1 2003: interview). To this writer, the parade of differences was not only arbitrary and insulting, but obscured the ongoing inequalities and racism of the city. The "One City, Many Cultures" project later evolved into the Cape Town Festival, an annual arts and culture festival in the city.

Other changes in the media since the Pagad controversy have been more substantial and lasting. Mahmood Sanglay notes that relations between the major media companies and independent and alternative media such as

Muslim Views have improved significantly since 1996 (2003: interview). A senior Cape Town-based journalist at a national newspaper observes another consequence of the stories. While before, Muslims were generally treated as "cultural curiosities" in South African newspapers, since the heightened profile of Islam with the Pagad stories,

> there has been a recognition that there is a Muslim section [of the population] that can be asked for comment on Iraq and Afghanistan. I honestly believe that if the Pagad story had not happened, nobody, not *The Argus*, not the *Cape Times*, would have bothered to think, hey, we've got a big Muslim population" (Anonymous 1 2003: interview).

The South African media encountered a defining test about Islam in reporting the Pagad stories. The test posed by the events, with their national and international resonances, was how to tell a story that was sufficiently specific. The association between Islam and militancy in the powerful international media idiom meant that consistent efforts were required to provide sufficient context and local detail. The challenge presented by this international idiom was deepened by the inconsistency of Pagad's own rhetoric. While denying that it was solely a Muslim group, it conveyed mixed signals about Islam by holdings its meetings in mosques and using Muslim prayers and religious rhetoric. Encountering a group that presented itself in contradictory ways as Muslim, combined with hostile conditions for journalists, deadly urban violence, and the power of a regressive international media idiom, the problem with the media's stories about Pagad was not negativity about the group. Rather, it was that, in many cases, the media did not sufficiently distinguish between the group and Islam. Nor did the reports consistently convey the fact that the Muslim community in South Africa is not monolithic. In the Pagad stories, the politics and economics of the international media clashed with well-established local stereotypes. The Pagad stories thus indigenised an international vocabulary about Islam, aided by the inadequacy of the home-grown South African idiom.

The Pagad events posed a potent and complicated challenge to the South African government, civil society and the media. At the level of representation, the Pagad stories were characterised by the encounter between an established South African Orientalist discourse of Islam, an international media idiom about extremist Islam and the manipulation of Orientalist stereoptypes by some Muslim groups themselves. The absence of a nuanced local media idiom for talking about Islam led to the adoption of anachronistic images drawn from the international media, and generated sensationalised news stories about the group. Certain aspects of Pagad's behaviour, such as its machismo, display of guns and the inflammatory language of some members of Pagad, exploited tropes about masculinity and Islam and held a clear appeal for the media, while the group's lower profile anti-crime activities and female members gained scant attention. Moreover, the contradictory emphasis which Pagad spokespeople placed on Islamic iconography obscured the similarities between Pagad and other vigilante groups operating in South Africa at the time. Pagad was suspicious about the motives of the media, and journalists reported hostility from members of Pagad, yet they also collaborated uneasily with each other and reinforced each other's interests. In many ways, the media can be faulted for its coverage, yet it was also on the receiving end of an unusual combination of pressures.

The masked Pagad figure came to serve discursive needs for both the media and the group itself. However, the image of the masked man in these articles was a vehicle through which an anachronistic discourse of Islam took hold in South Africa. The image evoked a ready-made, decontextualised vocabulary which made it harder to articulate a historically informed analysis that showed the use of drugs and gangs as political instruments by the apartheid regime in the 1980s, longstanding non-vigilante anti-crime initiatives within black communities, and complex responses to Pagad within Muslim communities. In the aftermath of the Pagad coverage, representations of Islam in the South African media have been profoundly changed. Interviews with journalists who work both in the mainstream South African media and in Muslim media provide an insight into the challenges of reporting on the Pagad stories. While these journalists have called for more nuanced and informed portrayals of Muslims, their larger aim is a media for the broader good.

CHAPTER 6

"The Trees Sway North-North-East":

Post-apartheid visions of Islam

We etch ourselves into … culture, in complex
palimpsests of knowledge and desire.

– Meena Alexander (1998: 152)

[A]nd what we said about it became a part of what it is.

– Wallace Stephens (1965 [1954]: 159)

Novel spaces

This last chapter considers the multifaceted visions of Islam produced in recent South African drama, poetry, fiction, film and memoir. The texts I explore below amplify areas of complexity and subversiveness already present in performances of self, food practices and oral narratives (as discussed in previous chapters). They radically reimagine Muslim presence in South Africa.

As part of the great flowering of culture in the post-apartheid period, artists and writers have re-envisioned Muslim life.[1] Such experiments are evident in recognised genres such as theatre, film, music, literature and visual art, and also through newer avenues such as slam poetry, blogs, listserves, stand-up comedy, performance collectives and self-published novels and poetry. Many writers straddle both spaces, producing prize-winning publications and simultaneously charting new pathways for disseminating their work, including the playwright and poet Malika Ndlovu, the activist and slam poet Mphutlane wa Bofelo, the poet, essayist and blogger Rustum Kozain, the actor and comedian Riaad Moosa (who starred in the recent film *Material*), and Shabbir Banoobhai, the author of several influential poetry collections, who has more recently self-published new anthologies and a novel titled *Heretic*. In 2009, the activist group The Inner Circle published *Hijab: Unveiling Queer Muslim Lives*, a ground-breaking collection of autobiographical writing by members of lesbian, gay and transgender Muslims. Memoir has long been a radical form in which to portray dissident visions of Muslim life, as is demonstrated in Zackie Achmat's riveting memoir about his life as a gay Muslim man in *Defiant Desire* (1994). Achmat also has a significant profile on Facebook, where he publishes essays that continue this intersection of confession and politics.

Political memoirs have provided nuanced visions of political activism, filling an important absence. The 2003 memoir *Our Generation* by the activist and journalist Zubeida Jaffer is a supple account of the role of Muslims in the anti-apartheid struggle, and includes the political, intimate and religious aspects of her life. *Our Generation* attends to Jaffer's role as an activist and mother who was imprisoned and tortured by the apartheid government. She shares her doubts as well as the resoluteness of her faith during the struggle against political injustice.

The formally complex novel *The Silent Minaret* (2005), by Ishtiyaq Shukri, has as its protagonist a former anti-apartheid activist from Cape Town who moves to London to study. After the British authorities close the Finbury Mosque near his house, he disappears, creating the enigma of an absent centre around which the narrative revolves. In its contemporary London setting, *The Silent Minaret* decentres Islam and "provincialises" South Africa, present-day London and Palestine. Such "anti-picturesque" works in literature, visual art, film and drama have radically expanded the view of Muslim life in South African culture.

Shaida Kazie Ali's *Not A Fairytale* (2010) re-envisions the possibilities of Muslim life through a feminist, postmodern frame. The novel recounts the lives of Zuhra and Salena, Muslim sisters growing up in apartheid Cape Town, and is divided into separate sections written in distinct voices, interspersed with recipes and feminist retellings of familiar fairytales.

Not A Fairytale conveys apartheid's intimate impact on the family, or as Ali said in an interview, "the apartheid of *that* family" (2011). The novel shows how patriarchy colludes with both racism and the codes of femininity to sentence women to silence and self-erasure. The two young women find their worth measured through their complexion, hair and obedience to their parents.

However, Muslims are not presented solely as virtuous victims of apartheid in the novel. They are both at the receiving end of racism and purveyors of racism themselves, favouring light skin and straight hair in a private injustice that echoes the larger injustice of the apartheid system. Some Muslims pass easily through the system: "Papa's skin is … very white, like a real white man's" (17). However, his wife, the dark-skinned Hawa, rigidly polices her daughters' behaviour and despises people with skin like her own, in an unconscious show of self-hatred. Zuhra observes her mother's reaction to her friend Rukshana: "Ma doesn't trust her because she's dark-skinned" (24). Hawa is the source of cutting remarks about black skin and "kroes" [frizzy] hair (34), but when her husband dies, she is confronted with her own nonexistence in the eyes of the state. "Ma gets the death certificate with my father's name on it and it says 'Never Married' and she screams and screams and people explain that Islamic marriages are not legal, but she will not be calmed" (41). Ali shows us that to be favoured by an unjust system is itself a form of entrapment. Selena's empty life in the first section of the novel is the result of her light skin: "This face … dooms her to playing white" (107).

Not A Fairytale's tragedies take the form of the decades-long prison of obedience and conformity in which some Muslim women are caught, perpetuated by patriarchal notions of family honour and cultural authenticity. As the elder daughter, Selena is made to enter a soulless marriage arranged by her parents, in which she is trapped for over twenty years. However, the novel also shows how the characters eventually shatter their constraints. Zuhra, who has "grown up knowing I was dark and therefore ugly" (66), finds her way to independence and happiness through education, as well as the resilience she gains from her undaunted imagination. And even Selena eventually escapes the confines of her empty marriage. The women find refuge in education, loyalty to one another, time – some, like Hawa, by simply outliving their husbands, and, in Zuhra's case, by embracing the role of the dissident daughter. Selena, who recedes into silent dutifulness in the first part of the novel, regains the interest of readers in the second half, in which her long-suppressed anger shatters a mirror (and perhaps the spell that has trapped her). She steps through the shards into a new, self-created future.

The role of fairytales in the novel is ambiguous. They can function as patriarchal codes that train girls to wait to be rescued by men, but they can also be a space of invention and solace under intractable conditions. The secret stories that women tell one another in *Not A Fairytale* show acute insight into the injustices they experience and into which some women induct others. Perhaps the most affecting lines in the novel are found in Selena's tragic revelation to Zuhra about marriage: "our mother and other women like her are like Judas goats. They let girls follow them into the marriage-abattoir" (24). However, fairy stories also have at their core the mesmerising women who are usually cast as villains. Ali revealed that *Not A Fairytale* was born from an epiphany she had while watching a parade of villains at Disneyworld and realising how many of them were clever, unafraid women (2011: interview). Her postmodern fairytales invert the formula that exiles and punishes intelligent women. In *Not A Fairytale*, Cinderella is retold as a feminist tale in which a female jinn grants Cinderella her wish – which is not to marry a prince, but to study. Meanwhile, Red Riding Hood not only survives the predatory wolf but goes to university and graduates as a vet. In *Not A Fairytale*, clever women are the heroines, not the villains of the stories.

The characters in the novel live in a world in which the magical, the religious and the occult are in close proximity. Islam features in an ordinary and humorous manner in the internal fairy stories. The Wolf doesn't eat the Three Little Pigs because "I'm Muslim" – instead, he employs them to run his restaurants, which they do with great success, ultimately buying themselves a house (65). *Not A Fairytale* does not make the mistake of framing Muslim men only as villains or turning older women into stereotypical stepmothers who hound their innocent daughters. Instead, there are kind-hearted men like Rukshana's father, who exorcises jinns for a living. Hawa, the sisters' sumptuously cruel mother, is nonetheless an explicable villain, trapped in self-hatred for being dark-skinned and terrified of displeasing her more powerful and socially desirable light-skinned husband. Inequitable marriages are the source of many jokes in the novel. When Zuhra learns that nuns are called the "brides of Christ" (17), she overhears a girl in her class wonder if "Christ is Muslim and that's why he has so many brides" (18).

Ali's feminist novel followed the publication of Imraan Coovadia's wide-ranging oeuvre of comic and serious fiction. *Green-Eyed Thieves* (2006), his second novel (the first, *The Wedding*, was discussed in Chapter 3) deals with racism, forced removals in South Africa, the torture of activists, militarism in Pakistan, and 9/11 and its impact on immigrants in the United States – yet it is achingly funny. The novel features the twin brothers Firoze and Ashraf Peer, their father Mirza, their shop-lifting mother Sameera, and Uncle Ten Percent Farouk, members of a prominent Johannesburg crime family. Firoze and Ashraf are Muslim South Africans of Indian descent, and their light skin and green eyes confound the markers of race in South Africa. In the course of their criminal activities, they pass for Jewish, Arab, Hispanic, Pakistani and Scottish. The plot of the novel moves from Johannesburg to Peshawar to New York City, and also flits across time in a seamless sequence from the 1970s to the twenty-first century.

The novel is an incisive satire of the codes of race and religion in South Africa and the United States. The story of a successful criminal family illustrates the hypocrisy of apartheid South Africa, which conceived of itself as a Christian and law-abiding state at the end of an uncivilised continent, while disenfranchising and impoverishing its black citizens. The novel wields the weapon of the joke against the powerful, such as "[t]he Brixton squad is notorious for their efficiency, which in South African terms means their ability to find an African suspect to pay for any particular crime" (73). Venality is revealed as always lying close to the surface of the apartheid state. Sun City, was a gambling resort in the invented country of Bophuthatswana, one of the "homelands" created by the apartheid South African government in order to legally exile its own population. The homelands were also exempt from the Immorality Act, which criminalised interracial sex. As a result, the narrator slyly observes, "Sun City is where South Africans, particularly white Johannesburgers, come to relax from Calvinism" (69).

In their acute observation of these unstated rules of apartheid, the protagonists of *Green-Eyed Thieves* thus come close to "the centre of things, or to the centre's underbelly" (140). After carrying out the biggest theft in the history of Sun City, the family eludes capture by adopting the expected racial roles assigned to them as Indian South Africans: a submissive attitude, and assurances of their co-operation with the police "so as to forestall the chaos and banditry we observe in the rest of Africa" (60). As expected, the captain, on "[s]eeing these humble Indians, as ridiculous as can be with their awkward smiles and neatly pressed turbans, [feels] proud, once again, to be a Christian and a European" (61) and allows them to escape.

Through the broad family of black, white, local, immigrant, Muslim, Hindu, Jewish, Christian, and determinedly irreligious accomplices, lovers and friends that gathers around the Peers, *Green-Eyed Thieves* creates a utopian South Africa constituted by transgressive affiliations across race and religion. The novel presents a fantasy of South Africans who break the laws against interracial families and interracial sex with as much enthusiasm and naturalness as they do those against theft or the prohibition on alcohol in Islam.

By the time they arrive in the United States, the characters have already experienced the country second-hand through South Africa's long enchantment with American popular culture. Paradoxically, during the 1980s, when the apartheid government entrenched its rule through violent oppression and successive States of Emergency, the top-rated series on South African television was *The Cosby Show*. Period details are richly evoked through popular culture references to Dorothy Radebe, Hugh Masekela, the Ramones, Louis Armstrong, *Days of Our Lives* and Kojak. While America confounds certain South African expectations, in other ways, the protagonists find it reassuringly familiar: "Non-existent law, as in South Africa, or omnipresent law, as in the US, work out to much the same thing" (162).

At times, the Peers find the settings of apartheid South Africa and the post-9/11 United States to be completely different. For instance, the rigidity of South Africa's concepts of race renders those who believe in them both absurd and vulnerable to the trickster criminals who easily manipulate the prescribed categories for their own advantage. Mirza notes that "South Africans live to pin people down into boxes and categories". In America, however, they find a country of protean racial and religious performances, an environment to which they quickly adapt. Having confounded South Africa's racial codes, in the United States, Firoze and Ashraf find many people who look like them: "Part Hispanic, part Jewish and part Japanese" (105), and become "the perfect immigrant[s], devoid of shame, caste [and] internal borders" (197).

An American setting allows Coovadia to convey a nuanced picture of Islam, noting differences among Muslims concerning politics, levels of observance and the capacity for humour, as well as the difficulties they face in the post 9/11 world. Muslims are as much a target of satire as any other characters in the novel. Mirza says to his son, "Well, Firoze, for the first time in years you're going to set foot in a mosque. I know you swore you'd never go back after the Rushdie affair, but times have changed. We have to stick together" (109).

Green-Eyed Thieves shows that at their worst, South Africa and the United States have uncannily similar flaws. In a sympathetic view of mostly poor immigrants at the mercy of growing discrimination and targeted immigration laws, Coovadia's comparative perspective allows him to read the similarities between racial codes in South Africa and the United States: "The worshippers, I guessed, were from the practical and technical economy: taxi drivers and dispatchers, electricians, engineers, garment cutters. They must have been Pakistanis, Palestinians, Somalis, Malays, Egyptians, Jordanians. They were fearful, quiet. They were one mishap away from deportation, as we would have been had Ashraf not created our counterfeit green cards." Both in apartheid South Africa and post-9/11 America, the novel critiques systems of law that entrench privilege and prejudice, and which are ranged unerringly against the powerless.

The narrator reserves his most cutting criticism for those who traffic in thinly veiled racism. The least sympathetic character in *Green-Eyed Thieves* is a renowned scholar of Islam at an Ivy League university who welcomes Firoze into his circle with a pointed invitation: "this country wants definitions … [S]omeone like you, someone with a real way with words, is just the person to give it the right definition of a Muslim. Some kind of apology on behalf of the religion would be much appreciated" (163). In the novel's nuanced perspective, such rigid ideas are contrary to America's promised fluidity and dangerously close to apartheid South Africa's addiction to putting people into "boxes and categories".

As *The Silent Minaret* did with London and Palestine, *Green-Eyed Thieves* compares South Africa and the United States to enrich insights about both settings. Like earlier travellers to America, the narrator of Coovadia's novel finds that the experience of leaving home has deepened his understanding of both the place he has left and the one he has adopted. Modelling himself on a French forebear, Firoze embraces the multiplicity of his new country and becomes a hyphenated American: "a hemi-semi-demi-American, a de Tocqueville of the current era".

"Looking at me like you look at them": At Her Feet[2]

Nadia Davids's *At Her Feet*, a one-woman play consisting of the interlocking monologues of six Muslim women, deals centrally with the intersection of religion, race and gender. Davids decided that in post-apartheid South Africa "it was okay for me to deal with issues of gender. [Previously] the race question had subsumed everything" (2004: interview). Davids's focus on gender in *At Her Feet* allows her to explore fully the wariness, competitiveness, racial contempt, class differences and consumerism that can divide Muslim women, and it also elicits the empathy and humour of the play's characters.

The title *At Her Feet* refers to the hadith [saying of the prophet], "Paradise lies at the feet of the mother", and signals the value that Islam accords to women and that the men in the play are seen to betray. The play begins with a monologue by Azra al Jamal, a young Jordanian woman who has been stoned to death by the male members of her family; it ends with Azra's mother comforting her dead daughter, reclaiming her from the acts of the men who would otherwise speak in her and her daughter's names.

In finely textured scenes, *At Her Feet* explores the local and global tendrils of a South African Muslim identity, invoking themes long associated with Islam, such as veiling, cooking, burial, patriarchal men and suffering woman, but taking them in unexpected directions. It refuses a single, linear narrative, instead using poetry, memories and recurring images to create a complex view of Muslims within an intricately rendered world. Its poetic language unsettles a single meaning, whether in engaging with representations of Islam or tensions among Muslims. An excerpt from the poem "Cape Town, Jerusalem" by Rustum Kozain appears at the start of the play, and warns of the danger of simplification and repression *within* Islam:

> … I turn from the stone's articulate act
> and seek the sentence long enough to house my tribe
> while knowing of neither's existence.

Contemplating the clarity of "the stone's articulate act" and the unerring identity offered by his "tribe", the speaker embraces neither.

At Her Feet uses the technique of one actress playing six characters to show the contradictory yet intersecting nature of their identities. The characters are Azra (a young Jordanian woman who tells her story after she has been stoned to death); Sara (a South African student and the principal storyteller); Ayesha (a politically engaged friend of Sara's); Tahira (Sara's conservative cousin); Aunty Kariema (a housewife whose blunt conservativism and eclectic tastes make her the the play's funniest character, but who also delivers its most poignant line); and Azra's mother (who ends the play). The rhythms of Muslim life – fasting, praying and Eid celebrations – but also quotidian acts of cooking, work and conversation shape the women's days.

At Her Feet opens with Azra wearing a hijab and performing abrupt and wordless movements signalling the stoning that ends her life. This deadly dance ends with her lying prone and silent; then she rises, removes her burkha and speaks: "My name is Azra al Jamal and I have just been killed." After this striking opening, the play moves to its South African characters, who have watched a television documentary about Azra's death and agonise over her fate. Each character is signalled by specific clothing and music: tablah music plays over Azra's movements, Erykah Badhu accompanies Sara, Black Star announces Ayesha's appearance, James Ingram moves Tahira and the songs of Zayne Adams (a popular Muslim South African singer) play while Auntie Kariema speaks. The changes in music and scarves allow the actress (in South Africa, this challenging role was played by the gifted Quanita Adams) to augment the gestures and accents through which she embodies the six women.

After Azra's powerful introduction, the first South African character is Sara, the storyteller, whose opening words are a poem, "The Scarf" (in South Africa, the term encompasses the head covering that Muslim women wear). "It begins with geometry", Sara commences. The apparent promise to take the audience inside the veil through Sara's words is refracted through the language of poetry, which refuses to explain the scarf.

Davids is wary of the danger that "if you write something about Muslim women, you are now that margin's voice" (2004: interview) and declines the limitation of such a position. "I don't see myself as a Muslim playwright who has access to stories and who has the right to tell stories" (2004: interview). The play unsettles any insider claim to reveal secrets. Sara's monologue on the veil is haunted by the gaze of others:

[T]he world has gone a bit of veil crazy. Behind the veil. At the drop of a veil. To veil or not to veil. And I wonder sometimes why, with my love of fabric, and texture, colour and beauty, with my collection of scarves that I drape around my waist, or wrap like a bandana on my head, or loop through my belt holes, or throw around my shoulders, I wonder if I don't wear it just because I don't like what it says. Or maybe it's because I don't want you looking at me like you look at them.

The speech explores the interior meanings of the beauty and creativity of scarves, while Sara also acknowledges that as a Muslim woman, she is afraid of the way she is viewed when she wears a scarf. Tahira, who works at a travel agency and is criticised by Ayesha for her consumerism at Eid, gives a moving account of being instructed by her employer, in the aftermath of 11 September, that she can no longer wear her scarf to work:

So, now I'm left holding my scarf in one hand, and unemployment in the other. I think about going out into the world with my head uncovered. I think about being at work, about people not being scared to buy plane tickets from me.

Rather than reveal the truth about why Muslim women do or do not wear the veil, these scenes explore multiple reasons for making the decision, from religious conviction, to the beauty of the fabric close to the skin, to Sara's acknowledgement that she fears the way she is perceived when she wears a scarf. Even as she quickly contests Auntie Kariema's racism within the family, Sara finds herself unable to cover her head in public. As in *Colour Me* and *Disgrace* (discussed in Chapters 1 and 3), the act of being looked at and looking back marks a crucial turning point in the play.

The vision of Islam and Muslim women's subjectivities conveyed in *At Her Feet* is therefore complex. The play unsettles entrenched images of Muslim women, but also declines to project a reassuring unity about them. It does not evade the difficulties of racism and of being a woman in often patriarchal Muslim communities. Indeed, *At Her Feet* illustrates that its Muslim characters are not exempt from contradiction or complicity with racism. For this, the critic Susana Molins Lliteras praised the play for "not fall[ing] into simple dichotomies between modern and traditional, liberated and suppressed", but creating characters of "unrivalled depth" (2003: 6).

Ayesha, the most overtly political character in the play, shares the name of a woman who was married to the Prophet and was herself a warrior and leader in the earliest Islamic community. Ayesha's feminist vision of Islam combines spirituality, politics, literary theory, poetry and music, in an eclectic list that the play treats with gentle amusement:

> I take Islam very seriously ... Islam blended with some Black Consciousness, Biko, Baraka, Malcolm, some feminist theory, big up to Spivak and Judith Butler, and of course my personal hero, Edward Said, with a little Lauren Hill in the mix.

In the play, Ayesha contests not only her fellow Muslims' racism (particularly Auntie Kariema's derogatory comments about blacks and Indian Muslims), but she conveys a view of Islam that is intimate with the West. Her vision combines the critical voices of Malcolm X and Edward Said in the United States, Steve Biko in South Africa, and the scholars Gayatri Spivak and Judith Butler, to create an erudite and radically feminist Islam.

However, it is the complex character Auntie Kariema, who holds racist views, yet is also funny and acute, who delivers the most powerful line of the play. Auntie Kariema reflects on Azra's fate, and her own:

> My mother died when I was ten. For five months she sat in a bed, wasting away slowly, while doctor did what he could. My father was in the background somewhere. ... And the day of her funeral was dark hey.... I stayed in the kitchen, near the stove, where it was warm not really wanting to move or think.... later, when she was wrapped in a white sheet, pressed with camphor and rose petals, and lifted above the men's shoulders, ready to be taken to the koebus [cemetery], I don't know what made me think I could go with them. But I followed the men out the door, and tried to tag along, maybe make myself unnoticeable ... because you see, I needed to bury my mother. And one of the men, a stranger who walked close by the coffin, turned to me and said "What are you doing? You know you're not allowed, go back to the house." But you see, I kept walking,

because I needed to bury my mother. I kept walking until my father, his face blurred with pain, picked me up and carried me to the stoep [veranda] by our house and left me with my aunties. I stood there crying, while the women went inside to make pies and tea and sandwiches with their grief. So this girl, this Arab girl. I suppose I can understand her ... I wanted to walk and she wanted to talk.

Auntie Kariema reveals that the rituals of closure offered by burying her mother are denied to her because of her gender. She learns from the other women present to channel the lingering pain of this exclusion into making "pies and tea and sandwiches", into which they translate their grief. The unforgotten and unassuaged pain of not being able to witness her mother's burial leads Auntie Kariema to the realisation of a direct connection between herself and Azra: "I wanted to walk and she wanted to talk".

Auntie Kariema's empathy with the young Jordanian girl is convincing not because they are both Muslim – in fact, her epiphany surprises her – but because she realises that they each felt a desire whose denial changed their lives. Like Kariema, all of *At Her Feet*'s characters are multi-faceted, flawed and holistic. Sara acknowleges that her artistic use of scarves is at least partly inspired by fear of how people see her when she wears them on her head. Tahira is forced to relinquish her scarf in order to keep her job, an act that is misread by Ayesha as hypocrisy. Despite her activist persona, Ayesha is profoundly hurt at being rejected by Auntie Kariema, the mother of her light-skinned boyfriend, for her dark skin and "kroes" hair. *At Her Feet*'s female characters acutely reflect their complex contemporary South Africa context.

Even as the play engaged directly and rivetingly with the difficulties for Muslim women posed by patriarchal men and internal differences of class, ethnicity and race, its attention to the intricacies of Muslim women's lives retriggered the continuing anxiety about race and Islam in South Africa. When Davids applied to the South African National Arts Council to support a nationwide tour of *At Her Feet*, her application was rejected because the Council determined that the play "does not represent the races and religions of South Africa". They invited her to reapply once she had revised the play to include "other races and religious groups" (Van Heerden 2008: 50). Davids addressed the racial and religious assumptions behind this demand in an open letter published in the *Sunday Independent* newspaper. She wrote:

> had I known that racial demographics were the determining factor,
> as opposed to artistic integrity, political relevance and public re-
> sponse, I would have worded my proposal differently ... The point of
> the production is to engage with the multiplicity of a single faith, in-
> terpreted by a variety of cultural, political and socio-economic para-
> digms. It also narrates an underwritten dimension of South African
> society which has been present in our country for over 300 years
> (Davids, quoted in Van Heerden 2008: 50–51).

Davids draws attention in her response to the troubling racialisation of
Muslims – which forecloses the right to explore the specificities of Islam in
South Africa. The intersection of race and gender continue to be of critical
importance in navigating the assumption that to focus on Muslims is to cater
to a minority which holds no interest for the general public.

Rustum Kozain's "Brother, who will bury me?"

Rustum Kozain's poem "Brother, who will bury me?," appeared in his first
collection, *This Carting Life* (2005), and speaks about Muslim burial with an
intimacy that claims a place for Islam in South Africa, yet resists a singularity
for Muslims. Instead, the poem insists that they belong alongside other communities in a landscape layered by history. Extensive in length at 151 lines, the
poem has a compelling, unpredictable speaker who delights in the implacable
desires forbidden to Muslims, such as the taste of ham and wine, and a sacri-
legious tattoo of a crescent and moon.

"Brother, who will bury me?" illustrates the ways in which Muslim burials
shape the South African landscape. The first part of the poem envisages an
orthodox Muslim burial, while the second half creates a vision of burial not
tied to Islam. These different endings redefine death as the possibility of a
homecoming anchored in the mutual history of all the people who have lived
in the landscape the narrator knows so intimately.

The poem starts with the speaker standing alone on Paarl Rock[3] with his
arms outstretched, a gesture that offers his body to the world in an open-ended

embrace. The poem speaks of an Islam located firmly in South Africa, with "branches plucked from bluegum trees, / lush with thin, long branches: our substitute / For olive." To be Muslim in South Africa means that one turns "north-north-east" to face Mecca. As though in response to the speaker, or perhaps promising a larger continuity of which he is a part, the "trees bend north-north-east in witness" (line 101).

Although initially simply a "dream" (line 5), the question "Brother, who will bury me, and where?" (line 13) precipitates the speaker into the future he has imagined. He asks not "who *would* bury me," but "who *will* bury me". We see his body being washed and rubbed with camphor, wrapped in soft white cloth, and hear the prayers of the men carrying the body. The speaker is profoundly attentive to the "grace" and intimacy of these masculine rituals (line 29). When his body is carried to the cemetery by relatives and friends who have gathered at his parents' home, what looks like "a stumble / Of obligation" is in fact the deliberate touching of the body, "my bier exchanged often / So everyone may find grace" (lines 28–29). Despite their intimacy with his body, he fears being seen as a "mock[er]" of his father's faith among those who remember that he left Islam (line 25).

In death, the speaker revisits the details of his life recorded by the angels on his shoulders – on the left, Israeel has noted all his sins, and on the right, Ismaeel has written down his good deeds. These two books, the accounting of his life, will determine whether he enters paradise or hell. Echoing them, the speaker faithfully revisits the details of his transgressions, the marks of which have been left on his body. As his memories take him beyond transgression and redemption, back to his childhood, he finds a site he can truly envision as a resting place.

The sumptuous details of memory are reflected in the speaker's recollections of childhood friends, who will drop his body on the way to the cemetery and create "[t]he disgrace of my corpse on tarmac". He vividly imagines the food served at the funeral, the requisite "sugar-bean stew" with gravy "thick and red as mud". The title refers to the speaker's brother, but we learn in the course of the poem that it also refers to the many Muslim brothers who carry and accompany his body and sing him into his final homecoming.

After the resonant description of a Muslim burial, the speaker's use of the word "or" in line 109 suddenly signals another, *equally possible* universe of death. "Or" appears three times in the poem, on each occasion lifting the speaker into an entirely different world, disavowing unity and calling several possible outcomes into existence.

In the second half of the poem, the speaker's vision opens from the Muslim grave, where the body is separated from soil only by a sheet, to a new perspective on the world. The speaker envisions other communities who have been "evicted" from the landscape; not only Muslims but other people who were "removed" during the years of apartheid: "Decades ago this graveyard was a jumble / of shacks. Migrant workers, their wives and children all without passes, lived here, called it / Bongweni, favourite place." Graveyards continue the divisions among the living, and the speaker might find himself "buried in some pauper's grave / in Paarl, where the unknown and the wretched lie." He insists on recalling other traumas on the same land against the erasure of "the unknown and the wretched" and feels a new sense of community among the dead of the place, who are "crouching still in rock / Like fossils waiting to spring into beginning." Yet, the thought of Muslim burial is not left entirely behind. Though they walk away, the men at the graveside will return to read prayers for the dead on predetermined days, months and even years apart. The speaker invites their prayers, during his "slow, final journey" (line 99).

Ultimately, the speaker finds rest in solitude. Remembering a childhood fight with his brother, he recalls running from him to sit alone next to a river "reek[ing] of laundry and decay" (line 132). In his grief and anger, he picks "veldflowers" [wild flowers], arranges them "[i]n a bleached Coke can", and, in a wordless gesture, offers them to his mother. He "sobbed in frustration, unable / to show her the solace in knowing / One's alone, even as that solace hurt more" (line 138). In this recollection of vulnerability and the comfort of beauty, the speaker finds his route to "solace". The poem ends with the image of the lone figure of the speaker deciding how he wishes to be buried – on those hills where flowers grow to offer future solace.

So in "Brother, who will bury me?" the speaker finds a homecoming in a new sense of history and place. The poem places a burial in the Muslim idiom alongside other idioms through the parallel possibilities created by the word "or."

Mr Chameleon: A long journeying to Africanness

Reflecting the powerful role of autobiography in creating images of Muslim life, I end this chapter with an analysis of a memoir by the late poet and activist Tatamkhulu Afrika. *Mr Chameleon* (2005), a beautifully written memoir, revisits the themes of race, politics and belonging that first intrigued me (and which are discussed in the Introduction).

By the time of his death in 2002 at the age of eighty, Afrika's unusual biography had become well known in literary circles in South Africa. He was born in Egypt in 1920 to a Turkish father and Egyptian mother, who moved to South Africa when Afrika was two. His parents died shortly after arriving in South Africa and Afrika was subsequently raised by white family friends. At the age of seventeen, he volunteered to join the Allied side in the Second World War and later also fought in the anti-apartheid struggle as a member of Umkhonto we Sizwe (the armed wing of the African National Congress – the term means "Spear of the Nation" in Zulu). In 1964, he converted to Islam and legally reclassified himself as "Malay" or Muslim, ceding the privileges of whiteness (as noted earlier, under apartheid Muslims could not be white). The last of Afrika's five names, Tatamkhulu Afrika, which means "Grandfather of Africa", was an honorific title given to him by fellow soldiers in Umkhonto we Sizwe and he adopted it officially as his final name.

Mr Chameleon is self-laceratingly direct about the slow, interior changes of Afrika's life. Recounting a particularly difficult period in the 1960s, when he was unemployed and lived on one pint of milk and half a loaf of bread a day for five months, Afrika lingers on the slow processes of time changing. *Mr Chameleon* conveys the pain and vertiginous moral shifts that result from a constant failure to find work and shows how Afrika withstands the hardship of self-doubt and hunger. During this testing period comes the beginning of a deeply felt return to Islam after Afrika reads a second hand copy of the Qur'an. *Mr Chameleon* conveys the unhurried growth of conviction that springs from this act of reading.

For Afrika, the arena of religion is not, however, solipsistic. He combines faith with a resolute insistence on political justice. The book also conveys how he avoids distancing himself from others. Even in childhood, he noted in himself a capacity for absolute imperviousness to others, as a defence against a fractured life filled with loss and change. The adult Afrika feels an unforgiving anger toward those from whom he differs politically; for example, after visiting the home of a coloured woman in Observatory[4] who is passing for white and witnessing her rigid self-policing to maintain the crucial fiction of whiteness, he resolves never to see her again.

As a child, he learns what cannot be spoken about, particularly the comfortless topic of his burgeoning sexuality. He also acknowledges the temptation to redeem himself through the narrative possibilities of autobiography; for instance, by lying about his sexuality or his unforgiving attitude to those who have hurt him. At one point, Afrika wonders whether he is "bragging" about his activities as a resistance fighter. The most moving moments in the book emerge when he perceives the vulnerability of others and reciprocates with openness in turn. During the 1960s, he treats gays in Cape Town generously and supportively at a time when they faced mostly violence and contempt. Afrika writes with unafraid directness about sexuality in *Bitter Eden*, based on his time as a German prisoner-of-war in North Africa.[5]

In contrast to Afrika's subtle reflections about his internal shifts, the viciousness and absurdity of apartheid's racial categories are fully displayed in *Mr Chameleon*: "[On] that night when they arrested us [they] at once separated me from my men because they thought that I was white – no, *insisted* that I was white" (2005: 406). Later on, the security police offer him the chance to have charges dropped against him if he betrays the rest of the group, and Afrika realises he has been made the offer because "after all, I was a white man, wasn't I?" (2005: 407). Under apartheid, the meanings of race stretch into every area of life. In jail, even the food reflects racial division: "pork for blacks, mutton and beef for the other races" (2005: 417). When Afrika is taken for interrogation to the Security Branch's office in Loop Street in Cape Town, the policeman

> handed a file with my name on it, saying I was an Egyptian, and the clerk, fluttering anxious hands, protest[ed] that there was no such racial classification, so where must he put the file, and the squat one said not to ask him but why not try 'Indians' because they were both pretty much the same thing, weren't they? (Afrika 2005: 411).

This scene demonstrates apartheid's own bureaucratic paralysis in the face of the unclear lines running through race and religion. Afrika exacerbates such confusion by refusing all given categories. His five successive name changes and racial reclassification from white to "Malay" confounded the certainties of apartheid. In prison, during Ramadan, he declines to break his fast with Sunni Muslims at sunset, but instead does so twelve minutes later, following the Shia requirement. Through his multiple forms of resistance, he embodies apartheid's anxiety about difference and change. In his refusals lie the threat that "the known [is] no longer known" (Afrika 2005: 401). Rejecting the "whiteness" which his upbringing and his light skin have given him, Afrika seeks Africanness through Islam, activism and empathy with other blacks.

For Afrika, an African identity does not reside in the skin, but is earned through activism, loyalty and recognition by fellow Africans:

> When [Chris Hani] was assassinated a short while later, I mourned over him as a black should – as the Africanness that he had accepted in me and to which after such a long journeying I had returned (2005: 406).[6]

To Afrika, these moments of recognition are the basis for a humanity that is not based on the privileges of race. Such moments mark crucial nodes throughout the book. When he first arrives at Victor Verster prison, although he cannot see him, Afrika recognises the voice of the poet and activist Sandile Dikeni shouting a greeting through a barred window.

What is most striking is where Afrika chooses to start and end his autobiography. Near the beginning of the book, Afrika recounts the childhood experience of seeing a chameleon changing colour to match its surroundings. He asks the woman he knows as Gran why this happens. "It's the way he gets what he wants, dear, and how he hides from those who want *him*" (Afrika 2005: 13). This became a manifesto that defined Afrika's life. By the end of the book, *Mr Chameleon* has changed his name five times, and been imprisoned both by the German army and the apartheid government.

Yet the memoir conveys something that exceeds even this hard-earned self-definition. What most distinguishes Afrika in a life of hardship and resistance are moments of deep recognition, of encounters between the otherwise inaccessible interior lives of human beings. The book ends not chronologically in 2002, but with an event that occurred during the anti-apartheid struggle in 1987 at the end of Afrika's imprisonment for acts of "terrorism". The last encounter Afrika recounts on leaving Victor Verster prison is not one with his fellow activists, but an interaction with a non-political prisoner, a rent-boy edging towards madness. During the months of his imprisonment, Afrika had watched the young man polishing a pair of red boots every day, "an inwardness about him precluding any approach" (Afrika 2005: 419). Eventually, through a series of encounters during which Afrika refuses either to abuse or ignore him, the boy "unlocked the door to himself" (Afrika 2005: 419). Afrika learns that "I was the only one who had ever asked about [the boots]" and that they "were for him to put on the day he made his break across the wall" (Afrika 2005: 419–420).

When the young man discovers that Afrika will be released while he will remain inside, he flings the red boots across the prison yard. On the day Afrika leaves the prison, just before stepping through the gates, he recrosses the yard to retrieve the boots, and places them again next to the young man. As he walks through the gates, Afrika hears a shout and glances back (in the memoir, across the inestimable distance of madness and now time that separates the two), and "slowly [the young man] raised his hand". In a long life in which political activism and Islam play central roles, it is the "unlocking" of the door to the self and the mutual recognition of another person's humanity, despite hopeless self-delusion and difference, that conclude *Mr Chameleon*.

The works by Ali, Coovadia, Davids, Kozain and Afrika have expanded the possibilities for envisioning Muslim presence in South Africa. Their writings display an acute reflexivity about the legacy of portrayals of Islam, which they mould into feminist, comic and dissident themes and forms. None of the writers see their work as correcting views on Islam, nor do they create a homogeneous insider's perspective. Their inventiveness disrupts any claim to authority over Muslim life. Embedded in the contemporary, the works portray the specificities of Muslim experience and embrace other communities with whom Muslims share a history and present. They consciously turn away from a single vision of Islam. The writers of these texts create complex and resonant perspectives on Muslim life, refusing simple outcomes or redemptive themes. They decentre Islam without marginalis-

151

ing it, and treat Muslims equally, not exceptionally. In doing so, their work unsettles the logic held in place by race. Instead, they craft a history attentive to slavery and its long aftermath, and a more inclusive national narrative and vision of Africanness.

Conclusion

The whole is always the untrue.

– Theodor Adorno, quoted in Hussein (2002: 233)

The photographs of Pagad on the front pages of South African news-papers in August 1996 created a shock of recognition by overturning the picturesque mode of representing Muslims and reviving the nineteenth-century image of the "fanatical" Oriental running "amok". Images of Pagad articulated both a new and an old vision of Muslims and intersected with an international idiom focused on militancy and alienation. It was this oscillation between the placid and the fanatical that prompted the writing of *Regarding Muslims*.

In this book, I have explored the long fascination with images of Muslims in South Africa. I have argued that the figure of the picturesque Muslim evokes not only what is to be remembered, but what to be forgotten – in fact, reliance on the picturesque or "kitsch" portrayal of Muslims, involving sentimental and reassuring tropes, *requires* the forgetting of certain histories.

This is manifested in a fascination with picturesque Muslim figures, at the same time that the violence of slavery has been erased, signs of which remain in popular culture in images that allude obliquely to slavery. I have argued that the charged play of visibility and invisibility in these images of Muslims in the popular realm holds a revealing diagnostic power.

Toni Morrison showed that the weighted tone of black characters in white American literature signalled subsumed meanings of race in the US, in which "black people ignite critical moments of discovery, change or em-phasis in literature not written by them" (1992: viii). Similarly, I have taken a lesson from the recurring image of the picturesque Muslim in popular culture and argue that this offers a diagnostic tool for eliciting a part of history that has disappeared – but *not* disappeared. The anxiety of remem-bering slavery is refracted in popular culture through a focus on festivity, beauty, submissiveness and placid religious observance. Where Morrison identified a "pervasive use of black images" in literature that contemplates the meaning of freedom and individuality in a context of systemic violence and enslavement (1992: x), I find that the most compelling themes in the South African instances I have analysed are belonging and indigeneity. "Visibility" in the picturesque mode literally makes Muslims disappear – but reappear as reassuring objects that allay the anxiety of belonging for the colonial gaze.

The manufacture of silence, placidity and distance refracts a long history of intimacy in the slaveholding household, as well as a colonial and national social and economic system that was founded on slavery. The violence and sexual abuse of slavery are obliquely conveyed through the occult powers of the enslaved: the physical allure of slave women, and their disquieting power in the kitchen to conjure and seduce through food and potions.

Such images of the charged intimacy of slavery have constructed the familiar figure of the exotic and submissive "Malay" who stands in for the violated figure of the slave. The placid "Malays" are therefore haunted figures whose meaning I have read obliquely. Such popular aesthetics can be seen as a barometer that reveals a tension of history, and in which we can observe the active forgetting of slavery.

A market for images: Muslims, the picturesque and the boundary

Paul Landau shows that a vast market for representations of colonial land-scapes and colonised bodies arose in the nineteenth century (2002: 4). J. M. Coetzee points to an explanatory and cataloguing imperative behind images of colonised people in the late nineteenth century (1988). Yet, although these images were proclaimed to be accurate accounts of colonial settings, dur-ing the process of production and printing in metropolitan centres such as London and Leiden, they were embellished with imagined and fantastic detail to enhance their exotic appeal (Klopper, 1989: 71). Thus, the colonised body and landscape had to enact a certain exoticism and distance even as the market for images drew them closer to the metropole into a consumerist intimacy. Colonised bodies were made to refract this contradictory desire for accuracy and fantasy. The figure of the native carried these fantasies and was transported to the metropole both in person, as in the case of Sarah Baart-man, and in images, as in Angas's *The Kafirs Illustrated* (1849).

In the Cape Colony, Muslim figures acted as markers of territorial, racial and ontological boundaries. In the landscape paintings I have analysed, Muslims formed a thin line between outside and inside. The focus of intense fascination, they acted as a border, an inoculation, a device of translation and, yet, also a threat. As picturesque figures, they retained an inherent relation to violence, erasure and unsettlement. It is by gazing continually at Muslim figures and keeping them close in popular paintings, cookbooks, cartoons – items one takes into one's home and looks at daily – that they did their ideological work.

While South Africa is known for the violence and institutionalised racism of apartheid, the tendency to underplay the complexity of the country's history supports the notion that it is exceptional, and therefore has no relevance to the rest of the continent or any other context. In contrast, I argue that it is critical to consider the place of Muslims in the history of race and sex in South Africa because the country's specificity promises to deepen understanding of the relation of race, religion and sexuality elsewhere in Africa and the rest of the world. Understanding better how slavery, colonialism, religion, gender and race work together in South Africa allows us to understand how they operate in other contexts. This can be seen in work by Pumla Gqola, Zine Magubane and Mahmood Mamdani, all of whom find South Africa's experiences of slavery, colonialism and apartheid to be illuminating instances of more general African and global patterns. Gqola has analysed the parallels between South Africa and other slavocratic societies to make sense of the former's contorted relation with its history of slavery (2010). Mamdani demonstrates that the way settler colonialism works in South Africa echoes the production of indigeneity and belonging in other parts of Africa (1996). *Regarding Muslims* therefore takes its place in existing conversations in African studies, feminist studies, studies of slavery and race, religious studies, Islamic studies, Indian Ocean studies, literary studies and cultural studies.

I did not write this book to proclaim a singularity for Muslims in South Africa, but to analyse the uses to which an abstracted and seductive convention of portraying Muslims as picturesque has been put. This will hopefully enable an informed and situated comparison with other contexts in several ways: the question of slavery and forced labour, the relation of race and religion in colonial settings, and how the presence of Muslim slaves helped to shape concepts of sexuality and gender in South Africa.

I have shown how the figure of the industrious "Malay" in colonial por-trayals of the Cape Colony was contrasted with the "idleness" of the Khoisan. The most obvious comparison is with the freighted portrayals of enslaved people in the United States, with its parallel history of colonial settlement, genocide of indigenous people, slavery and post-emancipation Jim Crow laws. The United States also has a history of oscillating images of Muslim subjects, including an era of fascination from the 1870s to the 1920s (Edwards 2000), followed by a period of obscurity ended by the precipitous changes in the aftermath of the oil crisis in 1973, the Iranian Revolution in 1979, the First Gulf War in 1991 and 11 September 2001.

Visibility, marginality and the creation of the centre

In this book, I have argued that South African images of Muslims form part of a sense-making mechanism that has generated a crucial sense of belonging for white settlers, and disarticulated the relation of indigenous Africans to the land. In chapters on food, visual art and literature, I have shown how a certain manner of looking at Muslims has rendered them marginal and invisible, and enabled the construction of a normative space in which whiteness has been central, and enslaved and enserfed people have been marginalised. In this mode of looking, Muslims were constructed as the boundary that enabled the centre to be formed.

I have termed this phenomenon the *ambiguous visibility* of Muslims in South Africa. They are rendered visible in a way that erases critical ele-ments of their history. The representation of Muslims is thus marked both by visibility and erasure. The picturesque portrayal of enslaved Muslims has had the effect of erasing the violence of slavery, producing an effect of in-visibility *through* visibility, in which slave bodies became an instrument of absence. Pumla Gqola identifies this phenomenon in relation to the highly visible figure of Sarah Baartman as "hypervisibility", or a form of display that echoes practices of capture and entrapment (2010). This is why the trope of returning the gaze is a powerful theme in *Regarding Muslims*, seen for example in the redirection of the gaze in art works such as Berni Searle's *Colour Me* series and the returned gaze of Soraya in *Disgrace*.

It is very important to understand the history of looking upon which this concept draws. As I showed in Chapter 1, the colonial period inaugurated a mode of looking, at Xhosaness, at Zuluness, at Khoisanness, at Muslimness – in short, at "nativeness" in South Africa – which is exemplified in Angas's *The Kaffirs Illustrated*. The figures in this book are objects of a mode of looking in which each type of "native" figure – the idle Khoisan, the festive Malay, the fierce Xhosa, the proud and warlike Zulu – is intricately linked to and builds on the other. While there has been extensive discussion of the assumed accuracy of Angas's attention to Zulu costume and ritual, his work on "Malays" has gone undiscussed. This inattention is suggestive. Aside from work by Shamil Jeppie and Pumla Dineo Gqola, there has been a paucity of serious attention among scholars of culture to this archive of images of Islam as part of the corpus of representations of forced labour. I address this lacuna in this book.

Certain responses to the convention of the picturesque have involved trying to reverse it, demonstrated in the mutual gendered performances at work in the masculine postures of Pagad portrayed in the media. However, simply to reverse the pattern of images is a limited response that obscures more important erasures.

Instead, my approach has been to foreground the presence of Muslim slaves who have been left out of the debates about landscape, forced labour and belonging inaugurated by J. M. Coetzee (1988), and expanded by David Bunn (2002) and Jessica Dubow (2000a; 2000b). In fact, the absence of Muslims in discussions of forced labour and the colonial landscape is highly revealing. *Regarding Muslims* addresses the curious dichotomy of a corpus of highly visible images of Muslims alongside a paucity of discussion of slavery in broader culture. It also shows that such images of Muslims helped to shape a brittle claim to belonging by white settlers in the South African colonies.

My method has been to trace the patterns amid the proliferation of images, as well as a counter-archive of narratives and practices marked by the accretion and intensification of stories; for example, the way Cass Abrahams and Achmat Davids expanded Leipoldt's image of the "free" use of spices by enslaved Muslim cooks, and Hedley Churchward's stories of a magical ring that connect Mecca and Table Mountain. Such oral accounts and jokes draw new maps and reorient the meanings of freedom and belonging. As Michel de Certeau alerted us, this is typical of colonised and conquered people. In these accounts, Table Mountain is reclaimed through bodily practices and oral narratives. Through burial and prayers, landscape is remade through sanctity as belonging.

Internal meanings and resistant frames cannot be the only frame for the discussions in this book, however, as both initial force and resistance mutually shape each other. There cannot be a pure resistance that redeems images of Muslims away from the history of South Africa.

Instead, I trace a series of responses to the entrapment of the picturesque, its power to abstract from history and context. One of the most suggestive tropes used by the Muslim cooks whom I interviewed, shows the gaze turned back, but obliquely, almost surreptitiously, in the ideas of "stealing with the eye" and "catching with the eye". This practice of looking back is one example of counter-narratives by the people under view.

Another is the subversive reclamation of the kitchen away from the space of silence and placidity through the publication of cookbooks that subvert the picturesque mode. These include the collectively written *Indian Delights* and *Cass Abrahams Cooks Cape Malay*, which identified "Malay" food as "food from Africa". The inventiveness and mixed genre of *Indian Delights* turns the expected "delight" of outsiders into an account of the complexity of the inside. Through their innovative approach, these recipe books seek to de-exoticise Muslim food by alluding to the history of poverty, violence and dislocation in which the food was made.

In Chapter 6, I discussed texts in which Islam is not artificially centred, and yet also not marginalised. *At Her Feet*, "Brother, Who Will Bury Me?" and *Mr Chameleon* are shaped by empathy and and the search for justice rather than religious or national loyalties. Shaida Kazie Ali's feminist vision in *Not a Fairytale* shows how racism and patriarchy recruit Muslim women and men into an "apartheid of the family". Ishtiyaq Shukri's novel *The Silent Minaret* places South African anti- and post-apartheid narratives alongside issues of Islamophobia in Europe and occupation in Palestine, subverting both South African and Muslim exceptionalism. Imraan Coovadia crafts a confident transnational satire in *Green-eyed Thieves*, comparing South Africa and the United States in an acerbic critique of racism in both countries. Nadia Davids's *At Her Feet* creates a feminist critique of nationalist South African narratives, ethnic differences among Muslims, and patriarchy within Islam in a politically ambitious and formally innovative play. Tatamkhulu

Afrika's poetry and memoirs meditate on the temptation of a "tribal" identity for Muslims, and instead assert an identity not based on religion, ethnicity or skin colour.

In such anti-picturesque texts, Muslims are no longer rendered visible through an oscillation between the picturesque and the menacing, but are subject to quotidian social and political processes, creating a critical and comparative perspective that integrates Islam into ordinary considerations of history, politics, satire and feminism. The value of these post-apartheid representations is to deepen earlier allusions to the complexities of the South African experience of being Muslim.

Why then is the South African case of portraying Muslims of interest both inside the country and beyond? The country's relationship with its Muslim citizens in many ways offers a model to the world, treating them as fully integrated members of a secular democracy that expressly protects religious expression. The South African state regards its relationship with minorities such as Muslims as a sign of the vibrancy of its democratic system. This has been seen, for instance, in Nelson Mandela's participation in the three-hundredth anniversary of Islam in South Africa in April 1994, just before the first democratic elections; the inclusion of Muslims in Thabo Mbeki's famous "I am an African" speech, which marked the birth of the new South African constitution in 1996; and sustained negotiations about integrating Muslim Personal Law into the country's secular legal system. This has allowed the South African state and civil society to deal with matters related to Islam in mostly mature and resilient ways. The challenge that Pagad posed to the country in the 1990s was met not with a discourse about civilisational difference between Christianity and Islam, but by subjecting those who were charged with violence to the normal processes of a secular criminal justice system, like any other citizens.

At the same time, both state and civil organs such as the media are complex entities that continue to reflect the tensions and fissures of a country shaped by apartheid and its aftermath. The making of a fully democratic and anti-racist South Africa is still in progress, as demonstrated by the National Arts Council's narrow refusal to sponsor performances of *At Her Feet* on the basis that it was not "racially representative enough". Therefore Tatamkhulu Afrika's metaphor of identity as a long journeying leading to a perpetually unfinished series of journeys and recognitions forms an apt climax to this book.

This book has dealt with the paradox of Islam in South Africa. It has shown that a conventional view of Muslim figures has played both a mediating and a translating role in the country from the colonial period to the present. This mechanism means that Muslim figures have been both liminal and powerful, invisible and hypervisible, exceptional and peripheral, and historical in the absence of history. The ideological work of the placid Muslim is a subtle and powerful device of meaning-making that holds lessons both for South Africa and elsewhere because of the relation of race to religion, and the way that the convention of hypervisible Muslim figures causes certain histories to be foregrounded and others to recede. The mechanism of invisibility through visibility, and distance through nearness, allows one to consider what the hypervisibilty of Muslims elsewhere might render invisible. The race of Muslims is always in question, as the failed attempt to create the racial category of "Cape Malays" and the loss of whiteness by whites who converted to Islam under apartheid make clear. The South African instance allows one to consider the ways in which Islam, slavery, sexuality and race are imbricated, as well as the place of Muslims as a minority in a secular democracy. Reading the South African example, how is Islam racialised and gendered, and made ordinary or exotic elsewhere?

Notes

Acknowledgements

1 I have used "Coloured" with an upper case "C" when referring to the official use of the term (such as under apartheid) and in other cases to "coloured" with a lower case "c" in the sense used by Zimitri Erasmus in her ground-breaking essay collection *Coloured by History, Shaped by Place* (2001), in which she reclaims the term away from its use under apartheid, which I discuss in the Introduction, and towards denoting a "kind of blackness" that declines apartheid's divisiveness, yet also draws on a specific and complex history of slavery, genocide, colonial rule and apartheid.

Foreword

1 It is important to note that South Africa has had two historical "settlements" of Muslims: the first via slaves from South-east Asia to the Cape during the seventeenth and eighteenth centuries; and the second via indentured labourers from India to mostly the eastern and northern parts of South Africa during the nineteenth century. These represent different versions of Sunni Islam, where secondary customs and rituals may differ, but with no fundamental devotional differences. More recent immigration from the Asian subcontinent, the Middle East, the Maghreb and a range of countries elsewhere in Africa will no doubt have an influence on Islam in South Africa in the years to come.

Introduction:
Beginnings in South Africa

1 This group was established in Cape Town in the early 1990s. Gangs and drug-related violence are particular concerns in working-class and poor neighbourhoods in the Cape.

2 I describe these images in detail in Chapter 5.

3 The importance of the oral tradition among Muslims at the Cape is something I discuss further in Chapter 3.

4 Kerry Ward writes, "Cape historians have long recognised that the Company's ways of categorising ethnicity and recording names that detail place of origin cannot be considered singular markers of identity. Concepts of ethnicity and identity for Southeast Asians were fluid and changed over time and place." (Worden 2012: 86). "Of course many of the forced immigrants from SE Asia were 'bandieten'." Personal communication, Patrick Harries, 26 April 2012.

5 The Act defined the three categories as follows:
A white person is one who in appearance is, or who is generally accepted as, a white person, but does not include a person who, although in appearance is obviously a white person, is generally accepted as a Coloured person
A native is a person who is in fact or is generally accepted as a member of any aboriginal race or tribe of Africa.
A Coloured person is a person who is not a white person nor a native.
The Population Registration Act, No. 30 of 1950, section 1(xv), (x) and (iii).

6 In later chapters, I discuss two examples of white men who converted to Islam:

Hedley Mobarek Churchward in Chapter 3 and Tatamkhulu Afrika in Chapter 6.

7   During archival research in the National Library, I found numerous newspaper articles about white men who married "pretty Malay girls" and therefore became Muslim.

8   Notable historians of Cape slavery include Nigel Worden, Vivian Bickford-Smith, Robert Shell, Pamela Scully, Timothy Keegan, Sue Newton-King, Richard Ross, Andrew Bank, Wayne Dooling, Clifton Crais, Kerry Ward, R. L. Watson and, not least, Shamil Jeppie.

9   Shula Marks discusses the continuing power of the "empty land" myth reflected in the assertion by Deputy Agriculture Minister Piet Mulder in March 2012 that Africans had not historically lived in the Northern and Western Cape and therefore had no claim to 40% of South Africa's land (2012). In addition to its fallacious claims about land ownership, this historically inaccurate statement renders the indigenous people of these territories *non-existent*, an assertion I discuss further in Chapter 1.

10 For example, Worden and Crais: "This work has been informed by the new literature on the nineteenth century that has emerged in disciplines such as cultural history and literary theory, and on topics ranging from slavery to sexuality, the state and the body" (1994: 3).

11 Susie Newton-King (2012) analyses recently discovered letters written by slaves.

12 Desirée Lewis writes that Bessie Head's fictional "versions of the past consequently become both a critique of mainstream history and a celebration of memories, processes and subjects which this mainstream excludes or silences" (Woodward et al. 2002: 268).

13 Exemplary works are discussed in Chapter 4.

Chapter 1
Ambiguous Visibility:
Muslims and the making of visuality

1   Reproduced in Gordon-Brown's *Pictorial Africana*, 5. For a discussion of other early landscape paintings of the Cape, see Antonia Malan's essay "The Cultural Landscape" (Worden 2012: 1–25).

2   The Mayibuye Photographic Centre at the University of the Western Cape includes a photograph of an apartheid-era sign that reads "Any kaffir caught trespassing will be shot."

3   The Promotion of Equality and Prevention of Unfair Discrimination Act of 2000 declares the use of words such as "kaffir," "hotnot" and "coolie" to be hate speech.

4   Robert Ross notes in *Beyond the Pale* that "many of the initial accounts whites gave of the Xhosa or Tswana were far from derogatory" (1993: 85).

5   Alimatul Qibtiyah, an Indonesian Islamic scholar, provided me with an exegesis of the Islamic use of the word "kaffir".

6   All transliterated words of Arabic origin in English are approximations due to the non-congruence of English and Arabic script.

7   The *Standard Swahili-English Dictionary* (1963 [1939]) denotes the word "*kafiri*" as meaning "unbeliever, non-Moslem". The *Swahili-English Dictionary* (1967) includes *Kufuru*: 1. to offend, 2. to abandon a religion, turn apostate. 3. sacrilege, atheism. The Portuguese dictionary, *Novo dicionario da lingua portuguesa* (1939) has two definitions of *cafre*. The first is an inhabitant of Cafraria, or the language of Cafraria, with the additional figurative meaning of "an uncivilised man". The *Dicionario da lingua portuguese contemporanea de Academia das Ciencias de Lisboa* (2001) defines the word *Cafraria* as "the former designation of a large

part of southern Africa, inhabited by non-Muslim peoples, and that today corresponds to two regions of South Africa." This dictionary offers three definitions of "cafre" (1). (from the Arabic *kafr* infidel) That which belongs to Cafraria ... [continues with definition of Cafraria given above]. (2) The same Arabic derivation. A black person from the western coast of Africa, not Muslim, who used to live in the so-called Cafraria ... (2) A barbarous, crude or ignorant person. (3) A greedy or miserly person. (3) Same derivation from Arabic. *Ling.* Language belonging to a group of southern Bantu languages, spoken in Cafaria. According to these dictionaries, the difference between the use of the derivations of "kafir" in Swahili and Portuguese is that in Portuguese, the word included derogatory connotations of "race," whereas in Swahili, the word referred to religious designation as believer or non-believer. According to Mark Rosenberg, Swahili derivations of "kafir" do include derogatory meanings, but these appear to be associated with "ignorance" rather than "race" (2004: personal communication).

8   Examples include "kaffir almanac", "kaffir appointment", "kaffirboom" [tree], "kaffirbread", "kaffir buck", "kaffir cabbage", "kaffir cat", "kaffir cherry", "kaffir coffee", "kaffircorn", "kaffir plum", "kaffir fever", "kaffir finch", "kaffir fowl", "kaffir hoe", "kaffir honeysuckle", "kaffir horse", "kaffir hut", "kaffir manna", "kaffir mushroom", "kaffir path" and "kaffir pot".

9   The title of R. Godlonton's *A narrative of the irruption of the kaffir hordes, into the Eastern Province of the Cape of Good Hope 1834–1835* (1835) shows the fear that inhered in the term during the nineteenth century.

10 Shula Marks's well-known essay "The Myth of the Empty Land" outlines this

argument, which still has currency today. In her analysis of colonial and apartheid histories, Desirée Lewis points out that the assertion that the land was unoccupied before colonisers arrived "denies the physical existence of an indigenous population and allows the Voortrekkers to encounter 'empty land'" (Woodward et al. 2002: 269).

11 See S. Dubow, "Ethnic Euphemisms and Racial Echoes" (1995). In addition, I discuss J. M. Coetzee's formulation of the "idleness" of the "native" in Chapter 3.

12 In reality, as Nigel Worden argues, the "isolation of many farmsteads in a society in which male slaves greatly outnumbered male colonists led to a level of control and coercion which, at local levels, could be violent and extreme" (1985: 4).

13 I discuss the problem of silence around slavery and sexuality in South Africa in Chapter 4.

14 Michael Godby, personal communication, June 2003.

15 The term used at the time for the Khoi.

16 Amuck a. and adv. Also amock, amok, 1663. [ad. Malay] A frenzied Malay. To run amuck, to run viciously, frenzied for blood. Wild, or wildly. *The Oxford Universal Dictionary* (1933).

Chapter 2
"Kitchen Language":
Muslims and the culture of food

1   This is a phrase ascribed to C. Louis Leipoldt by Laurens van der Post (1977: 129): "Ayah" means female servant. The fact that "Ayah" is a Hindi word indicates the origins of South African Muslims in South Asia as well as East Africa and South-east Asia.

2   Variations on this idea of complex encounters across boundaries include the

trope of the "seam" by de Kock (2001: 263–98), "complicities" by Sanders (2002) and "entanglement" by Nuttall (2009).

3   For a discussion of the complex racial and gender dynamics of *The Slave Book*, see Pumla Dineo Gqola (2001).

4   For a related discussion on discourses of poison in colonial South Africa, see Jane Taylor (1996) and David Bunn (1996).

5   Robert Ross writes: "It is a measure of the genuine importance attached to the franchise [for Africans and coloureds] that regular attempts were made to change or dilute it. There were plans to give the vote to white (but not black) women, so that the relative weight of African and coloured voters would be diminished. In 1930, this indeed happened" (1999: 174).

Chapter 3
"The Sea Inside Us":
Parallel journeys in the African oceans

1   As noted in Chapter 1, the oldest slave graveyard in South Africa was named "Tana Baru", which means "new place" in Behasa Melayu.

Chapter 4
"Sexual Geographies of the Cape":
Slavery, race and sexual violence

1   For a discussion of sexual violence in the American colonial context, see Smith 2005.

2   For an analysis of the structures which sustain such patterns of violence, see Gqola 2007: 111–124.

3   The play *Reclaiming the P…Word* declines to use the word in full in its title as a gesture of sensitivity, but uses the word in its dialogue as part of its project of reclamation. I follow the latter practice.

Chapter 5
Regarding Muslims:
Pagad, masked men and veiled women

1   The *Cape Times*, first published on 27 March 1876, is the second oldest newspaper in South Africa. *The Argus* (later known as the *Cape Argus*), which I also discuss in this chapter, is the oldest newspaper in the country, and first appeared in 1857.

2   A fatwa was passed by Ayatollah Khomeini in Iran, sentencing the author Salman Rushdie to death for blasphemy for his novel *The Satanic Verses* (1988). This was revoked in 1998 by the-then Iranian president Mohammad Khatami.

3   The use of the term *vigilante* in this case is a sensitive issue, as is indicated by the strenuous and at times violent objections to the designation by Pagad members and supporters. I use the word because I connect Rashaad Staggie's death and other actions associated with Pagad to the increased phenomenon of vigilantism by a number of groups in South Africa. On this phenomenon, see Dixon and Johns 2001; Buur and Jensen 2003.

4   See, among others, Botha (2001) and Tayob (1996).

5   The group also inspired artworks such as the play *Blood Brothers* by Mike van Graan.

6   The *Cape Times* is positioned as a quality paper with an emphasis on upper-income readers. In contrast, *The Argus*, owned by the same company, and which has the higher circulation of the two, is more populist, and is often characterised by a "sensationalistic" tone (Green 2000: 10).

7   Gool's professional career spans more than twenty years as one of the ground-breaking black photographers in Cape Town. His work includes an unprecedented documenting of seven years in the life of Nelson Mandela However, it tends to be dominated by the prominence of the Staggie

photographs (Samie 2003: online).
In one interview, Gool said after the
photographs "my life has never been the
same" (Gondwe 2001: online). Another
indication of the impact of the Pagad
story on journalism itself is that Francois
Nel, author of a South African textbook
for journalists (1998), discussed the
ethics of photojournalism by using the
Cape Times' coverage of the murder of
Rashaad Staggie.

8   "Mecca scarves": these are often brought
back as gifts by pilgrims returning from
Mecca.

9   *The Argus* appears five times a week on
Monday to Friday, and in 1996 also had
a single weekend edition, which covered
both Saturday and Sunday. At present, the
renamed *Cape Argus* produces two
separate editions on the weekend, the
Saturday Argus and *Sunday Argus*.

10   Examples of the Muslim media include
Africa Perspectives, *Al-Ummah*, *Al-Qalam*
and *Muslim Views* newspapers, as well
as smaller publications such as *Crescent*;
Muslim Woman; and *Islam Today*. Radio
channels include Radio Islam, Radio
786, Voice of the Cape, Channel Islam
International and Radio Al-Ansaar. On
the internet, some of the journalists I
interviewed have written for the Cairo-
based IslamOnline.net. Television stations
include Al-Jazeera and ITV and, during
Ramadaan, both the South African
Broadcasting Corporation (SABC) and
the television channel etv broadcast
religious programmes.

Chapter 6
"The Trees Sway North-North-East":
Post-apartheid visions of Islam

1   See, for example, Pallavi Rastogi's
Afrindian Fictions (2008) for an excel-
lent analysis of fiction by South African
Indian authors.

2   For discussions of the play, see Blumberg
(2011: 20–34) and Cloete(2011: 45–53).

3   A granite mountain near Paarl shaped
like a pearl, after which the town is
named.

4   An officially "white" suburb of Cape
Town that was nevertheless informally
racially mixed.

5   For discussions of the theme of sexuality
in Afrika's writing, see Stobie (2007a and
2007b: 148–65).

6   Chris Hani is a revered anti-apartheid
figure who at the time of his murder was
the leader of the South African Com-
munist Party. Since his death, and in
light of deepening disillusionment with
the African National Congress, Hani has
become even more widely admired.

Glossary

affal – offal, the discarded parts of an animal, cheaper cuts of meat.

Afrikaans – the language formed as a slave creole in the Cape during colonial times and later adopted by Afrikaner nationalists fighting Dutch and British imperialism.

Afrikaners – the name of the creole community that developed at the Cape Colony out of a convergence of Dutch, Portuguese, French and other settlers, and later laid claim to a white Afrikaner nationalist identity.

amok – frenzied, uncontrollable attack.

Arafat doeke – see Makka doeke; often worn by Palestinians, hence the name.

Asiatic, Other Asiatic, Indian, Griqua – terms used to denote sub-categories of "Colouredness" by the Extension of the Population Registration Act of 1959.

atchar – a spiced chutney.

athaan – Arabic for "call to prayer".

Ayah – "servant" in Hindi.

Bahasa Melayu – the Malay language, a lingua franca around the Indian Ocean region.

blatjang – a cooked chutney, often made with fruit and a combination of sweet, hot and sour flavours.

boeber – in the Cape "Malay" tradition, a heated milk drink made with spices such as cardamom, cinnamon and sugar.

Boer – the Dutch and Afrikaans word for "farmer". It became a synonym for the Afrikaans white nationalist ruling class under apartheid.

boerekos – literally, farmers' food; refers to typical Afrikaner dishes and recipes.

Bongweni – Xhosa for "favourite place".

bredie – a stew.

caffre – an archaic version of "kaffir" (see below).

Cape "Malay" – this was a name first used for Muslims at the Cape. Later it became a racial category established under the 1959 Extension of the Population Registration Act, and remains a term used by some Muslim people today. Pumla Gqola and Muhamed Haron argue that the term alludes to the history of slavery.

Coloured – in South Africa, the use of this term has a long history. It was first used for a community of free blacks, manumitted slaves and Khoisan people during the early days of the Cape Colony. After emancipation, former slaves were also included in this group. During apartheid, it became one of three legal racial categories established by the Population Registration Act of 1950.

Coloured/coloured – the term "Coloured" appears in this book both with an upper case "C" when referring to the official use of the term (such as under apartheid) and in other cases to "coloured" with a lower case "c" in the sense used by Zimitri Erasmus in her ground-breaking essay collection *Coloured by History, Shaped by Place* (2001), in which she reclaims the term away from its use under apartheid, and toward denoting a "kind of blackness" that declines apartheid's divisiveness, yet which draws on a specific and complex history of slavery, genocide, colonial rule and apartheid.

curry – any stew flavoured with a combination of spices that give warmth and "bite"; developed in colonial settings where Asian, European and African cuisines intersected.

doek – Afrikaans for "scarf" (see also Makka doeke).

Eid – the Muslim celebration of the end of the month of fasting (Ramadan).

gatvol – literally, Afrikaans for "arsehole full" but connotes "fed up".

gool – to make magic, conjure.

hadith – saying of the Prophet Mohammed.

Hajj – Arabic for "pilgrimage" to Mecca.

Hajji – person who has completed the pilgrimage to Mecca.

hartseer – Afrikaans for "heartsore".

Hertzoggie – a biscuit or cookie iced in such a way as to encode the political betrayal of Muslims by General Hertzog in 1936.

hijab – Arabic for veil or shelter or screen, used for scarves and various other kinds of head coverings.

Hottentots – a name with derogatory overtones the Dutch gave to the indigenous people of the Cape.

Israeel and Ismaeel – according to Islamic belief, angels on the left and right shoulders, who record all the actions of human beings.

jinn – supernatural being, sometimes translated as "demon", but which may have positive powers.

Jou ma se poes – literally "Your mother's vagina"; an extremely vulgar phrase commonly used in the Cape.

Kaap – Dutch and Afrikaans for "Cape".

kaffir – the word is infamous as a particularly heinous racial epithet in South Africa, but it has several other meanings, including "non-Muslim" or "infidel".

kaffirboetie – a derogatory name, which literally means little brother of kaffirs, given to white people who are seen by other whites as being too close, or corrupted by their closeness, to black people.

kafir – this is another archaic version of the word "kaffir" – since the word is transliterated from Arabic script, there are several possible versions in English.

Khoisan – a composite name for two groups, the Khoi and the San, indigenous people of southern Africa.

koebus – Muslim burial ground.

koples book – book for recitation lessons reflecting the importance of learning and reciting Arabic in local "Malay" schools or madressas.

kramat – burial place for Muslim leaders, often also a shrine.

kroes – curly hair, but with derogatory and usually racially offensive connotations.

kwaito – a popular musical form in South Africa.

Makka doeke – scarves brought from Mecca.

"Malay" – during the colonial period this was used as a racial designation for Muslim people.

melkkos – an Afrikaans version of boeber (see above), often made with less spices.

merrang – a prayer meeting held on a Thursday night.

moer – Afrikaans for "womb", also used as a colloquial and violent word for "beat" or "kill".

mulatto – word used in the Americas for a woman of mixed-race descent.

naai – Afrikaans for "sew", used as a swearword.

niyaat – Arabic for "intention".

Nguni – a name for a language group that includes Xhosa and Zulu. People who spoke these languages formed polities that resisted Dutch and British expansion during the colonial period.

poes – Afrikaans for "vagina", used as a swearword.

poesie – literally Afrikaans for "little vagina", but connotes contempt.

poeslik – an adjective based on the Afrikaans word for "vagina"; connotes weak or contemptible.

ratiep – a ritual piercing of the skin.

sambal – a salad.

Seur – Sir.

slawe – Afrikaans for "slaves".

State/s of Emergency – periods of martial law declared by the apartheid government during the 1980s.

stoep – veranda or porch.

Sufi – strand of Islamic practice based on internal purity, reflection and transcendence.

sugar-bean – a bean grown in South Africa, used to make stew.

tablah – small drum often used in Arab music.

Tana Baru – "New Place" in Malay; the name of the oldest slave graveyard in South Africa.

Tatamkhulu Afrika – Xhosa for "Grandfather of Africa".

toering – characteristic pointed hat worn by male "Malay" slaves in eighteenth- and nineteenth-century Cape Town.

Umkhonto we Sizwe – the armed wing of the African National Congress during the struggle against apartheid (the term means "Spear of the Nation" in Zulu).

veldflowers – wildflowers ("veld" means "field").

vleis – meat.

VOC – these initials stood for the Verenigde Oostindische Compagnie (the Dutch East India Company).

Xhosa – a broadly spoken Nguni language in South Africa, spoken particularly in the Eastern and Western Cape.

Bibliography

Primary materials

Interviews (all conducted by the author, unless stated otherwise)

Abrahams, Cass. Cookbook author. Interview on food, 20 July 2002, Cape Town.

Ali, Shaida Kazie. Novelist. Interview on images of Islam, 27 July 2011, Cape Town.

Anonymous 1. Journalist. Interview on images of Islam, 25 July 2003, Cape Town.

Anonymous 2. Journalist, the *Cape Times*. Interview on images of Islam, 17 July 2003, Cape Town.

Anonymous 3. Journalist, the *Cape Times*. Interview on images of Islam, 17 July 2003, Cape Town.

Auntie Galiema [pseudonym]. Interview on pilgrimage, 2008, Cape Town.

Davids, Nadia. Playwright, author of *At Her Feet*. Interviews on her play, 31 March and 4 April 2004, Cape Town.

Davidson, Patty. Cook and museum owner. Interview on food, 23 July 2002, Cape Town; interview on the hajj, 9 May 2012, Cape Town.

Fakier, Yazied. Freelance journalist, former Deputy Editor, the *Cape Times*.

Interview on images of Islam, 30 September 2000; interview on food, 4 June 2002, Cape Town.

Fick, Rose. Housewife. Interview on food, 23 July 2003, Cape Town.

Francis, Zainab. Caterer. Interview on food, 18 June 2002, Cape Town.

Jacobs, Rayda. Novelist and journalist. Interview on her novel and films, 29 July 2003, Cape Town.

Jaffer, Zubeida. Journalist. Interview on images of Islam, 24 June 2003, Cape Town.

Jardine, Imran. Caterer. Interview on food, 21 April 2002, Cape Town.

Johaardien, Ashraf. Playwright and author of *Salaam Stories*. Interviews on his play, 21 and 24 March 2004, Cape Town.

Jonker, Ghalib. Journalist, the *Cape Argus*. Interview on images of Islam, 22 November 2003, Cape Town.

Kozain, Rustum. Lecturer, poet and cook. Interview on his poetry, 20 September

2000; interview on food, 4 June 2002, Cape Town.

Minty, Zayd. Arts manager and curator. Interview on images of Islam, 6 June 2002; interview on food, 17 July 2003, Cape Town.

Qibtiyah, Alimatul. Islamic scholar. Interviewed on Islamic texts, 2 August 2004, State College, Pennsyvlania.

Reddy, San and Gamiet, Ghalib. Journalists, etv. Interview on images of Islam, 24 July 2003, Cape Town.

Sanglay, Mahmood. Journalist, *Muslim Views*. Interview on images of Islam, 22 November 2003, Cape Town.

Searle, Berni. Conceptual artist. Interview on her art, 6 August 2004, Cape Town.

Shaikh, Mohamed. Journalist, *Die Burger*. Interview on images of Islam, 21 July 2003, Cape Town.

1886 burial uprising

Note: Because newspaper conventions in 1885–86 did not include authors' bylines, the following material is listed alphabetically by article title.

The Death-rate. *Cape Times* (17 May 1886).

The Malay Burying-Ground: Deputation to Mr Tudhope. *Cape Times* (14 November 1885).

The Malay Burial Ground (Maitland board of management report to parliament). *Cape Times* (17 May 1886).

The Malay Cemetery Question. *Cape Argus* (20 May 1886).

The Malays and the Cemeteries. *Cape Argus* (18 January 1886).

The Malays and the Cemeteries. *Cape Times* (19 January 1886). [Separate articles published on two consecutive days]

The Moslem Cemetery (petition by Muslim community to parliament). *Cape Times* (20 May 1886).

The proposed Dutch Reformed Church cemetery. *Cape Times* (8 June 1886).

Green, L. G. 1950. Abdol Burns had a Scottish father. *Cape Times* (31 August): page number unrecorded.

Pagad

Enickl, M. 1996. Too late for talks – time for solutions. Letter to editor. *Cape Times* (8 August): 10.

Blignaut, C. 1996. Staggie died as he lived. *Cape Times* (5 August): 3.

Brown, B. 1996. 2 000 protesters kept from confronting "dealers" in Lenasia. Item from Centre for Contemporary Islam Archives. Unsourced, unpaginated.

Bruce, D. 2003. We need a new anti-terror law, but not this one. *Mail & Guardian* (25 April): 8.

Campbell, C. 1996. The "gent and the psycho". *Cape Times* (6 August): 3.

"Carlos". 1996. Sad end to a lifetime of causing sadness. Letter to editor. *Cape Times* (9 August): 8.

De Beer, Mrs. 1996. Staggie photos a strong warning for criminals. Letter to editor. *Cape Times* (9 August): 8.

Fisher, R. 2001. One City Many Cultures. *Cape Times* (27 March). http://www.rylandfisher.com/archives/showitem.asp?ID=46. Accessed 23 June 2002.

Friedman, R. 1996. Gatesville mosque under siege. *Cape Times* (2 August): 1.

Friedman, R. 1996. Pagad leader warns of suicide bombs. *Cape Times* (6 August): 1.

Friedman, R. 1996. Mass march by defiant, armed crowd. *Cape Times* (7 August): 1.

Friedman, R. 1996. "Ready for peace, ready for war." *Cape Times* (9 August): 1.

Friedman, R. 1996. Editor rejects police requests for pictures of gangster's slaying. *Cape Times* (9 August): 2.

Friedman, R. 1996. Police clamp down on Pagad. *Cape Times* (12 August): 1.

Friedman, R. and E. Ntabazalila. 1996. Pagad member shot dead. *Cape Times* (8 August): 1.

Gilmore, I. 1996. Muslim mob kills drug boss in Cape "jihad". *The Times* [UK] (6 August): 6.

Gilmore, I. 1996. Gang declares war on Cape Town vigilantes. *The Times* [UK] (7 August): 11.

Johnson, A. 1996. Dullah Omar's house invaded. *Cape Times* (18 March): 1.

Kimani, S. 2003. Bill finds a terrorist under every bed. *Mail & Guardian* (25 April): 3.

King, S. C. 1996. Pictures were important to show justice done. Letter to editor. *Cape Times* (9 August): 8.

Malan, P. 1996. Guns pulled on newsmen at burial. *Cape Argus* (9 August): 5.

Mgxashe, M. 1996. Pagad plans huge rally on "D-Day". *Saturday Weekend Argus* (10/11 August): 3.

Moosa, E. 1996. Islam against the world: flawed radicalism will hurt the Muslim faith. *The Argus* (26 November): unpaginated.

Muslim Judicial Council. 1996. "Struggle against evil of drugs will continue." *Cape Times* (9 August): 2.

Own correspondent. 1996. Vigilantes declare "holy war" on gangsters. *The Star* (12 August): 1.

Ranwell, C. 1996. Ghoulish way to boost circulation. Letter to editor. *Cape Times* (9 August): 8.

SAPA. 1996. "Mob killing shocked SA." *Cape Times* (8 August): 2.

Salie, A. 1996. Staggie's slaying was "not Islamic". *Cape Times* (8 August): 2.

Schronen, J. 1996. Muslim schools close after threats. *The Argus* (6 August): 1.

Schronen, J. and S. Isaacs. 1996. Vigilante war. *The Argus* (5 August): 1.

Smith, A. 1996. The Cape media and Pagad. *The Argus*. Item from Centre for Contemporary Islam Archives. Unpaginated.

Smith, A. 1996. Mass action on gangs. *The Argus* (7 August): 1.

Splash coverage for lynching in UK press. *Cape Times* (9 August): 2.

Staff writer. 1996. Police officer threatened with death. *Cape Times* (6 August): 3.

Templeton, L. 1996. Vigilantes reacting to justice system perceived as "soft". *Cape Times* (6 August): 2.

Templeton, L. 1996. "I hope the police gun them down one by one, including my own son." *Cape Times* (8 August): 3.

Thamm, M. 1999. In the beginning: the magic of birth. *Cape Times* (1 February): 13.

Underhill, G. 1996. Pagad unmasked – Aslam Toefy. *Saturday Weekend Argus* (16/17 November): 24.

Van Breda, Y. 1996. Fear. *Sunday Times* (11 August): Item from Centre for Contemporary Islam Archives. Unpaginated.

Vongai, C. 1996. Killing photographs draw praise, condemnation. *Cape Times* (6 August): 2.

Vongai, C. 1996. "One gangster, one bullet." *Cape Times* (12 August): 2.

Whitlock, A. 1996. …and PE may be next, says police chief. *Saturday Weekend Argus* (10/11 August): 4.

Younghusband, P. 1996. Flames of Vengeance. *Daily Mail* (6 August): unpaginated.

Secondary material

A Lady. 1963. *Life at the Cape a Hundred Years Ago*. Cape Town: C. Struik.

Abrahams, C. 2000. *Cass Abrahams Cooks Cape Malay: Food from Africa*. Cape Town: Metz Press.
- - -. 1995. *The Culture & Cuisine of the Cape Malays*. Cape Town: Metz Press.

Abrahams, Y. 2003. Colonialism, Dysjuncture and Dysfunction: Sarah Baartman's Resistance (remix). *Agenda* 58: 12–25.

- - -. 2000. Colonialism, Dysjuncture and Dysfunction: The Historiography of Sarah Baartman. Unpublished PhD thesis. University of Cape Town.

- - -.1998. Images of Sara Bartman: Sexuality, race, and gender in early-nineteenth-century Britain. In R. R. Pierson and N. Chaudhuri (eds), *Nation, Empire, Colony: Historicizing gender and race*. Bloomington and Indianapolis: Indiana University Press.

Abreu, M. 2005. *Mulatas, Crioulos*, and *Morenas*: Racial Hierarchy, Gender relations, and National Identity in Postabolition Popular song, Southeastern Brazil, 1890–1920. In P. Scully and D. Paton (eds), *Gender and Slave Emancipation*. Durham: Duke University Press.

Abu-Lughod, L. 1986. *Veiled Sentiments: Honor and Poetry in a Bedouin Society*. Berkeley and London: University of California Press.

Achmat, Z. 1994. My childhood as an adult molester, A Salt River moffie. In M. Gevisser and E. Cameron (eds.), *Defiant Desire: Gay and Lesbian Lives in South Africa*. London: Routledge.

Afrika, T. 2005. *Mr Chameleon: An Autobiography*. Johannesburg: Jacana Media.

Agha, O. H. 2002. Islamic Fundamentalism and its Image in the Western Media: Alternative views. In K. Haifez (Ed.) *Islam and the West in the Mass Media:*

Fragmented Images in a Globalizing world. New York: Hampton Press.

Ahmed, L. 1992. *Women and Gender in Islam*. New Haven and London: Yale University Press.

Aitken, T. 2004. The Lords Seventeen. *Times Literary Supplement* (28 May): 22.

Alatas, S. 1977. *The Myth of the Lazy Native: A Study of the Image of the Malays, Filipinos and Javanese from the 16th to the 20th Century and its Function in the Ideology of Colonial Capitalism*. London: Cass.

Alexander, M. 1998. Alphabets of Flesh. In E. Shohat (ed.), *Talking Visions: Multicultural Feminism in a Transnational Age*. Cambridge, MA and London: MIT Press.

Ali, S. K. 2010. *Not a Fairytale*. Cape Town: Umuzi.

Ali, Y. 1945. *The Holy Quran: Translation and Commentary*. Lahore: Islamic Centre International.

Allison, S. and M. Robins. 1997. *South African Cape Malay Cooking*. London: Absolute Press.

Alloula, M. 1986. *The Colonial Harem*. Minneapolis: University of Minnesota Press.

AlSayyad, N. and M. Castells (eds). 2002. *Muslim Europe or Euro-Islam: Politics, culture and Citizenship in the Age of Globalization*. Lanham: Lexington Books.

Altorki, S. and F. El-Solh. 1989. *Arab Women in the Field: Studying your Own Society*. Cairo: The American University of Cairo Press.

Appadurai, A. 2006. *Fear of Small Numbers: An Essay on the Geography of Anger*. Durham: Duke University Press.

- - -. 1988. How to Make a National Cuisine: Cookbooks in Contemporary India. *Comparative Studies in Society and History* 30 (1): 3–24.

Angas, G. F. 1974 [1849]. *The Kafirs Illustrated: in a series of drawings taken among the Amazulu, Amaponda, and Amakosa Tribes. Also, portraits of the Hottentot, Malay, Fingo, and other races inhabiting Southern Africa together with sketches of landscape scenery in the Zulu country, Natal and the Cape Colony*. Cape Town: A. A. Balkema.

Ashcroft, B. and P. Ahluwalia. 1999. *Edward Said*. London and New York: Routledge.

Ashcroft, B., G. Griffiths and H. Tiffin. 1998. *Key Concepts in Post-Colonial Studies*. London and New York: Routledge.

Attwell, D. 2002. Race in *Disgrace*. *Interventions: International Journal of Postcolonial Studies* 4 (3): 331–341.

Baderoon, G. 2007. Catch with the Eye: Change and Continuity in Muslim Cooking in Cape Town. In S. Field, F. Swanson

and R. Meyer (eds), *Imagining the City: Memory, Space and Culture in Cape Town*. Cape Town: HSRC Press.

- - -. 2006. *A Hundred Silences*. Roggebaai: Kwela/Snailpress.

- - -. 2005. Pagad, Islam and the Challenge of the Local. *Ecquid Novi Journal: African Journalism Studies* 26 (1): 85-107.

- - -. 2004. *Oblique Figures: Representations of Islam in South African Media and Culture*. Unpublished Doctoral thesis. English Department. University of Cape Town.

- - -. 2003. Covering the East – Veils and Masks: Orientalism in South African Media. In H. Wasserman and S. Jacobs (eds). *Shifting Selves: Post-apartheid Essays on Media, Culture and Identity*. Cape Town: Kwela.

- - -. 2002. Everybody's Mother Was a Good Cook: Meanings of Food in Muslim Cooking. *Agenda* 51.

- - -. 2000a. What Does Islam Want: The New Geography of News. *African Gender Institute Newsletter* 9 (December).

- - -. 2000b. Art and Islam in South Africa: A Reflection. *Annual Review of Islam in South Africa* 4 (December).

- - -. 2000c. Review: New Media in the Muslim World: The Emerging Public Sphere. *Journal for Islamic Studies* 20.

- - -. 1999. Muslims in the Media. *Annual Review of Islam in South Africa* 2 (December). http://www.uct.ac.za/depts/religion/arisa2.htm.

Badroodien, A. 2004. Rac(e)ing Poverty and Punishment in South Africa, 1920–1970. *Safundi: The Journal of South African and American Comparative Studies* 13/14: April.

Baily, D. A. and G. Tawadros. 2003. *Veil: Veiling, Representation and Contemporary Art.* London and Oxford: Institute of International Visual Arts in association with Modern Art Oxford.

Bain, K. 2003. Hypertheatrical Performance on the Post-apartheid Stage. In H. Wasserman and S. Jacobs (eds), *Shifting Selves: Post-apartheid essays on mass media, culture and identity.* Cape Town: Kwela.

Baker, J. 1999. The Malay Kitchen – Cellars-Hohenort, Constantia. *Wine* 6 (6): 58–66.

Bangstad, S. 2007. *Global Flows, Local Appropriations: Facets of Secularization and Re-Islamicisation among contemporary Cape Muslims.* Amsterdam: Amsterdam University Press.

- - -. 2002. Revisiting PAGAD: Machoism or Islamism? *Institute for the Study of Islam in the Modern World Newsletter,* 11 December 2002.

- - -. 2001. The *Social Functions of Food in a Muslim Community.* Unpublished paper presented at the Centre for Contemporary Islam, 10 October.

Bank, A. 1995. Slavery without Slaves; Robert Shell's *Social History of Cape Slave Society. South African History Journal* 33 (33): 182–193.

Banoobhai, S. 2012. *Heretic.* Cape Town: Shabbir Banoobhai.

Barber, K. 2006. *Africa's Hidden Histories: Everyday Literacy and Making the Self.* Indianapolis: Indiana University Press.

Barrell, J. 1980. *The Dark Side of the Landscape: The Rural Poor in English painting 1730–1840,* Cambridge: Cambridge University Press.

Berlant, L. (ed.). 2000. *Intimacy.* Chicago: University of Chicago Press.

Bhabha, H. 2004. Keynote address, *The Black Body Conference.* DePaul University, Chicago, 23 April.

- - -. 1994. *The Location of Culture.* London and New York: Routledge.

- - -. 1986. Remembering Fanon: Self, Psyche and the Colonial Condition. Foreword to F. Fanon [1952], *Black Skin, White Masks.* London: Pluto.

Bickford-Smith, V. 1995. *Ethnic Pride and Racial Prejudice in Victorian Cape Town.* Cambridge: Cambridge University Press.

Blumberg, Marcia. 2011. Lifting the Veil, Breaking Silences: Muslim Women in South Africa Interrogate Multiple Marginalities. *Contemporary Theatre Review,* Special Issue: Making Theatre in Africa: Reflections and Documents 21 (1): 20–34.

Boehmer, E. 1995. *Migrant Metaphors: Colonial and Postcolonial literature.* Oxford: Oxford University Press.

Borges, J. L. 1962. *Labyrinths: Selected stories and Other writings.* New York: New Directions.

Bose, S. 2006. *A Hundred Horizons: The Indian Ocean in the Age of Global Empire.* Cambridge, Massachusetts: Harvard University Press.

Botes, E. 1996. Condensing the Media: a Retrospective of 1996. *Stellenbosch Journalism Insight.* http://www.sun.ac.za/journalism/sji/1996/condensing96.htm. Accessed 10 July 2004.

Botha, A. 2001. The Prime Suspects? The Metamorphosis of Pagad. In Boshoff, H., A. Botha and M. Schonteich, *Fear in the City, Urban Terrorism in South Africa.* Institute for Security Studies Monograph, July. http://www.iss.co.za/Pubs/Monographs/No63.Content63.html.

Botha, C. G. 1969 [1928]. *The Public Archives of South Africa: (1652–1910).* New York: Burt Franklin.

Bourdieu, P. 1996. *Photography: A Middle-brow Art.* Trans. S. Whiteside. Palo Alto: Stanford University Press.

Bradlow, F. R. 1981. Islam at the Cape of Good Hope. *South African Historical Journal* 13 (1): 12–19.

Bradlow, F. R. and M. Cairns. 1978. *The Early Cape Muslims: A Study of their Mosques, Genealogy and Origins.* Cape Town: A. A. Balkema.

Bridge, G. and S. Watson. 2002. Lest Power be Forgotten: Networks, Division and Difference in the City. *The Sociological Review* 50 (4): 505.

Bunn, D. 2002. The Sleep of the Brave: Graves as Sites and Signs in the Colonial Eastern Cape. In *Images and Empires: Visuality in Colonial and Postcolonial Africa.* Berkeley: University of California Press.

- - -. 1996. The Brown Serpent of the Rocks: Bushman Arrow Toxins in the Dutch and British imagination, 1735–1850. In B. Cooper and A. Steyn (eds), *Transgressing Boundaries: New Directions in the Study of Culture in Africa.* Cape Town and Athens: University of Cape Town Press and Ohio University Press.

- - -. 1994. "Our Wattled Cot": Mercantile and Domestic Space in Thomas Pringle's African landscapes. In W. J. T. Mitchell (ed.), *Landscape and Power.* Chicago: University of Chicago Press.

Burdett, C. 2002. Reading Imperialism: Complexity vs Hybridity. *New Formations: A Journal of Culture/Theory/Politics* 46 (Spring): 176–77.

Butler, J. 2004. *Precarious Life: The Powers of Mourning and Violence*. London and New York: Verso.

Buur, L. and S. Jensen. 2003. Vigilantism and the Policing of Everyday Life in South Africa. http://www.server.law.wits.ac.za/workshop/workshop03/buur_jensen.doc. Accessed 22 June 2004.

Carter, P. 1996. Turning the Tables – or, Grounding Post-Colonialism. In K. Darian-Smith, L. Gunner and S. Nuttall (eds), *Text, Theory, Space: Land, Literature and History in South Africa and Australia*. New York: Routledge.

Cannadine, D. 2001. *Ornamentalism: How the British Saw their Empire*. New York: Oxford University Press.

Chomsky, N. 2003. *Power and Terror: Post-9/11 Talks and Interviews*. New York: Seven Stories Press.
- - -. 2001. *9-11*. New York: Seven Stories Press.
- - -. 1989. *Necessary Illusions: Thought Control in Democratic Societies*. New York: South End Press.

Chrisman, L. 2003. *Postcolonial Contraventions: Cultural readings of Race, Imperialism and Transnationalism*. Manchester and New York: Manchester University Press.

Christiansë, Y. 2009. *Imprendehora*. Roggebaai: Kwela/Snailpress.

- - -. 2006. Selections from Castaway. In S. Pierce and A. Rao (eds), *Discipline and the Other Body: Correction, Corporeality, Colonialism*. Durham, North Carolina: Duke University Press.
- - -. 2003. Passing Away: The Unspeakable (Losses) of Post-apartheid South Africa. In D. Eng and D. Kazanjian (eds), *Loss: The Politics of Mourning*. Berkeley: University of California Press.
- - -. 1999. *Castaway*. Durham: Duke University Press.

Clendinnen, I. 2002. *Every Single Document: London Review of Books*. 24 (10) http://lrb.co.uk.contribhome.php?get=clen01. Accessed 30 June 2004.

Coetzee, J. M. 1999. *Disgrace*. New York and London: Penguin.
- - -. 1988. *White Writing: On the Culture of Letters in South Africa*. New Haven and London: Yale University Press.

Coetzee, R. 1977. *The South African Culinary Tradition: The Origin of South Africa's Culinary Arts during the 17th and 18th centuries and 167 Authentic Recipes of this Period*. Cape Town: C. Struik Publishers.

Coombes, A. E. 2003. *History After Apartheid: Visual Culture and Public Memory in a Democratic South Africa*. Durham: Duke University Press.

Coombes, A. E. and S. Edwards 1989. Site Unseen: Photography in the Colonial Empire, Images of Subconscious Eroticism. *Art History* 12: 510–16.

Cooper, B.M., 1999. The Strength in the Song: Muslim Personhood, Audible Capital and Hausa Women's Performance of the Hajj. *Social Text*, 60 Globalization ?, (Autumn, 1999): 87–109.

Cooper, F. and A. L Stoler (eds). 1997. *Tensions of Empire: Colonial Cultures in a Bourgeois World*. Berkeley: University of California Press.

Coovadia, Imraan. 2006. *Green-Eyed Thieves*. Cape Town: Umuzi.
- - -. 2001. *The Wedding*. Cape Town: Umuzi.

Cloete, N. 2011. Gendering Performance in *At Her Feet. South African Theatre Journal* (1): 45–53.

Creedon, J. 1989. Towers of the New Gods. *New Internationalist* 202 (December). http://www.newint.org/issue202/towers.htm.

Curry, D. 2003. Review: Deep hiStories: Gender and Colonialism in Southern Africa, W. Woodward, P. Hayes and G. Minkley (eds.), H-South Africa, H-Net Reviews, November. http://www.h-net.msu.edu/reviews/showref.cgi?path=16453 1074895250. Accessed 4 June 2004.

Da Costa, Y. and A. Davids. 1994. *Pages from Cape Muslim History*. Pietermaritzburg: Shuter and Shooter.

D'Arcy, M. C. 2002. Art for All: Postcards Peeking into the Past. *Muslim Views* (June): 19.

Davids, A. 2011. *The Afrikaans of the Cape Muslims: From 1815–1915*. Cape Town: Protea.
- - -. 1990. On Cape Muslim Cooking. *Boorhanool Islam Newsletter* 25 (2): 44–48.
- - -. 1989. The Words the Slaves Made. Unpublished conference paper, Slavery and After. Department of History, University of Cape Town.
- - -. 1985. *History of the Tana Baru*. Cape Town: Committee for the Preservation of the Tana Baru.
- - -. 1980. *The Mosques of Bo-Kaap*. Cape Town: SA Institute of Arabic and Islamic Research.

Davids, L. 2003. Positioning Muslim Women: A Feminist Narrative Analysis. *Annual Review of Islam in South Africa* 6 (December): 35–40.
- - -. 2002. "At Her Feet": Interview with Nadia Davids. *Annual Review of Islam in South Africa* 5 (December): 8–10.

Davids, N. 2006. *At Her Feet: A Play in One Act*. Cape Town: Oshun.
- - -. 2001. At Her Feet. Unpublished theatrical script provided by playwright to the author.

Davenport, R. and C. Saunders. 2000. *South Africa: A Modern History*. London: Macmillan Press.

De Certeau, M. 1984. *The Practice of Everyday Life*. Trans. S. F. Rendall. Berkeley and London: University of California Press.

De Kock, L. 2001. South Africa in the Global Imaginary: An Introduction. *Poetics Today* 22 (2): 263–98.

De Lange, L., T. Kruger and I. Verster. 1996. Transformation Times: Moegsien Williams speaks. *Stellenbosch Journalism Insight* (1996). http://www.sun.ac.za/journalism/sji/1996/moegsien.htm. Accessed 14 June 2004.

De Lange, L. and J. Versfeld. 1996. Is your Press Card Bullet-proof? *Stellenbosch Journalism Insight*. http://academic.sun.ac.za/journalism/sji/1996/bulletproof.htm, Accessed 14 August 2004.

Den Besten, H. 2013. South African Khoekhoe in Contact with Dutch/Afrikaans. In R. Vossen (ed.), *The Khoesan Languages*. Abington: Routledge.

Dennie, G. 1997. The Cultural Politics of Burial in South Africa 1884–1990. Unpublished PhD thesis. Johns Hopkins University.
- - -. 1992. One King, Two Burials: The Politics of Funerals in South Africa's Transkei. *Journal of Contemporary African Studies* 11: 76–87.

Desai, A. and G. Vahed. 2008. *Inside Indenture*. Durban: Madiba Press.

Dicionario Da Lingua Portuguese. 2001. Lisbon: Contemporanea De Academia Das Ciencias De LisboaVerbo.

Dixon, B. and L. Johns. 2001. Gangs, Pagad and the State: Vigilantism and Revenge Violence in the Western Cape. *Violence and Transition Series* 2 (May): unpaginated.

Dodd, A. 1996. The Women of Pagad. In R. Galant and F. Gamieldien (eds), *Drugs, Gangs, People's Power: Exploring the Pagad Phenomenon*. Claremont: Claremont Main Road Masjid.

Dolan, J. 2010. *Theatre and Sexuality*. New York: Palgrave Macmillan.

Dooling, W. 2007. Slavery, Emancipation and Colonial Rule in South Africa. Athens: Ohio University Press; Pietermaritzburg: UKZN Press.

Driver, D. 1988. "Woman" as Sign in the South African Colonial Enterprise. *Journal of Literary Studies* 4 (1): 3–18.

Du Plessis, I. D. 1981. *Tales from the Malay Quarter*. Cape Town: Howard Timmins Publishers.
- - -. 1972. *The Cape Malays: History, Religion, Traditions, Folk Tales of the Malay Quarter*. Cape Town: A. A. Balkema.

Du Plessis, I. D. and C. A. Lückhoff. 1953. *The Malay Quarter and Its People*. Cape Town: A. A. Balkema.

Dubow, J. 2000a. From a View on the World to a Point of View in It: Rethinking Sight, Space and the Colonial Subject. *Interventions: International Journal of Postcolonial Studies* 2 (1): 87–102.

- - -. 2000b. Colonial Space, Colonial Identity: Perception and the South African Landscape. Unpublished PhD thesis. Royal Holloway College, University of London.

Dubow, N. 1991. *Paradise: The Journal and Letters (1917–1933) of Irma Stern*. Diep River: Chameleon Press.

Dubow, S. 1995. *Scientific Racism in Modern South Africa*. Cambridge: Cambridge University Press.

- - -. 1994. Ethnic Euphemisms and Racial Echoes. *Journal of Southern African Studies* 20 (3): 355–70.

Duckitt, H. 1902 [1978]. *Hilda's Diary of a Cape Housekeeper: Being a chronical [sic] of daily events and monthly work in a Cape household, with numerous cooking recipes, and notes on gardening, poultry keeping, etc.* London: Chapman and Hall.

- - -. 1891 [1966]. *Hilda's "Where Is It" of Recipes: Containing, amongst other practical and tried recipes, many old Cape, Indian, and Malay dishes and preserves; Also directions for polishing furniture, silk, etc., and a collection of home remedies in case of sickness*. Cape Town and Amsterdam: A. A. Balkema.

Duff-Gordon, Lady. 1921. *Letters from the Cape*. London: Humphrey Milford.

Ebrahim, M.H. 2009. *The Cape Hajj Tradition: Past and Present*. Cape Town: International Peace College of South Africa.

Edwards, H. (ed). 2000. *Noble Dreams, Wicked Pleasures: Orientalism in America, 1870–1930*. Princeton: Princeton University Press.

Erasmus, Z. 2001a. Introduction: Re-imagining Coloured identities in Post-apartheid South Africa. In Z. Erasmus (ed.), *Coloured by History, Shaped by Place: New Perspectives on Coloured Identities in Cape Town*. Cape Town: Kwela Books.

- - -. 2001b. Some kind of Black: Living the Moments of Entanglement. In B. Hesse (ed.). *Un/Settled Multiculturalism: Diasporas, Entanglement, Transruptions*. London: Zed Books. 185-208.

Erickson, J. 1998. *Islam and Postcolonial Narrative*. Cambridge: Cambridge University Press.

Esack, F. 1996. Pagad and Islamic Radicalism: Taking on the State? *Indicator South Africa* 13 (4): 7–11.

Fanon, F. 1986 [1952]. *Black Skin, White Masks*. London: Pluto.

- - -. 1967 [1961]. *The Wretched of the Earth*. Trans. C. Farrington. London: Penguin.

- - -. 1965. *A Dying Colonialism*. New York: Grove Weidenfeld.

Fine, M. 1995. *Disruptive Voices: The Possibilities of Feminist Research*. Michigan: Michigan University Press.

Fisher, R. 2000. Pushing the Paradigm. *Rhodes Journalism Review* 19. http://journ.ru.ac.za/rjr/Fisher_story.html. Accessed 23 June 2003.

- - -. 1999. Section 205 Cry "Halt"! *Rhodes Journalism Review* 17. http://www.rjr.ru.ac.za/rjr17/section_205.php. Accessed 10 May 2004.

Fonow, M. and J. Cook (eds). 1999. *Beyond Methodology: Feminist Scholarship on Lived Research*. Bloomington: Indiana University Press.

Foucault, M. 1977. *Discipline and Punish: The Birth of the Prison*. Trans. Alan Sheridan. London: Allen Lane.

Frankenberg, R. and L. Mani. 1993. Crosscurrents, Crosstalk: Race, "Postcoloniality" and the Politics of Location. *Cultural Studies* 7: 2 (May): 292–310.

Galant, R. and G. Fahmi (eds). 1996. *Drugs, Gangs, People's Power: Exploring the Pagad Phenomenon*. Claremont: Claremont Main Road Masjid.

Gane, G. 2002. Unspeakable Injuries in *Disgrace* and *David's Story*. *Kunapipi: Journal of Postcolonial Studies* XXIV (1 & 2): 101–13.

Garton, B. 2003. The Forgotten Compass of Death: Apocalypse Then and Now in the Social History of South Africa. *Journal of Social History* 37 (1): 199–218.

Gass, W. and L. Cuoco. 2000. *The Writer and Religion*. Carbondale and Edwardsville: Southern Illinois University Press.

Gerber, H. 1957. *Traditional Cookery of the Cape Malays: Food Customs and 200 old Cape Recipes*. Amsterdam and Cape Town: A. A. Balkema.

Gilman, S. 1985. Black Bodies, White Bodies: Towards an Iconography of Female Sexuality in late Nineteenth-century Art, Medicine and Literature. *Critical Inquiry* 12 (1): 204–42.

Glancey, J. 2003. The Divided City. *The Guardian* (17 February). http://www.guardian.co.uk/arts/critic/feature/0,1169,897163,00.html.

Glaser, D. 2000. The Media Inquiry Reports of the South African Rights Commission: A Critique. *African Affairs* 99: 373–393.

Godlonton, R. 1965 [1835]. *A Narrative of the Irruption of the Kaffir Hordes into the Eastern Province of the Cape of Good Hope 1834–1835*. Cape Town: Struik.

Gondwe, T. 2001. The Full Picture – Benny Gool. *Design Indaba Magazine*. http://www.designindabamag. com/2001/3rd/artical0103 gool.html. Accessed 14 August 2004.

Goody, J. 1982. *Cooking, Cuisine and Class: A Study in Comparative Sociology*. Cambridge: Cambridge University Press.

Gordon-Brown, A. 1975. *Pictorial Africana: A survey of old South African paintings, drawings and prints to the end of the nineteenth century with a biographic dictionary of one thousand artists*. Cape Town and Rotterdam: A. A. Balkema.

Govinden, D. 2008. *"Sister Outsiders": The Representation of Identity and Difference in Selected Writings by South African Indian Women*. Pretoria: Unisa Press.

Gqola, P. D. 2010. *What is Slavery to Me?: Postcolonial/Slave memory in Post-apartheid South Africa*. Johannesburg: Wits University Press.

- - -. 2004. Shackled Memories & Elusive Discourses? Slave Pasts and the Contemporary Cultural and Artistic Imagination in South Africa. Unpublished PhD thesis. University of Munich.

- - -. 2001. "Slaves Don't Have Opinions": Inscriptions of Slave bodies and the Denial of Agency in Rayda Jacobs's *The Slave Book*. In Z. Erasmus (ed.), *Coloured by History, Shaped by Place: New Perspectives on Coloured Identities in Cape Town*. Cape Town: Kwela Books.

Graham, L. V. 2002. A Hidden Side to the Story: Reading Rape in Recent South African Literature. *Kunapipi: Journal of Postcolonial Studies* XXIV (1 & 2): 9–24.

Grebe, M. 2003. *Cape Malay Cooking: The Cape Malay Influence in South African Cooking*. http://www.inmamaskitchen. com/FOOD_IS_ART/reference/capeMalayart.html. Accessed 21 June 2003.

Green, N. 2000. South African Media a Motley Mix. *Inside Journalism* Spring 2000: 10–14.

Greenberg, Clement. 1939. Avant-Garde and Kitsch. *Partisan Review* 6 (Fall): 34–49.

Grosz, E. 1990. *Jacques Lacan: A Feminist Reader*. London: Routledge.

Haefele, B.W. 1988. Islamic Fundamentalism and Pagad: An Internal Security Issue for South Africa. *Crime and Conflict* 8: 8–13.

Hafiz, K (ed.). 2000. *Islam and the West in the Mass Media: Fragmented Images in a Globalizing World*. Cresskill: Hampton Press.

Hall, M. 2003. *Cape Town's District Six and the Archaeology of Memory*. http://www.

wac.uct.ac.za/croatia/hall.htm. Accessed 27 June 2003.

- - -. 2002. Blackbirds and Black Butter-flies. In C. Hamilton et al. (eds), *Refiguring the Archive*. Dordrecht: Kluwer Academic Publishers.

- - -. 2000. *Archaeology and the Modern World: Colonial Transcripts in South Africa and Chesapeake*. New York and London: Routledge.

- - -. 1992. *People in a Changing Urban Landscape: Excavating Cape Town*. Inaugural Lecture, University of Cape Town. 25 March 1992.

- - -. 1991. Fish and the Fisherman, Archaeology and Art: Cape Town seen by Bowler, D'Oyly and De Meillon. *South African Journal of Art and Architectural History* 2 (3 & 4): 78–88.

Hall, S. 1997. *Representation: Cultural Representation and Signifying Practices*. Newbury Park, CA: Sage.

- - -. 1981. The Determinations of News Photographs. In S. Cohen and J. Young (eds), *The Manufacture of News*. London: Constable.

Hamilton, C., V. Harris and G. Reid. 2002. Introduction. In C. Hamilton et al. (eds), *Refiguring the Archive*. Dordrecht: Kluwer Academic Publishers.

Harley, J. B. 2001. *The New Nature of Maps: Essays in the History of Cartography*. Baltimore: Johns Hopkins University Press.

Haron, M. 2001a. The Making, Preservation and Study of South African "Ajami" Mss and Texts. *Sudanic Africa* 12: 1–14.

- - -. 2001b. *Conflict of Identity: The Case of South Africa's Cape Malays*. Unpublished conference paper, Malay World Conference. Kuala Lumpur, 12–14 October 2001.

Harris, M. 1997. The Abominable Pig. In C. Counihan and P. Van Esterik (eds), *Food and Culture: A Reader*. London and New York: Routledge.

Harrison, R. P. 2003. *The Dominion of the Dead*. Chicago: University of Chicago Press.

Hartley, J. 1996. *Popular Reality*. London and New York: Routledge.

Haupt, A. 2001. Black Thing: Hip-hop nationalism, race and gender in Prophets of da City and Brasse vannie Kaap. In Z. Erasmus (ed.), *Coloured by History, Shaped by Place: New Perspectives on Coloured Identities in Cape Town*. Cape Town: Kwela Books.

Head, B. 1974. *A Question of Power*. London: Heinemann.

Hendricks, P. 2009. *Hijab: Unveiling Queer Muslim Lives*. Wynberg: The Inner Circle.

Hermansen, M. 1999. Roads to Mecca: Conversion Narratives of European and Euro-American Muslims. *The Muslim World*, 89 (1), 56–89.

Hewitt, A. G. 1973 [1890]. *Cape Cookery: Simple yet Distinctive*. Cape Town: David Philip.

Higgins, J. 2003. The Sole Measure of Poetic Value: A Response to Kelwyn Sole. *Pretexts: Literary and Cultural Studies* 12 (1): 97–102.

Hofmeyr, I. 2007. The Black Atlantic Meets the Indian Ocean: Forging New Paradigms of Transnationalism in the Global South – Literary and Cultural Perspectives. *Social Dynamics* 33 (2): 3–32.

Hussein, A. 2002. *Edward Said: Criticism and Society*. London: Verso.

Images of the East. 1999. Videotaped discussion with Abdulkader Tayob, Jane Bennett, Yazeed Fakier and Lesley Fordred, chaired by Gabeba Baderoon. University of Cape Town.

Insoll, T. 2003. *The Archaeology of Islam in Sub-Saharan Africa*. Cambridge and Cape Town: Cambridge University Press.

Jacobs, E. M. 1991. *In Pursuit of Pepper and Tea: The Story of the Dutch East India Company*. Amsterdam: Netherlands Maritime Museum / Walburg Pers.

Jacobs, Rayda. 2005. *Mecca Diaries*. Cape Town: Jacana.
- - -. 1998. *The Slave Book*. Cape Town: Kwela Books.

Jacobs, S. 2004. Media and Policy Debates in Post-apartheid South Africa. Unpublished PhD thesis. Birkbeck College, University of London.
- - -. 2002. Review of Sarah Nuttall and Cheryl-Ann Michael (eds), *Senses of Culture: South African Culture Studies*. H-South Africa. H-Net Reviews. (September). http://www.h-net.msu.edu/reviews/showrev.cgi?path=135601034387654. Accessed 11 November 2002.

Jaffer, M (ed.). 1996. *Guide to the Kramats of the Western Cape*. Cape Town: Cape Mazaar (Kramat) Society.

Jaffer, Z. 2003. *Our Generation*. Cape Town: Kwela Books.

Jaggi, M. 2003. Stance of Pride. *Mail and Guardian* (12 December) http://www.chico.mweb.co.za/art/2003/2003dec/031212-toni.html. Accessed 15 December 2003.

Jamal, A. 2004. The Bearable Lightness of Tracey Rose's *The Kiss*. www.chimurenga.co.za. Accessed 12 July 2004.

Jameson, F. 1981. *The Political Unconscious: Narrative as a Socially Symbolic Act*. Ithaca, N.Y.: Cornell University Press; London: Methuen.

Jeenah. N. 1996. Pagad: Aluta Continua. In R. Galant and F. Gamieldien (eds), *Drugs, Gangs, People's Power:*

Exploring the Pagad Phenomenon. Claremont: Claremont Main Road Masjid.

Jeenah, N. and S. Shaikh. 2000. *Journey
of Discovery: A South African Hajj*. Ocean
View: Full Moon Press.

Jeppie, S. 2001. Reclassifications: Coloured, Malay, Muslim. In Z. Erasmus
(ed.), *Coloured by History, Shaped by
Place: New Perspectives on Coloured Identities in Cape Town*. Cape Town: Kwela
Books.

- - -. 1998. People Against Gangsterism
  and Drugs. *Annual Review of Islam in
  South Africa* 1. http://web.uct/ac.za/
  depts/religion/IE/institutes/institutes_
  ARISA_Pagad.html. Accessed 4 June
  2003.

- - -. 1996. Introduction. In R. Galant and
  F. Gamieldien (eds), *Drugs, Gangs,
  People's Power: Exploring the Pagad
  Phenomenon*. Claremont: Claremont
  Main Road Masjid.

- - -. 1988. I. D. du Plessis and the "Reinvention" of the "Malay", c. 1935–
  1952. Unpublished seminar paper.
  Centre for African Studies, University
  of Cape Town. 28 September 1988.

Johnson, D. 2012. *Imagining the Cape
Colony: History, Literature and the South
African Nation*. Cape Town: UCT Press.

Joseph, B. 2004. *Reading the East India
Company, 1720–1840: Colonial Currencies
of Gender*. London: University of Chicago
Press.

Kabbani, R. 1986. *Europe's Myths of
Orient: Devise and Rule*. Basingstoke and
London: Macmillan.

Karan, M. 2003. Muslim Community
Radio. http://www.sun.ac.za/journalism/
muslim.doc+%22voice+of+the+cape%2
2&hl=en. Accessed 30 May 2004.

Keegan, T. 1996. *Colonial South Africa and
the Origins of the Racial Order*. Charlottesville: University Press of Virginia.

Kennedy, R. F. 1967. *Catalogue of Pictures
in the Africana Museum*. Johannesburg:
Africana Museum.

Kennedy, V. 2000. *Edward Said: A Critical
Introduction*. Cambridge: Polity Press.

Khan, S. 1998. Muslim Women: Negotiations in the Third Space. *Signs: Journal
of Women in Culture and Society* 23 (2):
463–94.

Klopper, S. 1989. George French Angas's
(Re)presentation of the Zulu in *The
Kafirs Illustrated*. *South African Journal of
Cultural Art History* 3 (1): 63–73.

Kornhaber, D. 2004. Presenting the Past,
Performing the Future: Theatre in New
York and Cape Town Ten years after
Apartheid. *Safundi: The Journal of South
African and American Comparative Stud-
ies* 13/14 (April).

Kozain, R. 2005. *This Carting Life*. Cape
Town: Kwela/Snailpress.

- - -. 2002. The Old in the New. *Pretexts:*

Literary and Cultural Studies 11 (2): 197–203.

Krige, H. 1998. Review: Everyday Cape Malay Cooking. *Wynboer* August: 87.

Lagardian, Z. 1995. *Everyday Cape Malay Cooking*. Cape Town: Struik Publishers.

Landau, P. S. 2002. Introduction: An Amazing Distance: Pictures and People in Africa. In P. Landau (ed), *Images and Empires: Visuality in Colonial and Postcolonial Africa*. Berkeley: University of California Prress.

Lane, C. (ed.). 1998. *The Psychoanalysis of race*. New York: Columbia University Press.

Laxton, P. (ed.). 2001. *The New Nature of Maps: Essays in the history of cartography*. Baltimore: Johns Hopkins University Press.

Leipoldt, C. L.1976. *Leipoldt's Cape Cookery*. Cape Town: W. J. Fleisch.

Lewis, D. 2005. Against the Grain: Black Women and Sexuality. *Agenda*, 63: 11-24.

- - -. 2004. Review: It All Begins: Poems from Postliberation South Africa. *Chimurenga Online*, www.chimurenga.co.za. Accessed 4 July 2004.

- - -. 2002. Self-Representations and Reconstructions of Southern African Pasts: Bessie Head's *A Bewitched Crossroad*. In W. Woodward, P. Hayes,

G. Minkley (eds), *Deep Histories: Gender and Colonialism in Southern Africa*. Amsterdam: Rodopi.

- - -. 2004. Review: It All Begins: Poems from Postliberation South Africa. *Chimurenga Online*, www.chimurenga.co.za. Accessed 4 July 2004.

- - -. 2001. The Conceptual Art of Berni Searle. *Agenda* 50: 108–113.

- - -. 1999. Thomas Baines: Tracing the Present in the Past. In M Stevenson (ed.), *Thomas Baines: An Artist in the Service of Science in Southern Africa*. Cape Town: Fernwood Press.

Lewis, S. 2003. Interview with Kelwyn Sole. *Wasafiri* 38: 5–10.

Lichtenstein, H. 1928 [1812]. *Travels in Southern Africa in the Years 1803, 1804, 1805, and 1806*. Trans. A. Plumptre. Cape Town: Van Riebeeck Society.

Lliteras, S. M. 2002. Taking the Gender-Jihad to the Stage. *Annual Review of Islam in South Africa* 5 (December): 6–7.

Loomba, A. 2002. *Shakespeare, Race and Colonialism*. New York: Oxford.

- - -. 1998a. *Colonialism / Postcolonialism*. London: Routledge.

- - -. 1998b. *Of Queens and Spices: Race in Renaissance Drama*. Lecture. University of Cape Town, 14 May.

- - -. 1989. *Gender, Race, Renaissance Drama*. Manchester: Manchester University Press.

Lowe, Lisa. 2006. The Intimacies of Four Continents. In A.L. Stoler (ed.), *Haunted by Empire: Geographies of intimacy in North American history*. Durham: Duke University Press.

Maake, N. 1996. Inscribing Identity on the Landscape: National Symbols in South Africa. In K. Darian-Smith, L. Gunner and S. Nuttall (eds), *Text, Theory, Space: Land, Literature and History in South Africa and Australia*. New York: Routledge.

MacKenzie, J.M. 1995. *Orientalism: History, Theory and the Arts*. Manchester: Manchester University Press.

Magubane, Z. 2004. *Bringing the Empire Home: Race, Class and Gender in Britain and Colonial South Africa*. Chicago and London: University of Chicago Press.

Mamdani, M. 2004. *Good Muslim, Bad Muslim: America, the Cold War and the Roots of Terror*. New York: Pantheon.
- - -. 1996. *Citizen and Subject: Contemporary Africa and the Legacy of Late Colonialism*. Princeton: Princeton University Press.

Marks, S. 2012. South Africans Ignorant about Land Struggle. *Mail & Guardian*, 2 March. http://mg.co.za/article/2012-03-02-sa-ignorant-about-its-land-struggle.
- - -. 1980. South Africa: The Myth of the Empty Land. *History Today* 30 (1): 150–55.

Maseko, Z. 1998. *The Life and Times of Sara Baartman "The Hottentot Venus"*. Documentary film. New York: First Run/ Icarus Films.

Mason, J. E. 2003. *Social Death and Resurrection: Slavery and Emancipation in South Africa*. Charlottesville: University of Virginia Press.

Mbeki, T. I Am An African. http://www.gov.za/speeches/leaders/former.html

Mbembe, Achille. 2002. The Power of the Archive and its Limits. *Refiguring the Archive*, 19–26.

McClintock, A. 1995. *Imperial Leather: Race, Gender and Sexuality in the Colonial Contest*. New York and London: Routledge.

McCole, J. J. 1993. *Walter Benjamin and the Antinomies of Tradition*. Ithaca: Cornell University Press.

Menninghaus, W. 2009. On the "Vital Significance" of Kitsch: Walter Benjamin's Politics of "Bad Taste". In A. Benjamin and C. Rice (eds), *Walter Benjamin and the Architecture of Modernity*. Melbourne: re:press.

Michael, C. A. 2006. On the Slipperiness of Food. In S. Nuttall (ed.), *Beautiful/ Ugly: African and Diaspora Aesthetics*. Durham: Duke University Press.

Miller, E. 2002. Spreading Flavours. *Leadership* (November): 45–47.

Minkley, G. and C. Rassool. 1999. Photography with a Difference? Leon Levson's camera studies and photographic exhibitions of native life in South Africa, 1947–1950. Unpublished conference paper, Encounters with Photography: Photographing People in Southern Africa, 1860–1999. Cape Town: South African Museum, 14–17 July 1999.

Mitchell, W. J. T. 2002 [1994]. Imperial Landscape. In W. J. T. Mitchell (ed.), *Landscape and Power: Space, place, and landscape*. Chicago: University of Chicago Press.

Mkhize, N., J. Bennett, V. Reddy and R. Moletsane 2010. *The Country We Want To Live In: Hate Crimes and Homophobia in the Lives of Black Lesbian South Africans*. Cape Town: HSRC Press.

Morphet, T. 1999. Personal traits: The work of Eaton and Biermann in Durban. In Hilton Judin and Ivan Vladislavić (eds.), *Blank: Architecture, Apartheid and After*. Rotterdam: Nederlands Architectuur-instituut.

Morrison, T. 1992. *Playing in the Dark: Whiteness and the Literary Imagination*. Cambridge and London: Harvard University Press.
- - -. 1987. *Beloved*. New York: Knopf.

Morton, T. 2000. *The Poetics of Spice: Romantic Consumerism and the Exotic*. Cambridge: Cambridge University Press.

Murray, N. 2001. Breaking "New Ground" – The Case of Cape Town's Tana Baru Burial Ground. www.archafrica.uct.ac.za/mappingalternatives/Papers/murray.rtf. Accessed 23 June 2003.

Mutman, M. 1994. Pictures from Afar: Shooting the Middle East. *Inscriptions*: 3–44.
- - -. 1992. Under the Sign of Orientalism: The West vs. Islam. *Cultural Critique*, 1992–93: 165–197.

Narayan, U. 1997. *Dislocating Cultures: Identities, Traditions and Third-world Feminism*. New York: Routledge.

Ndlovu, M., B. Boswell and R. Khan. 2002. *Voices of Nisaa*. Green Point: New Moon Ventures.

Nel, F. 1998. *Writing for the Media in South Africa*. Johannesburg and Detroit: International Thomson Publishing.

Newton-King, S. 2012. Family, Friendship and Survival Among Freed Slaves. In N. Worden (ed.), *Cape Town between East and West: Social Identities in a Dutch Co-lonial Town*. Johannesburg: Jacana Media.

Nochlin, L. 1983. The Imaginary Orient. *Art in America* (May): 119–191.

Novo Dicionario da Lingua Portuguesa. 1939. Lisboa: Livraria Bertrand.

Nuttall, S. 2009. *Entanglement: Literary and Cultural Reflections on Post-apartheid*. Johannesburg: Wits University Press.

Nuttall, S. (ed.). 2006. *Beautiful/Ugly: African and Diaspora Aesthetics*. Durham: Duke University Press.

Nuttall, S. and C. A. Michael (eds). 2000. *Senses of Culture: South African Culture Studies*. Oxford and New York: Oxford University Press.

Nyezwa, M. 2000. *Song Trials*. Pietermaritzburg: UKZN Press.

Odendaal, L. 1995. Cass: A Mixed Bredie. *De Kat* 10 (12): 116–ay).

Oppelt, R. 2012. C. Louis Leipoldt and the Role of the "Cape Malay" in South African Cookery. *Journal of Literary Studies* 28 (1): 51–68.

Osman, L. Forthcoming in 2015. *The Kitchen Dweller's Testimony*. Lincoln: University of Nebraska Press and Senegal: Amalion Press.

Pechey, G. 2002. Coetzee's Purgatorial Africa: The case of Disgrace. *Interventions: International Journal of Postcolonial Studies* 4 (3) 20: 374–383.

Penn, N. 1999. *Rogues, Rebels and Runaways: Eighteenth-century Cape Characters*. Cape Town: David Philip.

Penney, J. 1998. Uncanny Foreigners: Does the Subaltern Speak through Julia Kristeva? In Christopher Lane (ed.), *The Psychoanalysis of Race*: 120–38.

Perumal, J. and D. Pillay. 2002. The Bina Gumede Story: Exploring the Ethics of Researching the Other, *Agenda* 51: 92–100.

Peterson, B. 2002. The Archives and the Political Imaginary. In C. Hamilton et al. (eds), *Refiguring the Archive*. Dordrecht: Kluwer Academic Publishers.

Pillay, S. 2003. Experts, Terrorists, Gangsters: Problematising Public Discourse on a Post-apartheid Showdown. In H. Wasserman and S. Jacobs (eds), *Shifting Selves: Post-apartheid Essays on Media, Culture and Identity*. Cape Town: Kwela.
- - -. 1999. One City, Many Prejudices. *Mail & Guardian* (1 October).

Pityana, B. 2000. South Africa's Inquiry into Racism in the Media: The Role of National Institutions in the Promotion and Protection of Human Rights. *African Affairs* 99: 525–32.

Poole, E. 2002. *Reporting Islam: Media Representations of British Muslims*. London: I. B. Tauris.

Posel, D. 2001. What's in a Name? Racial Categorisations under Apartheid and their Afterlife. *Transformation* 47: 50–74.

Pratt, G. and V. Rosner, (eds.). 2012. *The Global and the Intimate: Feminism in Our Time*. New York: Columbia University Press.

Pratt, M. L. 1992. *Imperial Eyes: Travel writing and Transculturation*. London and New York: Routledge.

Shathley, Q. 2002. Not Unlike Kafka. *Annual Review of Islam in South Africa* 5 (December): 11–12.

Radio 786 ... Is Here to Stay. 2000. Pamphlet. Cape Town.

Raditlhalo, S. 2005. "The Travelling Salesman": A Tribute to K. Sello Duiker: 1974–2005. *Feminist Africa* (5): 96–104.

Rahman, F. 1981. *Islam and Modernity: Transformation of an Intellectual Tradition*. Chicago: The University of Chicago Press.

Rai, A. S. 1998. "Thus Spake the Subaltern ...": Postcolonial Criticism and the Scene of Desire. In C. Lane (ed.), *The Psychoanalysis of Race*.

Rasool, E. 1995. "Fundamentalist Faith." *Agenda* 25: 38–46.

Rastogi, P. 2008. *Afrindian Fictions: Diaspora, Race and National Desire in South Africa*. Columbus, OH: Ohio State University Press.

Read, A. (ed). 1996. *Frantz Fanon and Visual Representation*. London: Institute of Contemporary Arts.

Reddy, T. 2001. The Politics of Naming: The Constitution of Coloured Subjects in South Africa. In Z. Erasmus (ed.), *Coloured by History, Shaped by Place: New Perspectives on Coloured Identities in Cape Town*. Cape Town: Kwela Books.

Richards, T. 1993. *The Imperial Archive: Knowledge and the Fantasy of Empire*. London: Verso.

Riding, A. 2001. Sudden Resonance for an Iranian Film about Afghanistan. *New York Times*, 5 November.

Rood, B. 1977. *Maleier-Kookkuns*. Cape Town: Tafelberg Publishers.

Rosenthal, Eric and Hedley Churchward. 1981 [1931]. *From Drury Lane to Mecca – Being an Account of the Strange Life and Adventures of Hedley Churchward, etc.* Cape Town: Howard Timmins.

Ross, Robert. 1999. *Status and Respectability in the Cape Colony 1750–1870*: A Tragedy of Manners. Cambridge: Cambridge University Press.
- - -. 1983. *Cape of Torments: Slavery and Resistance in South Africa*. London: Routledge & Kegan Paul.

Ryen, A. 2000. Colonial Methodology? Methodological challenges to cross-cultural projects collecting data by structured interviews. In C. Truman, D. M. Mertens and B. Humphries (eds), *Research and Inequality*. London: University College London Press.

Said, E. W. 2003a. *Freud and the Non-European*. London and New York: Verso.
- - -. 2003b. *Culture and Resistance: Conversations with Edward W. Said*. Cambridge: South End Press.

- - -. 1997. *Covering Islam: How the Media and the Experts Determine How We See the World.* New York: Vintage.

- - -. 1993. *Culture and Imperialism.* London: Chatto & Windus.

- - -. 1979. *The Question of Palestine.* Vintage: New York.

- - -. 1978 [1991]. *Orientalism.* London: Penguin.

- - -. 1975. *Beginnings: Intention and Method.* New York: Columba University Press.

Salie, A. 1994. Imam's Detention Portrayed in Play. *Athlone News* (13 July): unpaginated. Baxter Theatre Archives.

Samie, N. 2003. Eat, Sleep, Drink Photography. *Careers at Iafrica.com.* 9 November. http://careers.iafrica.com/topjobs/mediaarts/284177.htm. Accessed 4 August 2004.

Samuelson M. 2007. *Remembering the Nation: Dismembering Women: Stories of the South African Transition.* Pietermaritzburg: UKZN Press.

- - -. 2002. The Rainbow Womb: Rape and Race in South African Fiction of the Transition. *Kunapipi: Journal of Postcolonial Studies* XXIV (1 & 2): 88-100.

Sanders, M. 2002. Ambiguities of Mourning: Law, Custom and Testimony of Women before South Africa's Truth and Reconciliation Commission. In D. Eng

and D. Kazanjian (eds), *Loss: the Politics of Mourning.* Berkeley and London: University of California Press.

- - -. 2002. *Complicities: The intellectual and Apartheid.* Durham: Duke.

Searle, B. 1999. *Colour Me: Conceptual Art and Photographic Installation.* Cape Town: Mark Coetzee Fine Art Cabinet.

Schick, I. C. 1990. Representing Middle Eastern Women. *Feminist Studies* 16: 345–80.

Settler, F. 1998. Funerals: Sites of Conversion and Resistance. Unpublished conference paper, Coloured by History, Shaped by Place: Identities and cultural practices in the city. University of Cape Town, 21–23 June 1998.

Shathley, Q. 2002. Not Unlike Kafka. *Annual Review of Islam in South Africa* 5 (December): 11–12.

Shaw, G. 1975. *Some Beginnings: The Cape Times (1876–1910).* London: Oxford University Press.

Shell, R. 1994. *Children of Bondage: A Social History of the Slave Society at the Cape of Good Hope, 1652–1838.* Hanover: Wesleyan University Press.

Shell, R. C. H. 1997. Between Christ and Mohammed: Conversion, Slavery and Gender in the Urban Western Cape. In R. Elphick and T. R. H. Davenport (eds), *Christianity in South Africa: Political,*

Social and Cultural History. Berkeley: University of California Press.

Shukri, I. 2005. *The Silent Minaret*. Johannesburg: Jacana Media.

Silva, P., W. Dore, D. Mantzel, C. Muller and M. Wright. 1996. *A Dictionary of South African English on Historical Principles*. Oxford: Oxford University Press, in Association with the Dictionary Unit for South African English.

Sinha, M. 1995. *Colonial Masculinity: The "manly Englishman" and the "effeminate Bengali" in the late nineteenth century*. Manchester: Manchester University Press.

Skotnes, P. 1996. (ed.). *Negotiating the Presence of the Bushmen*. Cape Town: University of Cape Town.

Smith, C. 2001 (ed.). *Returning the Gaze*. Catalogue. Cape Town: One.

Smith, G. 2002. Fetching Saartjie. *Mail & Guardian* (20 May). http://www.chico.mweb.co.za/art/2002/2002may/020520-saartjie.html. Accessed 30 April 2003.

Sole, K. 2001–2002. The Witness of Poetry: Economic Calculation, Civil Society and the Limits of Everyday Experience in a Liberated South Africa. *New Formations* 45: 24–53.

- - -. 1985. Review: South African Theatre. *Critical Arts* 3 (4). http://www.und.ac.za/publications/criticalarts/v3n5a5.htm. Accessed 13 May 2004.

Sontag, S. 2004. Regarding the Torture of Others. *The New York Times Magazine* (23 May). www.nytimes.com. Accessed 23 May 2004.

- - -. 2003a. *Regarding the Pain of Others*. New York: Farrar, Straus and Giroux.

- - -. 2003b. The Telling Shot. *The Guardian Review* (1 February): 4–6.

South Africa – a Culinary Rainbow. 1995. *African Panorama* 40 (3): 30–33.

South African Human Rights Commission. 1999. *Research Report Commissioned by the South African Human Rights Commission as Part of Its Inquiry into Race and Media*. Pretoria: South African Human Rights Commission.

Spivak, G. 1988. Can the Subaltern Speak? In C. Nelson and L. Grossberg (eds), *Marxism and the Interpretation of Culture*. Urbana-Champaign: University of Illinois Press.

Standard Swahili-English Dictionary. 1963 [1939]. Oxford and New York: Oxford University Press.

Stevens, W. 1965 [1954]. *The Collected Poems of Wallace Stevens*. New York: Alfred Knopf.

Strelitz, L. 2001. Where the Global Meets the Local: Media Studies and the Myth of Cultural Homogenization. *Transnational Broadcasting Studies* 6 (http://www.tbsjournal.com/Archives/Sprin1g01/strelitz.html. Accessed 4 July 2004.

Stoler, A. L. 2002. Colonial Archives and the Arts of Governance: On the Content in the Form. In C. Hamilton et al. (eds), *Refiguring the Archive*. Dordrecht: Kluwer Academic Publishers.

- - -. 1997. Sexual Affronts and Racial Frontiers: European Identities and the Cultural Politics of Exclusion in Colonial Southeast Asia. In F.Cooper and A.L. Stoler (eds), *Tensions of Empire: Colonial Cultures in a Bourgeois World*. Los Angeles: UCLA Press.

- - -. 1995. *Race and the Education of Desire: Foucault's History of Sexuality and the Colonial Order of Things*. Durham and London: Duke University Press.

Stromsoe, A. 1962. *Aagot Stromsoe's Fish Book*. Cape Town: Howard Timmins.

Super, J. C. 2002. Food and History. *Journal of Social History* 36 (1): 165–78.

Swahili-English Dictionary 1967. New York: Catholic University of America Press.

Switzer, L. (ed.). 1997. *South Africa's Alternative Press: Voices of protest and resistance, 1880s–1960s*. Cambridge: Cambridge University Press.

Tagg, J. 1993. *The Burden of Representation: Essays on Photography and Representation*. Minneapolis: University of Minnesota Press.

Taylor, J. 1996. The Poison Pen. In B. Cooper and A. Steyn (eds), *Transgressing Boundaries: New Directions in the Study of Culture in Africa*. Cape Town and Athens: University of Cape Town Press and Ohio University Press.

Tayob, A. 2002. The South African Muslim Communities Response to September 11th. *Annual Review of Islam in South Africa* 5 (December): 20–25.

- - -. 1999. *Islam in South Africa: Mosques, Imams and Sermons*. Gainesville/Miami: University Press of Florida.

- - -. 1996. *Jihad against Drugs in Cape Town: A Discourse-centred Analysis*. Cape Town: Department of Religious Studies.

Theal, G. M. 1905. *Records of the Cape Colony from February 1793, Volume 34 by Cape of Good Hope (South Africa)*. Great Britain: Public Record Office.

Thompson, J. B. 1995. *The Media and Modernity: A Social Theory of the Media*. Cambridge: Polity Press.

Tomaselli, K. 2000. *Cultural Studies as Psycho-babble: Post-litcrit, Methodology and Dynamic Justice*. Keynote Address, Third Crossroads Conference on Cultural Studies. University of Birmingham.

Twine, F. W. and J. W. Warren (eds). 2000. *Racing Research, Researching Race: Methodological Dilemmas in Critical Race Studies*. New York and London: New York University Press.

Van der Post, L. 1977. *First Catch Your Eland: A Taste of Africa*. London: Hogarth Press.

- - -. 1970. *African Food*. New York: Time-Life Books.

Van Heerden, J. 2008. Theatre in a New Democracy: Some Major Trends in South African Theatre from 1994 to 2003. Unpublished PhD thesis, Stellenbosch University.

Van Heyningen, E. 2008. Costly Mythologies: The Concentration Camps of the South African War in Afrikaner historiography. *Journal of Southern African Studies*, 34 (3): 495–513.

- - -. 1989a. Agents of Empire: The Medical Profession in the Cape Colony 1880–1910. *Medical History* 33: 450–71.

- - -. 1989b. *Public Health and Society in Cape Town, 1880–1910*. Unpublished PhD thesis, University of Cape Town.

Van Graan, M. 2004. Looking in, Watching out. *Mail & Guardian* (23 April).

Versveld, M. 1991 [1983]. *Food for Thought: A Philosopher's Cookbook*. Cape Town: Carrefour Press.

Visel, Robin. 1990. "We Bear the World and We Make It": Bessie Head and Olive Schreiner. *Research in African Literatures* 21 (3): 115–24.

Viswanathan, G. (ed.). 2001. *Power, Politic, and Culture: Interviews with Edward W. Said*. New York: Pantheon.

Waern, K. A. 2004. *Revision: MAMA on the Construction of History*. Exhibition catalogue. Stockholm: Arkitekturmuseet/Swedish Museum of Architecture. 14 February–16 May.

Ward, K. 2012. Southeast Asian Migrants. In N. Worden (ed.). *Cape Town between East and West: Social Identities in a Dutch Colonial Town*. Johannesburg: Jacana Media.

Watson, H. 1994. Women and the Veil: Personal responses to global process. In A. Ahmed and H. Donnan (eds), *Islam, Globalization and Postmodernity*. London and New York: Routledge.

Westra, P. and J.C. Armstrong, (eds). 2006. *Slave Trade with Madagascar. The Journals of the Cape Slaver Leijdsman, 1715. /Slawehandel met Madagascar. Die Joernale van die Kaapse Slawerskip Leijsman, 1715*. Cape Town: Africana.

Wicomb, Z. 2000. *David's Story*. Cape Town: Kwela.

- - -. 1998. Shame and Identity: The Case of the Coloured in South Africa. In R. Jolly and D. Attridge (eds), *Writing South Africa – Literature, Apartheid and Democracy, 1970–1995*. Cambridge: Cambridge University Press.

- - -. 1996. To Hear The Variety of Discourses. In M. J. Daymond (ed.), *South African Feminisms: Writing, Theory and*

Criticism, 1990–1994. New York and London: Garland Publishing.

Williams, F. 1988. *The Cape Malay Cookbook.* Cape Town: Struik.

Williams, R. 1975. *The Country and the City.* Oxford: Oxford University Press.

Willoughby, G. 2003. Bristling Energy. *Mail & Guardian Online* (19 June) http://www.mg.co.za.

Winter, T. 2004. Outside the Community. *The Times Literary Supplement.* January 30: 25.

Witz, L. 2000. Beyond Van Riebeeck. In S. Nuttall and C. Michael (eds), *Senses of Culture: South African Culture Studies.* Oxford and New York: Oxford University Press.

Wolfe, Michael. 1997. *One Thousand Roads to Mecca: Ten Centuries of Travellers Writing about the Muslim Pilgrimage.* New York: Grove Press.

Woodward, W., P. Hayes and G. Minkley. 2002. Introduction. In *Deep hiStories: Gender and Colonialism in Southern Africa.* Amsterdam and New York: Rodopi.

Worden, N. (ed.). 2012. *Cape Town between East and West: Social Identities in a Dutch Colonial Town.* Johannesburg: Jacana Media.

- - -. 1994. *The Making of Modern South Africa: Conquest, Segregation and Apartheid.* Oxford: Blackwell.

- - -. 1985. *Slavery in Dutch South Africa.* London: Cambridge University Press.

Worden, N. and C. Crais (eds). 1994. *Breaking the Chains: Slavery and its Legacy in the Nineteenth-century Cape Colony.* Johannesburg: Wits University Press.

Worden, N., E. van Heyningen and V. Bickford-Smith. 1998. *Cape Town: The Making of a City.* Claremont: Verloren Press.

Yegenoglu, M. 1998. *Colonial Fantasies: Towards a Feminist Reading of Orientalism.* Cambridge: Cambridge University Press.

Young, R. 1995. *Colonial Desire: Hybridity in Theory, Culture and Race.* London and New York: Routledge.

- - -. 1990. *White Mythologies: Writing, History and the West.* London and New York: Routledge.

Index